It has been claimed that organization theory is in a state of 'crisis'. This book traces the history of the orthodox systems theory paradigm in organization studies from its foundations in positivist sociology, through its theoretical and empirical development under structural-functionalism, to its recent deconstruction by postmodernists. The analysis offers general support for the 'sociology-in-crisis' thesis, but takes issue with one of its main propositions, that paradigms are incommensurable. It is argued that paradigms are porous rather than hermetic phenomena, a fact which has profound implications for the theory building process. Based on language-game philosophy, a dialectical theory is developed to illustrate how seemingly exclusive idioms can be mediated. Two products from this enquiry are a pluri-paradigm method for organizational research and an epistemological framework for postmodern organizational analysis.

Cambridge Studies in Management 20

Sociology and organization theory

Cambridge Studies in Management   20

Formerly Management and Industrial Relations series

Editors
WILLIAM BROWN, *University of Cambridge*
ANTHONY HOPWOOD, *London School of Economics*
and PAUL WILLMAN, *London Business School*

The series focuses on the human and organizational aspects of management. It covers the areas of organization theory and behaviour, strategy and business policy, the organizational and social aspects of accounting, personnel and human resource management, industrial relations and industrial sociology.

The series aims for high standards of scholarship and seeks to publish the best among original theoretical and empirical research; innovative contributions to advancing understanding in the area; and books which synthesize and/or review the best of current research, and aims to make the work published in specialist journals more widely accessible.

The books are intended for an international audience among specialists in universities and business schools, undergraduate, graduate and MBA students, and also for a wider readership among business practitioners and trade unionists.

For a list of titles in this series, see end of book

Sociology and organization theory

Positivism, paradigms and postmodernity

John Hassard

CAMBRIDGE
UNIVERSITY PRESS

Published by the Press Syndicate of the University of Cambridge
The Pitt Building, Trumpington Street, Cambridge CB2 1RP
40 West 20th Street, New York, NY 10011–4211, USA
10 Stamford Road, Oakleigh, Melbourne 3166; Australia

First published 1993
Reprinted 1994
First paperback edition 1995

Printed in Great Britain at the University Press, Cambridge

A catalogue record for this book is available from the British Library

Library of Congress cataloguing in publication data

Hassard, John, 1953–
Sociology and organization theory: positivism, paradigms and
postmodernity / John Hassard.
    p.   cm.
Includes bibliographical references and index.
ISBN 0 521 35034 4
1. Organizational sociology. 2. Paradigms (Social sciences)
I. Title.
HM131.H3346   1993
302.3'5 – dc20   92–28988 CIP

ISBN 0 521 35034 4 hardback
ISBN 0 521 48458 8 paperback

To Roisin

Contents

List of figures and tables   *page* x
Acknowledgements   xi

Introduction   1

1   Foundations of orthodoxy   4

2   The hegemony of systems   19

3   From functionalism to fragmentation   49

4   Closed paradigms and analytical openings   76

5   Multiple paradigm research   88

6   Postmodernism and organization   111

Notes   139
Bibliography   147
Author index   159
Subject index   163

Figures and Tables

FIGURES

1 Mechanical equilibrium model (Roethlisberger and Dickson 1939; Scheme for interpreting complaints and reduced work effectiveness) *page* 35
2 Four paradigm model of social theory (Burrell and Morgan 1979) 66
3 Scheme for analysing assumptions about social science (Burrell and Morgan 1979) 67
4 Sociology of regulation and the sociology of radical change (Burrell and Morgan 1979) 67
5 Route of the research investigation 91
6 Job characteristics model (Hackman and Oldham 1980) 93

TABLES

1 Analysis of variance 95
2 Means and standard deviations 96

Acknowledgements

I should like to thank my teachers Gibson Burrell (Warwick University), Peter Clark (Aston University), Robert Cooper (Lancaster University) and Gareth Morgan (York University, Ontario) for providing invaluable tuition relevant to the project.

I am fortunate to have Ian Atkin, Paul Forrester, Louise McArdle and Nelson Tang as colleagues within the Department of Management and John Law and Susan Leigh Star as fellow organizational researchers within the Faculty of Social Sciences at Keele University. Each has in some way influenced my thinking. Of my colleagues, however, I owe the greatest debt to Stephen Procter, especially for the time and effort he has spent commenting on various drafts of the volume.

I would also like to thank Michael Rowlinson (Southampton University) and Martin Parker (Staffordshire University) for their comments on earlier drafts of this book. I must of course add the customary rider that none of the above is in any way responsible for any shortcomings the volume may have.

Thanks are also due to our departmental secretary, Debbie Pointon, for her help with the preparation of the manuscript.

Finally, throughout the writing of this book my partner Roisin Hutchinson has provided invaluable encouragement, support and ideas. She has been a caring companion for fifteen years and it is to her that the book is dedicated.

Note

The author is grateful for permission to reproduce material from his articles 'Overcoming Hermeticism in Organization Theory' (*Human Relations*, 1988, 41 (3): 247–59) and 'Multiple Paradigm Research in Organizations: A Case Study' (*Organization Studies*, 1991, 12 (2): 275–99).

Introduction

Since the early 1970s, there have been numerous attempts to define the professional community structure of social science. Writers have catalogued a range of alternatives to the apparently declining but still dominant theoretical paradigm of structural-functionalism. The process of specifying new paradigms has been predicated mainly on Thomas Kuhn's (1962) work in the history of science, in which he distinguishes between periods of 'normal' and 'revolutionary' activity. In line with Kuhn's thinking, sociologists have argued that the emergence of new influential perspectives signals sociology is currently experiencing a period of scientific revolution, or 'science-in-crisis'.

The book examines this 'crisis' thesis as it applies to the branch of sociology concerned with organizations. We trace the history of the influential systems-theory approach to organizational analysis from its origins in positivist and evolutionary philosophy, through its development under sociological functionalism, to its deconstruction by radical structuralists and postmodernists. In highlighting the often acrimonious debate between the systems theorists and the critics of organization theory, we offer support for the crisis theory perspective.

This position, however, cannot be given unqualified support. In particular, we question its contention that paradigms are 'incommensurable'. Rather than advocate the hermetic sealing of systems theory or other discourses, we suggest that – as paradigms – they are ultimately pervious phenomena. We argue that seemingly incommensurable theoretical positions can be mediated, notably through recourse to language-game philosophy. Two tangible outcomes of this inquiry are a research methodology which employs a plurality of sociological paradigms and an epistemology which forms the basis for a postmodern approach to organizational analysis.

The 3 Ps – Positivism, Paradigms and Postmodernity

The structure of the book is as follows: In Chapter 1, we trace the orgins of systems theory in social science and document the influence of writers on

1

positivism and evolution, notably Auguste Comte, John Stuart Mill, Herbert Spencer and Emile Durkheim. The analysis shows how the social systems approach has recourse to metaphors that suggest conceptual parallels between societies and organisms. It is argued that positivist and evolutionary principles are translated into modern social theory through sociological functionalism and most importantly through the method known as structural-functionalism.

Having described the positivist and evolutionist roots of sociological functionalism, we illustrate in Chapter 2 how functionalist theory forms the basis for characterizing organizations as 'open systems'. In concert with renewed interest in Talcott Parsons' work, we detail the structural-functional approach to organizations. Thereafter we document how sociological functionalism was joined with general-systems theory to form an equilibrium model for organizational analysis, and how this approach attained an intellectual hegemony in organization theory for almost half a century. We outline finally how the systems metaphor came to direct research based on, *inter alia*, the human relations, socio-technical and contingency approaches to organizational analysis, and how it has formed the theoretical basis for best-selling textbooks on management and organization.

In Chapter 3, we argue that the power of the generic social systems approach has diminished as new paradigms for sociology and organization theory have emerged. We describe how the conceptual limitations of systems theory provided openings for the development of new perspectives. We then explain how the Kuhnian revolution which swept across sociology in the late 1960s and early 1970s found expression in organization theory during the late 1970s and 1980s. The development of new intellectual perspectives in organization theory thus gave rise to a community structure characterized by paradigm heterodoxy. The chapter documents the growth of crisis theory and paradigmism in social and organizational analysis and examines specific cases from this history.

Analysis of the paradigm concept continues in Chapter 4, but at a more philosophical level. The chapter assesses the correspondence between paradigm models and the philosophical principles upon which they are based. The discussion suggests that many attempts to describe community structure are based on a shallow reading of Kuhn. We also argue that the logic which underpins these attempts is ambiguous on the central issue of paradigm mediation. To develop a theory of paradigm mediation, we reject both Kuhn's (1962) 'strong' incommensurability thesis and Popper's (1970) notion of liberal transitions, in favour of a philosophy which holds absolutism and relativism in greater tension – Wittgenstein's (1953) 'everyday language-game' philosophy.

In Chapter 5, this argument forms the logical justification for an exploration of multiple paradigms in organizational research. We outline a research programme in which four paradigms – functionalism, phenomenology, critical theory and structuralism – form the basis for an empirical study of work organization. The aim is to develop a methodology that is compatible with the view that organization theory comprises a plurality of competing perspectives. Details of the fieldwork are given, research findings are presented, and the validity of the method is discussed.

The analysis of paradigm heterodoxy is brought to a close with discussion of a new approach to organizational analysis – postmodernism (Chapter 6). Initially we contrast modern and postmodern forms of explanation and explore a family of terms derived from these two concepts. In so doing, we discuss whether postmodernism is best described as an 'epoch' or an 'epistemology', a distinction which underpins current debates. Through reference to the works of Jean Baudrillard, Jacques Derrida and Jean-François Lyotard, we then produce an inventory of postmodern concepts for social theory. When combined with the distinction between epoch and epistemology, this inventory provides a framework for a nascent postmodern theory of organization.

1   Foundations of orthodoxy

Introduction

In this chapter we trace the origins of functionalism and systems theory in social science. We illustrate how the social systems approach draws inspiration from writings which suggest conceptual parallels between societies and organisms. The way is prepared for a deconstruction of this approach by establishing the foundations upon which its mode of theorizing rests.

To achieve this, we first examine the work of some of the founding fathers of social science. The majority of the chapter is devoted to an appreciation of the influence of Auguste Comte, John Stuart Mill, Herbert Spencer and Emile Durkheim on the development of social systems thinking. We document how this influence is derived mainly from their writings on principles of positivism and evolution.

At the end of the chapter we suggest that these principles are translated into modern social science through the approach known as structural-functionalism. It was through developments in sociological functionalism that an 'orthodoxy' of systems analysis was established in organization theory.

Founding fathers of social science

Our account of sociological orthodoxy begins with the antecedents of sociological positivism. Although elements of a positivist heritage can be found in the philosophy of the ancient Greeks, we begin where for many sociology itself begins, with the writings of Auguste Comte (1798–1857).

Auguste Comte

As students of sociology know, there are four things for which Comte is famous: he gave 'sociology' its name; he propounded sociological positivism; he placed sociology at the apex of a hierarchy of the sciences; and he developed the 'law of the three stages'. While each of these claims is a

4

topic for discussion in itself, we will content ourselves with the second of them, the view that Comte was a major figure in the development of a 'positive' approach to scientific knowledge. In the shadow of Henri de Saint-Simon (1760–1825) it was Comte who assembled a positivist philosophy of science founded upon principles of empirical certainty (Comte 1853, 1865).

Context

To place Comte's philosophy of science in context, we note that in the chaos and anarchy of post-Napoleonic Europe the desire for a new basis of intellectual and moral life saw the surety of scientific claims hold sway (Keat and Urry 1975). In particular, the problems facing an emergent industrial society were felt to be soluble through scientific analysis. In this milieu, Comte was to discover that the time was ripe for advancing the scientific study of society. He believed that social problems should be answered by reference to what was scientifically possible. The discovery of the 'laws of social physics', or 'sociology', would ensure that the processes of social change were ones which were scientifically inevitable (Aron 1968). The laws of social physics would reconcile order and progress, and the labouring classes, in particular, would become convinced of the rightful ethos of science and production. Social physics would be based upon established scientific methods of observation, experiment and comparison.

Theses

If we explore deeper into Comte's science we find that his arguments for positivism are founded on two main theses. The first is the suggestion that in 'abstract history' there is a progression in the development of the human mind from the theological, through the metaphysical, to the positive mode of thought.

The second thesis is that there is a hierarchy of sciences within which mathematics is placed at the bottom while sociology is at the top, with each science passing, sequentially, through the three phases: theological, metaphysical, positive. By describing these phases it becomes clear how the positive departs markedly from the other forms of knowing. It also becomes clear how Comte's ideal of a new science of sociology is based on positivist beliefs.

When we examine the 'law of the three stages', we find that the theological phase is one in which worldly phenomena are explained in terms of supernatural forces (for example, spirits or gods); in the metaphysical stage, in terms of abstract forces or personified entities; and in the positive stage, through the stating of normative, systematic and law-like relations between empirically observable data. Whereas in the first two phases inquiry centres upon implicit, unseen and underlying essences, in the last it focuses on explicit and open relations. Positive science is concerned only with what can be observed – with establishing law-like relations between observable phenomena through the accurate accumulation of empirical data. This is achieved by way of observing, experimenting, controlling and predicting. It is Comte's view that the closer a form of knowledge gets to the positive stage, the more general, simple and independent of other sciences it becomes (Keat and Urry 1975). As sociology is the most individual, complex and dependent of the sciences, Comte felt it would be the last to reach this phase.

Positivism

The crux of positivist inquiry is that we can only have true knowledge of explicit phenomena and the relations between them. Scientists should not make hypothetical inferences about the essence of the implicit structure of phenomena: they should instead identify phenomena which are systematically connected to one another by way of invariable and universal laws. Comte claimed that every systematic relation discovered between any two phenomena enables us both to explain them and foresee them, each by means of the other (Comte 1844, Aron 1968). Meaningful statements are ones which can be tested and possibily refuted. It is this quality which most clearly differentiates positivism from theology or metaphysics. We must construct hypotheses and test them against our observations. Scientific theories are generated from conjoining facts relating to observed phenomena in terms of regular theoretical sequences of their coexistence. For science, unobservable factors are at best only heuristic fictions; they may be of some use in modelling relationships, but the real issue is whether we can observe systematic connections.

Pragmatism

As well as advancing positivism, Comte also advanced pragmatism. For Comte the main strengths of positive science lay in its practical application: a prime criterion is that it should be of value in everyday affairs (Andreski 1974). Positivist knowledge is a practical and objective arbiter which must exercise control over both physical and social states. Positive science has the ability to influence changes in our basic beliefs of social organization. So deep is his commitment to pragmatism that he rejects, as metaphysical, work on the theory of probability, the structure of matter and the theory of evolution.

Method

In terms of method, Comte starts from the position that society is the fundamental reality: it is the social which is basic, given and real. In adopting this position Comte argues against any form of scientific reductionism. He claims that differing sciences concentrate their analyses at different phenomenal levels, and that each possesses its own independent character, arguing, for example, that there are distinct differences between the 'organic' and 'inorganic' sciences. In the simpler inorganic sciences the individual elements are much more familiar to us than the whole which they constitute; thus, we must proceed from the simple to the compound. However, the reverse is true in the study of man (biology) and society (sociology), where we must consider each element in the light of the whole (Andreski 1974). Therefore, while social physics takes recourse to other sciences – both for empirical data and methodology – it is not reducible to these other sciences. Comte resists any reduction of the social to some other level.

Comte and sociological orthodoxy

In Comte, therefore, we find an apostle of scientific rationality: he advocates 'reasoning and observation combining as the means of know-ledge' (Comte 1853, p. 1). Comte propounds a social theory in which scientific rationality is dominant; a positive approach which provides the key to human destiny and the one, absolute and valid society. His project is for a science of social physics – sociology – founded on models and methods from the natural sciences. It is a science which addresses itself to the discovery of laws explaining both the various elements of society – 'social statics' – and the manner in which they change through time – 'social dynamics'. In developing this analysis Comte highlights the link between biology, the study of man, and sociology, the study of society. Notable here is that biology marks a point of transition between the sciences: it marks the distinction between the organic and the inorganic, and places emphasis upon a systematic understanding of the totality of the living whole. In this analysis, Comte lays many of the foundations for the social systems approach in sociology and organization theory. His positivist method draws upon models from the natural sciences, and it uses both mechanical and organismic analogies to develop a systematic and holistic approach to social analysis.

John Stuart Mill

A second major figure in the development of sociological orthodoxy is John Stuart Mill (1806–73). Although Mill did not produce any sociological analysis himself, he is nevertheless important in that he wrote explicitly about the 'proper' character and methodology of social science.

Mill and Comte

Of particular interest to us is Mill's contact with Comte. As a young man, Mill was in close contact with Comte and the Saint-Simonians. He shared their belief that effective reform must be based upon a knowledge of the laws governing the concomitance and succession of social facts; that is, upon 'social statics' and 'social dynamics' (Keat and Urry 1975). Unlike Saint-Simon and Comte, however, Mill saw his task as primarily an intellectual one; of clearing away any archaic doctrines and inherited prejudices which might obstruct the course of progress. While the direction in which Mill hoped progress would be made differed from that of Comte and Saint-Simon, his belief that sociology offered a firm foundation for controlled progress remained undaunted (Thomas 1985). Although in *Auguste Comte and Positivism* (1866) we see Mill offering a critique of the Comtean system, this is a critique motivated by the belief that Comte had not lived up to his own positivist ideals.

Induction and deduction

At the heart of Mill's analysis lies the belief that nothing can be the object of knowledge except our direct experiences and what can be inferred from them. For Mill, such sense-experience yields a series of specific facts about discrete occurrences. He wished to create rules governing the logics of induction and deduction. For the former, we see rules of inductive inference, Mill's methods, from which we can infer general propositions from individual facts (Thomas 1985). Thereafter, rules of deductive inference are used to explain specific cases by deducing them from the laws and antecedent conditions. Mill claims that we can deduce lower-level laws from higher laws, and pragmatic policies from general principles. For Mill, as for many modern positivists, scientific progress is signalled by a reduction in the number of laws coupled with an increase in the number of phenomena which the laws can explain.

The principles of induction and deduction are in fact of generic applicability. Mill argues that all phenomena belong to a unitary natural world, and that the same forms of scientific procedures are appropriate throughout. In particular, for the study of man in society, Mill argues that a social science should be modelled upon the principles of Newtonian mechanics (Acton 1972). It is here that Mill's own reductive positivism is apparent, for he suggests that a social science should allow us to predict events in order that they can be judiciously controlled.

Mill also, and in contrast to Comte, takes an atomistic view of the world, this being most evident in his individualist interpretation of the social sciences. Mill believes that laws governing the behaviour of people in social interaction can be inferred from the laws which govern people away from society. As the basic atoms in society are individual people, it will be from the laws of psychology that the laws relating to social life can be deduced (Keat and Urry 1975). The law-like relations between social phenomena cannot be observed in any simple sense. The laws of psychology are, for both ontological and epistemological reasons, the only secure foundation for a social science. Mill's positivism advances a form of theoretical reductionism which we do not find in Comte.

Mill and sociological orthodoxy

Mill's work on methodology is central to the development of sociological orthodoxy. His criteria for what makes science 'scientific' have long been part of the intellectual toolkit for the social theorist. When Weber (1949) in *Methodology of the Social Sciences* confronts the question of whether sociology is a science, he is querying whether sociology can satisfy the conditions which Mill suggests a science should satisfy.

It was indeed Mill who gave concrete form to the demand that all sciences fit a similar pattern. He was a firm believer in the formal structuring of procedure and the uniformity of adequate explanations. Explanations, he felt, should fit one basic logical pattern; which involves the deduction of what is to be explained from the dual premises of one or more casual laws and the description of a series of primary conditions. No other forms are to be considered – either an explanation fits with this pattern or else it is incomplete. A discipline becomes more scientific as its laws become more general, cover a wide variety of eventualities and have fewer exceptions. In brief, disciplines become more scientific the closer their logical structures resemble that of Newtonian mechanics, which is the long-time scientific paradigm of the empiricists.

Herbert Spencer

A third figure whose ideas underpin the development of sociological orthodoxy is Herbert Spencer (1820–95). Although Spencer distances himself from Comte and the positivists – see for example his *Reasons for Dissenting from the Philosophy of A. Comte* (1864) – a closer look at his work reveals several affinities with positivism, notably in his analysis of evolution. It is these affinities which serve to make Spencer a landmark contributor to sociological orthodoxy, especially as he lays foundations for structural-functional analysis.

Themes

The two main themes of Spencer's work are his analysis of the organismic analogy and his processes of evolution (Goldthorpe 1969). It can be argued that in his writings on these topics we find a positivist at work.

In Spencer's development of organismic theory we find an analogy between the social body and the human organism. Spencer argues, however, that this is never a pure and direct analogy, an error he claims was made by both Plato and Hobbes. Instead, Spencer argues that there are simply some similarities in the development of animal and social organisms; in particular, both start as small aggregates and increase in mass, both develop a more complex infrastructure as they grow, and both see undifferentiated parts become progressively interdependent.

These analogies are a product of Spencer's concerns for the processes of evolution and their relevance for the study of societies. The origins of these interests lie in *A Theory of Population* (1852) in which he puts forward functionalist ideas on the development of human society. In an anticipation of Darwin's theory of natural selection (published six years later), Spencer describes how the principle of the 'survival of the fittest' is of paramount importance in the evolutionary process (Goldthorpe 1969).

Following a second and more thorough volume, *The Principles of Psychology* (1872), in which he extends this analysis to mental phenomena, Spencer takes evolutionism to its ultimate conclusion in *Progress: its Law and Cause* (1857). Spencer argues that the concept of evolution is of universal applicability: it is the key to conceptualizing all phenomena, whether inorganic, organic or 'superorganic' (i.e. social). He argues that the laws of the sciences can, in principle, be subsumed and unified under the one supreme law of 'evolution and dissolution' (Low-Beer 1969). This law offers a systematic, genetic account of the whole cosmos: 'an account of the transformation of things' and of 'the ultimate uniformities they represent'. Secular change can be accounted for through a process of increasing differentiation on the one hand and increasing integration on the other. Whereas unevolved structures are internally homogeneous, with parts cohering only loosely, evolved structures are heterogeneous, with their parts tightly knit. This is true, Spencer argues, whether the process under consideration is the formation of the earth out of a nebular mass, the evolution of the species, the embryological growth of an individual animal, or the development of human societies.

Societies and organisms

For sociological orthodoxy, the single most important aspect of Spencer's thesis is his concept of societies as 'superorganisms'. Spencer suggests that the evolution of societies is a process akin to the evolution of species. The object, however, is not simply to illustrate that the pattern of change is the same in the two cases – progressive differentiation and integration – but that such change is effected through analogous 'mechanisms'. While Spencer concedes that social change can result from a plethora of factors, his model of social evolution is based on immutable first principles: principles validated by the biology of his day.

The two major influences here are Lamarck and Darwin (Goldthorpe 1969). From Lamarckian theory, Spencer argues that within human societies we witness a process of continual and mutual interaction between the various institutions of social control and the characteristics of individuals. As such, the dynamic of societies is for them to become, by consensus, more integrated, even while the division of labour (differentiation) is increasing. In contrast, from the Darwinian extension of the 'survival of the fittest', Spencer underlines the part played in the evolution of societies by social conflict, and especially by war. In the formative stages of social evolution, warfare and conquest are of crucial importance both in the development of larger and more complex social systems, and in the strengthening of their internal cohesion.

Individual in society

The main thrust of Spencer's analysis, therefore, is to illustrate analogical similarities between society and the living organism. In particular, Spencer cites the functional interdependence within the living organism – in which there is an integration of functionally differentiated parts – as the basis for his model of society.

Spencer, however, is also an individualist, both in his belief that the free spontaneous development of the individual is a primary political and social goal, and in the view that the social world is explicable in terms of the beliefs and values of individual members of a given society. By suggesting that we should think of the elements of society – which correspond to the parts of the living body – as individual actors, Spencer is able to reconcile the functional organization of the whole with the primacy of the individual (Low-Beer 1969). Indeed, Spencer sees industrial society as comprising a population of private individuals who enter freely into mutually beneficial contracts, the consequence of which is a state of social and political consensus – a functional integration of differentiated parts which is enacted spontaneously (Keat and Urry 1975). Again, at the heart of Spencer's analysis is the metaphor of the organism rather than the mechanism. The model revolves around the notion of self-generated growth rather than artificial and external construction.

Positivism and the organic metaphor

We have suggested that Spencer's approach is a positivist one. To argue this, we must locate Spencer's organismic model of society within his general wish to establish the law-like regularities of social life which exist between empirically observable phenomena. It has been argued that the organismic model is chosen not because it will provide the means to describe the underlying mechanisms which produce observable regularities, but rather because the organismic metatheory produces a model of society as a set of law-like relations between observables. Indeed, Spencer regards this parallelism between organisms and society as 'scaffolding to help in building up a coherent body of sociological inductions' (Spencer 1893, p. 581, quoted in Keat and Urry 1975, p. 80). When we finally remove this scaffolding the general law-like relations will stand alone to be judged against empirical observations.

Positivism and evolution

We have also said that positivism is at the heart of Spencer's theory of evolution. Spencer argues that with evolution he has developed a new philosophy based upon scientific fact and inductive procedure (Goldthorpe 1969). For Spencer, evolution represents a unique process which can be seen in all elements of nature, a process of specialization of function (progressive differentiation) combined with mutual interdependence of structurally differentiated parts (progressive integration). Spencer's positivism aims to show how social phenomena are representations of the general laws of evolution; he wishes to show how evolution is a universal quality of existence which can be deduced from observations and he is, therefore, not concerned with articulating the underlying causal mechanisms driving species changes. The theory of evolution is based upon the observation, classification and ordering of facts relating to different species (Low-Beer 1969). Although for evolution in nature we can only observe the ontogenetic process of differentation and integration (egg to adult), in analysing social evolution we have records and actual experiences of phylogenetic development (species to species). Indeed, in the latter we are better able to ground our model upon observations of formal process.

Spencer and sociological orthodoxy

To summarize Spencer's contribution to sociological orthodoxy, we can say that it rests chiefly upon his input to the development of structural-functional forms of analysis. It is Spencer who first systematically employs the terms 'structure' and 'function' in ways approximating to current sociological usage. Spencer's development of biological analogies enables him to produce organic conceptions of society in a sophisticated way. It is Spencer who develops the notion of society as a self-regulating 'system'. This system should be understood through the study of its constituent parts and their patterns of interdependence, and through analysis of the contributions which each part makes towards the maintenance of the whole.

It can be argued, therefore, that Spencer's work anticipates sociological functionalism, for his theorizing emphasizes key axioms of the functionalist position. Spencer does not simply suggest that institutions are related: he goes further to argue that some institutional forms have a tendency to co-exist from society to society. Spencer not only reformulates the concept of societies as systems, but also directs us to the problems of understanding the limited ways in which societies can be patterned.

Linked to this concept of the patterning of social structures is Spencer's emphasis on the degree of 'resistance' such structures can exhibit when faced with attempts to induce change. Spencer suggests that if we can develop a science of society, and thus if social phenomena conform to 'laws' then it must follow that men and women cannot shape society entirely according to their own desires. There will always be barriers to what can be accomplished in any given phase of a society's evolution – the 'laws' of social development.

Spencer, however, avoids being ensnared by his model into a completely 'necessitarian' position – which would assert the futility of attempts at conscious social change. He argues, instead, that as institutions change the nature of individuals, so individuals in turn seek to mould institutions into closer conformity with their evolving needs. In this he is assisted by the fact that voluntarist action is incorporated into the Lamarckian aspects of his evolutionism.

Emile Durkheim

Our final landmark contributor to sociological orthodoxy is Emile Durkheim (1858–1917). Although in many ways a critic of the writings of Comte, Mill and Spencer, Durkheim was also deeply influenced by them. This is evident in his adoption of the Comtean notion of an external social reality which is capable of being investigated.

Positivism and sociological method

Apart from some epistemological oscillations in his later works – notably in *The Elementary Forms of Religious Life* (1915) where he focuses on the dialectic of the personal and the social – Durkheim's methodological position remains a straightforward positivist one. If we consult his *Rules of Sociological Method* (1938), *The Division of Labour in Society* (1947) and *Suicide* (1951) we find a thorough positivist at work. Durkheim considers himself a 'scientific rationalist', and cites as his goal the extension to the study of human behaviour of methods and procedures from the natural sciences. For Durkheim, the natural sciences are successful because they establish clear law-like relations of cause and effect, and he feels that social science should be concerned, similarly, with establishing law-like relations for social behaviour (Giddens 1978). Durkheim, in fact, believes that in time sociology will advance to the level that social theory governs practice: sociology will provide the rules of action for the future. For Durkheim, this position has not been arrived at, however, because of the inadequacies of sociological research activity. Indeed, a major problem has been the willingness of professional sociologists to develop complex systems and philosophies while at the same time neglecting the development of a body of well-established empirical findings about social phenomena. Durkheim feels that only by developing such a body of knowledge will sociology begin to address the task of integrating the existing social sciences into a ('synthesizing') science of society (Lukes 1973).

Social facts

Whereas Durkheim generally plays down the importance of philosophical doctrines, he feels that in Comte's 'positivist metaphysics' we have some epistemological foundations for a science of society. Although Durkheim notes that Comte failed to produce any formal sociological analysis, he argues that he identified the 'proper' method for the study of the social.

Similarly, for Durkheim, Spencer's contribution lies in his powerful organic analogy. This analogy compensates for his naive methodological individualism and his extravagent attempt to verify the grand law of evolution.

Durkheim feels, however, that neither Comte nor Spencer is sufficiently positivist when approaching social science. Recognizing this failing, Durkheim sees his own task as giving sociology 'a method and a body', and in particular of developing a 'scientific' method for discovering social 'facts'. Durkheim is consequently very self-conscious about the correctness of procedure, especially with regard to the definition and classification of phenomena. His methodology emphasizes the role of the social scientist as the passive receiver of sense impressions. Durkheim argues that the sociologist should define a phenomenon in terms of clearly visible external criteria for distinguishing membership of one class from another, for he feels that reality will yield itself to us in a direct and unproblematic way (Aron 1970). Durkheim argues that all which is subject to observation has the character of a 'thing', and that such observations form the basis for scientific analysis. His argument is that we should define a phenomenon in terms of external characteristics which class together the instances of the phenomenon under study. These instances will be produced by a single cause, it being the single cause which provides the essence of a phenomenon. Durkheim thus seeks to discover through Millian causes the essences of phenomena. The external facts which he takes as indices of internal facts are the sets of legal rules in a society (Lukes 1973). Durkheim argues that by looking at externally observable laws we can discern the nature of the underlying moral rules of a society and thus the basis of its social order or 'solidarity'.

Social trends

For establishing a 'body' for sociology, Durkheim is concerned primarily with the analysis of those social trends which form the basis for solidarity. Durkheim is concerned with obligations, contracts, duties and customs, the external social facts which constrain and regulate behaviour (Giddens 1978). When we confine ourselves to analysing such facts we are, he feels, truly studying 'society'. Durkheim emphasizes how individuals are often constrained by external facts which are vague and difficult to study. If we are analysing the legal determinants of human behaviour we have hard data (for example, written legal codes) ready at hand: yet if we wish to study, for example, the effects of a crowd on its members then it is not so obvious what form of evidence we should seek (Rex 1969).

For Durkheim, the analysis of social trends represents one of the major objectives for a science of society. He argues that if a social fact has no unique and observable existence of its own, then it is the sociologist's job to supply it with one. This is to be accomplished through discovering statistical rates which should be taken not merely as a counting of separate individual instances, but as indices of social currents.

The empirical application of this methodology forms the basis for two of Durkheim's greatest volumes: *The Division of Labour in Society* and *Suicide*. The latter is indeed the paradigm case of Durkheim's positivism: it remains the exemplar of the sociological application of statistics. The methodology Durkheim develops in *Suicide* suggests that by contrasting statistical rates for a phenomenon for differing social groups we are able to discover the specifically social nature of variations in the rate. From his discoveries on suicide Durkheim was able to draw his theoretical conclusions, which rest upon empirically tested, and thus retestable, hypotheses. Although today we may wish to reject some of his conclusions, his method and his hypotheses remain influential.

Durkheim and sociological orthodoxy

Although, outside France, Durkheim's ideas made little headway until the 1930s, from that point onwards they have influenced crucially the methodological basis of the discipline of sociology.

In the 1930s, in particular, two social anthropologists, Bronislaw Malinowski and A. R. Radcliffe-Brown, turned to Durkheim for developing the theoretical foundations of the functionalist method, a method which was developed into a dominant mode of analysis in both anthropology and sociology.

However, the main impact of Durkheim's ideas came when they were explored in detail by two major figures of modern sociology, Talcott Parsons and Robert Merton. Parsons, in particular, not only developed a brilliant analysis of the theoretical advances presented by Durkheim's approach, but also drew upon Durkheim in advancing the approach to social analysis which was to become the dominant paradigm for the discipline, that of 'structural-functionalism'.

Positivism, functionalism and social systems theory

We have examined those aspects of the works of Comte, Mill, Spencer and Durkheim which underpin the development of a systems-theory orthodoxy in organizational analysis. In Comte we see the most potent of modern influences, especially in his recommendation that sociology should examine the coexistence of social phenomena. At the heart of this recommendation lies the idea that the beliefs and values of a society are interconnected as a whole. The corollary is that in developing a method for explaining the essence of any one element we discover laws which prescribe how that element coexists with all others. For Comte, this method is the basis for developing a grand 'positive' scheme for planning the reconstruction of society, a scheme which specifies the combinations of social elements which are viable pragmatically. This positive approach will provide the key to human destiny, the key to the one valid form of society. The vision is of a world in which scientific rationality forms the basis for the regulation of social order. For this, the discipline base lies in sociology, a science of society based on models and methods from the natural sciences. Sociology will discover the scientific laws that explain the relations between parts of society.

This stress on a unitary, natural world-system, a totality in which all parts relate to a whole, is also seen in the writings of Spencer. It is Spencer who not only draws functional analogies between the processes of organisms and societies, but who also shows how sociology will analyse the structure of societies in order to identify how each part contributes to the functioning of the whole. Spencer develops an evolutionary typology of societies. He suggests that societies, like organisms, exhibit varying degrees of structural complexity, which can be measured in terms of the number of different forms of items of which the structure is composed. If a structure consists of a number of like items then each will tend towards self-sufficiency. However, if it consists of a number of disparate items, where the structure is internally differentiated, then it will display a greater degree of interdependence between parts. Spencer's argument is that greater differentiation of structure makes for greater integration of the whole, which in turn makes the structure more able to survive by reducing internal disharmony. In Spencer, therefore, we see the foundations of the analysis of social phenomena in terms of 'structure and function'. Society is a self-regulating system which can be understood through analysis of its various organs and the ways in which they are related.

Most recent functionalist thinking, however, owes more to Durkheim than Spencer. We have noted that, like Spencer, Durkheim was influenced strongly by biological thinking and particularly the concept of the structuration of function.

Durkheim though is also a methodologist. In particular, he believes that causal analysis is required in addition to functional analysis. Whilst, like Comte and Spencer, Durkheim borrows freely from the natural sciences, he wishes to advance not only an holistic methodology which distinguishes between overt functions and structures, but also one which explains less visible social phenomena, such as social trends. Durkheim argues that sociology should concern itself with understanding the 'collective conscience', or how the social is founded on shared values, norms and beliefs. In industrial society, with its extensive division of labour (functional differentiation), Durkheim sees an earlier 'mechanical solidarity', based on similarity of parts, being replaced by an 'organic solidarity' arising from interdependence of parts. The latter is a solidarity based on a normative belief system.

Through the above analysis, we can appreciate how the development of sociological positivism influenced the development of a sociological orthodoxy of systems analysis. We see emphasis on developing a true science of society, a science which, through controlled study, will yield law-like relations between social phenomena (the 'laws of social physics'). We also see the refinement of principles of induction and deduction, and the development of logical procedures for observation, experimentation and prediction. This scientific approach emphasizes direct experience of an external social reality, a concrete reality which lends itself to rational, empirical analysis. The aim of such analysis is to discover the motives for integration and solidarity – the motors of social order. Explanations emerge from many quarters, but notably via analogies from Darwinian biology and Newtonian mechanics. In particular, organismic analogies, based upon the holistic interdependence of living parts, are paramount. These analogies stress systems relations, and centrally the integration and differentiation of structures and functions.

Finally, for modern social science these principles, and especially the organic analogy, make their impact through the style of analysis commonly referred to as structural-functionalism. In structural-functionalism we witness the logical conclusion to the development of 'social physics'. This approach, which until the mid-1960s represented virtually a paradigm for sociology, incorporates concerns for holism, the interrelationships of parts, and the biological analogy within an overall mission to resolve the problem of social order. In Chapter 2, we discover how structural-functionalism operationalizes a 'systematic' approach to social analysis, a methodology for discerning the laws of functional relationships within a concrete social reality.

Conclusions

The aim of this chapter has been to prepare the ground for an analysis of the systems theory perspective on organizations by documenting the main influences on its mode of theorizing. In so doing, the works of several of the founding fathers of sociology have been assessed, and the assumptions and philosophies which underpin their positions have been described. The analysis has shown how the works of Comte, Mill, Spencer and Durkheim all influence the social systems approach, notably through the development of the principles of positivism and functionalism. We also noted how, for social science, the logical conclusion to this intellectual heritage is the development of structural-functionalist sociology. Overall we have seen how a systems approach draws conceptual parallels between societies and organisms, and accepts the view that the parts of society function in ways which contribute to the maintenance of the whole.

2 The hegemony of systems

Introduction

Having described how functionalism in social science has its roots in the writings of Comte, Mill, Spencer and Durkheim, we now illustrate how this approach offers a basis for characterizing organizations as 'open systems'.

We start by noting how functionalist thinking became influential in anthropology and sociology. Thereafter we describe how sociological functionalism was joined with general-systems theory to form a generic systems model for organizational analysis. Finally, we argue that the systems approach attained an intellectual hegemony in organizational theory for almost half a century, mainly through professing a prior claim to empirical explanation.

From this analysis, we see how the systems metaphor underpins the human relations, socio-technical and contingency theories of organization, and informs popular textbooks on business and management.

Functionalism in social science

We have outlined the contributions made to functionalist sociology by the founding fathers of social science. We note, however, that none of them uses the term 'functionalist' to characterize the philosophy of their own work. Instead the origins of an explicitly functionalist approach to social science lie in anthropology, and particularly in the works of Bronislaw Malinowski and A. R. Radcliffe-Brown.

Malinowski

It was Bronislaw Malinowski (1884–1942) who first developed a distinctly functionalist approach to social analysis (see Malinowski 1944). Malinowski suggests that the novel characteristics of a primitive society can be explained in terms of their function within that social system. He states that societies are complex wholes which should be comprehended in terms of the relationships between their constituent parts and the physical environment.

It is argued that to understand a cultural fact we must reference it both to general principles of social conduct and to those features in a society which provide the context within which it is located. In what he calls the functional analysis of culture, Malinowski contends that particular languages, religions or economies be evaluated in their own terms; that is, in respect of the functions they perform for that particular 'integral system of culture'.

If, for example, we wish to understand why a Trobriand man makes payments in kind to his sister's husband, we need to know not only the general principles of exchange which govern all societies, but also that Trobriand society is a matrilineal one (see Malinowski 1932). In Trobriand society, a man is succeeded by his sister's son, it being his sister who provides him with heirs. The said payments signify that women and their children have an interest in the property of the matrilineage.

In his time, Malinowski confronted the prevailing orthodoxy in anthropology, especially when arguing for systematic fieldwork, rather then armchair theorizing, as the basis for knowledge (Jarvie 1964). He suggested that only by gaining first-hand experience can we begin to make authoritative claims to understand primitive societies as systems of culture, a practice he feels is superior to offering historical and evolutionist conjectures. For Malinowski, the latter practice only 'tears items from their wider context'; it does violence to meaning (Cohen 1968). He argues that this functionalist form of analysis not only offers concrete descriptions of how primitive societies are structured, but also helps us dispense with speculations about stages of social development and evolution.

Radcliffe-Brown

While in Malinowski we see the origins of a functionalist approach to social analysis, it is in the work of A. R. Radcliffe-Brown (1881–1955) that the approach was developed into a distinctive form of explanation. Although rejecting claims that his approach should be described as 'functionalist', on constructing the concept of function in terms of analogies between social and organic life Radcliffe-Brown develops a doctrine which is in many ways similar to Malinowski's. In particular, like Malinowski, he eschews evolutionism and diffusionism, as instead he explains societies in the 'here and now'.

Radcliffe-Brown's functionalism is in fact analytically more sophisticated than Malinowski's. He draws upon social theory, and specifically upon Durkheim's work, to establish parallels between biological organisms and societies. Following Durkheim, Radcliffe-Brown argues that the nature of cultural phenomena can only be explained in social terms. His basic assumptions are Durkheimian ones, especially the claims that for societies to survive there must be some minimal solidarity between members (the function of social phenomena being to create social solidarity or to sustain the institutions which manage it), some minimal consistency in the relationship between parts of a social system, and some minimal structural features evident, with various practices being related to these in such a way as to contribute to their maintenance.

Radcliffe-Brown also suggests that the concept of function involves the assumption that there are necessary conditions of existence for human societies. Expanding the organic analogy, he argues that societies should be conceived of as structures whose dynamic is continuity. The difference between social and animal organisms lies in the concept of 'life cycle'. In normal circumstances societies do not die in the same way as organisms. Instead, the on-going life of a society is conceptualized in the 'functioning of its social structure'. Indeed, it is here that the notion of structural-functionalism emerges. As Radcliffe-Brown (1952) argues, the concept of function 'involves the notion of a structure consisting of a set of relations amongst unit entities, the continuity of the structure being maintained by life-processes made up of the activities of the constituent units' (p. 180). Thus, for Radcliffe-Brown, social phenomena should be explained in terms of their survival and continuity. Institutions are distinguished by their contributions to the integration, stability and maintenance of the social system as a whole.

Functionalism and sociology

While a structural-functionalist style of social analysis is evident in the works of Malinowski and Radcliffe-Brown, it is within the writings of the American sociologist Talcott Parsons that a definitive statement of sociological functionalism is found. Indeed, it is fair to say that Parsons is *the* structural-functionalist sociologist. Many of the principles and concepts he develops form axioms for an orthodoxy of functionalist sociology.

The work of Talcott Parsons

Above all else, Talcott Parsons (1902–79) is remembered for his attempt to construct a general-systems theory for analysing the social world. Parsons is indeed a 'grand' theorist, and in his first major work, *The Structure of Social Action* (1937), he attempts to develop a social theory capable of explaining all social life. In this work, his 'voluntaristic theory' of social action, he attempts to elucidate what he sees as the great convergence in social theory, that between Durkheim, Marshall, Pareto and Weber. In so doing, he wishes to provide a solution to 'the Hobbesian problem of order' by locating the motives of social action in normative aspects of social life. Here action is not free; it is, instead, grounded in and circumscribed by normative principles of action, that is, by 'values'.

The social system

While *The Structure of Social Action* is dominated by Weberian concerns, by the time of Parsons' second major work, *The Social System* (1951), it is the systems theory of Pareto which consumes the analysis. In the years between these two volumes Parsons gave increasing weight to the normative structure of 'the system', and thus *The Social System* is an attempt 'to carry out Pareto's intuition' (1951, p. vii).

In this work, Parsons takes as his point of departure the system as a whole and analyses the conditions necessary for its functioning, evolution and survival. For Parsons, the term 'function' refers to the various solutions a system must adopt in order to survive. As such, functional analysis concerns the classification of adaptation problems, and it is this task which leads Parsons to his notion of 'functional imperatives', or the actions which must be performed if a society is to survive.

The AGIL model

In *The Social System*, Parsons identifies the four functional imperatives which must be satisfied if social equilibrium is to be realized. These imperatives, which form the basis for his famous 'AGIL' model, are 'Adaptation', the acts which establish relations between system and environment; 'Goal Attainment', the acts which define the system's goals and mobilize resources to obtain goals; 'Integration', the acts which establish control and maintain coordination between parts; and 'Latency' (or 'pattern maintenance'), the acts which supply actors with the necessary motivation. In operationalizing this scheme, Parsons claims it is possible to integrate personality systems into cultural systems, and in turn cultural systems into the social system. Through this, he claims that much of the Hobbesian problem of order is resolved. The various motivations that exist in society can be integrated into an ordered model of the social system, with this process being contextualized through the medium of the 'central value system'.

The central value system

The concept of the central value system suggests that sub-systems possess shared orientations towards action: each sub-system 'functions' by striving toward the common goal. It is the central value system which Parsons feels is the basis for social integration, for it regulates the wider society by defining its social values and normative expectations. This notion implies that role relationships develop on the basis of shared expectations about the behaviour and attitudes of other individuals. Without this concept, Parsons feels that the attribution of functions to system parts would be impossible. To study the processes that exist in society we must first understand the values that determine the normative behaviour underlying those processes.

Parsons and sociological orthodoxy

Parsons' work is central to the development of the systems orthodoxy in sociological theory. For Parsons, the main task of sociology is to analyse society as a system of functionally interdependent variables. In line with a general systems approach, he suggests that the study of any social process is a study of 'boundary maintenance'. Parsons not only constructs a theory for the functional analysis of each social system, but also elaborates a set of functional prerequisites for the necessary operations of each system. These relate not only to the social system, but also to the personalities of individual actors. Every social system must cater for the needs of its members if it is to survive, and every system must possess certain central values which limit the range within which norms can develop. If the system fails in this, it is unlikely that individual personalities will internalize the need to conform. Every system must possess institutional means for ensuring that failures in organization are remedial. These institutional structures must be compatible with one another.

Functionalism and organization theory

Having described the impact of Parsons' functionalism on modern social theory, we now argue that although relatively little of his work is devoted specifically to organizations, nevertheless, he remains a major influence upon the social systems approach to the field.

Parsons on organizations

Parsons' contribution to a systems analysis of organizations is found in two theoretical articles in the inaugural volume of the *Administrative Science Quarterly* (1956), and in some remarks on the internal processes of organizations in his book *Structure and Process in Modern Societies* (1960).

In the former, he constructs a theory of organization on the basis of the principles laid down in *The Social System* (1951). Parsons defines organization in functionalist terms, and suggests that 'primacy of orientation to the attainment of a specific goal is the defining characteristic of an organization' (1956, p. 63). This analysis highlights both the wide variation in sub-unit goal-orientations and the numerous ways in which sub-units adapt to changing environments.

Parsons views organizations as systems both in their own right and as constituent parts of larger systems. He suggests that while organizations are sub-units of larger environments, they themselves possess several layers of, for example, individuals, groups and departments. The basic problem for organizations is to integrate, both vertically and horizontally, the functions which operate at different levels. This reductionism is justified on the basis that organizations possess many of the characteristics of social systems in general.

When we conduct analysis at the organizational level, Parsons feels we gain an exceptionally clear picture of social system properties. Indeed his thesis of the goal-directedness of social systems is undoubtedly more accessible when offered at the tangible level of the organization. Similarly, his analysis of the hierarchical relations and structures of modern societies achieves greater clarity when reduced to the more concrete level of the formal institution.

Systems analysis

As organizations are situated at the cultural/institutional level, the corollary, for Parsons, is that the systems analyst should determine the goals and values of formal organizations. The initial concern must be to determine the values associated with differentiated functional contexts for, in line with the concept of the central value system, organization goals must be legitimated by organizational values, which in turn must be consistent with societal values. Organizational goals will be judged according to whether they make a legitimate contribution to the functional requirements of the total social system. While the organization must federate its goals with those of the sub-systems which comprise the organization, its own goals must, in turn, federate with those of the wider system. Only when values and normative patterns are congruent are they able to regulate the processes through which the functional needs of the system are satisfied. It is indeed these processes which are at the heart of Parsons' analysis in *The Social System*.

AGIL and organization

We noted earlier how in *The Social System* Parsons outlines four functional problems which have to be solved for a system to survive. These problems concern the capacity to adapt, to attain goals, to integrate parts of the system, and to provide latency or pattern maintenance (i.e. motivation to maintain the central value system). If we examine these four problems in terms of system dynamics we find that adaptation and goal attainment are the most commercial in orientation, because they concern the ways in which the system relates to its environment. In contrast, integration and latency concern the internal operation of the system and are oriented toward maintaining functional stability.

On relating these problems to the analysis of organizations, we discover that the problem of adaptation is one of ensuring that an organization obtains the necessary resources to function adequately. These resources include human as well as material inputs. The adaptation problem is one which refers also to the normative patterns which regulate resource acquisition.

In contrast, goal attainment concerns the way the organization mobilizes its resources once secured. This process must be effected in a way which ensures that organizational goals can be achieved. In so doing, major institutional-level decisions are made and the organization's power structure is reproduced.

The remaining functional problems, integration and latency, find less explicit treatment in Parsons' analysis of organizations. This is a reflection of the fact that in the *Administrative Science Quarterly* articles Parsons places greater emphasis on the relations between system and environment – on the boundary exchanges of higher and lower order systems – than on the internal operating of systems.

These functional problems subsequently form the basis for Parsons' attempt to construct an organizational typology. Parsons argues that organizations can be classified according to the type of goals they pursue, or, put another way, the functions they perform for the higher order system, in this case, society. Parsons differentiates between economic organizations (adaptation problem), political organizations (goal attainment problem), integrative organizations (control problem) and pattern maintenance organizations (motivation problem). He argues that we must not only consider how organizations are differentiated at the system level, through being specialized to process one or other of these functional problems, but also how their internal functioning sees four separate sub-systems dedicated to processing four functionally related requirements.

Internal structures and processes

In his later *Structure and Process in Modern Societies* (1960) Parsons devotes more attention to the internal functioning of organizations. This he achieves through the differentiation of three sub-unit levels: the technical, managerial and institutional. The analysis here is directed against the formal principles of hierarchy associated with Weber's work. Parsons argues that defining organizations in terms of fixed pyramids of influence and authority is too simple an approach to take. He suggests that there are qualitative breaks in the line-structure and that when identified we can see these in terms of the technical, managerial and institutional levels.

Parsons describes the technical level as the basic level at which the work is organized. This is the level at which the general goals of the organization are translated into actions appropriate to their accomplishment. It is a matter of the processing of both people and materials, with the main constraint at this level being the functioning of the technology.

The managerial level is, by definition, concerned with the administering of the organization. Its function is to obtain the resources required by the technical level, and to act as an intermediary between the technical system and the organization's clients. In concrete terms, we are talking about the actions of administrators, managers and executives.

Finally, Parsons argues that every organization engages in activities which functional for society as a whole – the necessary integration of goals and the central value system. Thus, at the institutional level we witness attempts to ensure concord and uniformity between the organization and the wider social system. The institutional level is able to mediate between both the technical and managerial levels and the wider society; its role is to integrate the organization with its environment.

Structure and Process in Modern Societies, therefore, although still fairly abstract and general, represents a more tangible account of organizational processes from the Parsonian perspective. In particular, it offers an assessment of the internal structures of the organization and outlines many problems of integrating the organization with its environment. In so doing, Parsons succeeds in defining some of the main research foci for an open systems approach to organization analysis.

Robert Merton and Philip Selznick

We have noted that Parsons is generally regarded as the central figure in the development of structural-functionalist ideas. Several other writers, however, have also made important contributions to the development of a structural-functionalist approach to organizational analysis. Two figures who stand out in this respect are Robert Merton and Philip Selznick.

Merton From Robert Merton's work, we find that not all functionalists develop 'grand' theories in which all components and their interrelations are traced to the wider social system. His 'theories of the middle range' attempt to explain the consequences of one institutional level for another, yet avoid the problems of assuming an organic analogy in all natural systems (see Merton 1949).

Merton constructs his middle-range theories by introducing three new concepts to the functionalist perspective: 'dysfunctions' (in contrast to functions), 'latent' or unintended functions (in contrast to manifest ones) and 'functional alternatives' (in contrast to the conservative notion that because a social system is working successfully, it could not work just as well or even better with a different pattern of relationships) (Silverman 1970).

These concerns are applied to organizations in his article 'Bureaucratic Structure and Personality' (1940), in which he shows how changes can occur in the personality of employees simply through the impact of features of organization structure (Clegg and Dunkerley 1980). Merton develops this analysis through a set of sequential propositions which suggest that: members at the top of the organization always make demands for control of the organization; these demands result in an emphasis on reliable behaviour on the part of organization members; this explains the desire for accountability and predictability in organizations; and, to achieve predictability, formal methods for establishing control are introduced through techniques of scientific management and classical administrative theory (see March and Simon 1958).

The crux of this analysis is Merton's description of three particular consequences of this overemphasis on reliability and predictability. First, he notes how personal relationships are reduced. Bureaucratic actors are considered as role incumbents rather than individuals with personalities. They become the objects of organization, not the subjects. Second, he notes how the rules of the organization can become overinternalized by organization members. Although rules are designed to achieve the organization's goals, they can often develop into phenomena which are prized independently of this objective. Merton talks of 'goal displacement', and suggests that when rules take on an instrumental value of their own we encounter undesirable and unanticipated social consequences. And third, Merton suggests that in the drive for predictability we transform categorization into a decision-making technique. We witness a form of decision-making myopia in which, as categories become restricted, we fail to explore the full search-potential of problem-solving activity.

Merton suggests, therefore, that although these processes make actors' behaviour more predictable, they also make it more rigid. There is a tendency for organization members to develop a defensive culture in which it is normative to use rules as a barrier against outside threats and pressures.

Although such rule-bound behaviour satisfies the organization's demand for reliability, this normative defensiveness sees an increase in difficulty with clients. Merton thus illustrates how the consequences of action may be in conflict with the manifest intentions.

Selznick Merton's work is often coupled with that of another functionalist sociologist, Philip Selznick. In the latter's work, however, we find a different emphasis, for as March and Simon (1958) point out, while Merton places emphasis on the demand for control within organizations, Selznick stresses the delegation of authority. Nevertheless, Selznick's aims are essentially similar to Merton's, in that Selznick wishes to illustrate how delegation, like the demand for control, can give rise to unanticipated consequences.

If we consult an early paper by Selznick (1943), we find that his is a systems analysis: it can be reduced to a series of systems propositions about the consequences of delegation. In this work, Selznick suggests that when delegation occurs in organizations, it tends to bring with it an increase in the amount of training in specialized competences. Delegation leads to departmentalization and increases the bifurcation of interests lower in the organization. Such bifurcation can lead to greater conflict among sub-units so that the content of decisions depends upon the internal strategy being pursued. This is especially so if the overall goals of the organization have not been internalized by its members. As differences between the organization's goals and the sub-units' achievements increase, further delegation results (see March and Simon 1958, p. 43).

Selznick developed these ideas in a subsequent theoretical paper (Selznick 1948) and in a book based on empirical work, *TVA and the Grass Roots* (1949). It is especially in the latter that Selznick develops a structural-functionalist framework for organizational analysis. Indeed, for many, this work represents the earliest systematic attempt to develop a functionalist perspective to the study of organizations.

In the study of the Tennessee Valley Authority (TVA), Selznick embarks upon a theoretical systems course by using the 'needs' of the organization as his basic conceptual tool. He argues that every organization has a specific set of needs which have to be satisfied in order for it to survive. However, in the process of satisfying these needs, Selznick recognizes that there may be some resistance or 'recalcitrance' from within the organization. Selznick argues that organization members tend to be recalcitrant because of the diverse roles they occupy, only one of which is an organizational role. Recalcitrance, though, is also witnessed at the institutional level, due to the fact that the organization has to deal with other elements in its environment in terms of the general rather than the specific. As the general has little chance of covering all contingencies and situations, the position may be that the organization is faced with a hostile environment as well as friction from within. One way the organization may resolve this problem is by referring constantly to its legitimacy. For the organization to survive, the kind of response it receives will be of paramount importance.

At the time that Selznick was conducting this study the Tennessee Valley Authority had a particularly positive and high profile image: it was regarded as a symbol and product of Roosevelt's 'New Deal' policy and thus, as a model of democratic organization. Drawing upon Robert Michels' work, Selznick's study exposes the bureaucratic oligarchy beneath the democratic ideal. At the heart of Selznick's analysis is Michels' concept that all organizations are shaped by influences which are tangential to their ordered structures and stated goals. Also, after Pareto, Selznick illustrates how the formal aspects of organization never succeed in conquering the non-rational aspects of human behaviour. This is demonstrated through an in-depth analysis of administrative processes both within the organization and in its relations with the environment. Above all, he illustrates not only how the delegation of authority leads to specialization within increasingly limited spheres of action, but also how groups of individuals become oriented to narrow sub-goals associated with these specialized interests. The logic of the bureaucratic division of labour is of a progression toward operational goals which are in conflict with each other and which thus detract from the overall purposes of the organization as a system. *Esprit de corps*, for example, becomes a medium which generates unintended consequences. The battle for control which emanates from these conflicts of loyalty is seen to further the division of organization and commitment to sub-unit goals and ideologies. As in Merton's analysis, dysfunctional consequences are found to be cumulative and self-perpetuating; they become implanted increasingly within the logic of the organization, the result being a continuing diversion from its formal goals.

Selznick's work is important, therefore, in suggesting that structural-functionalism represents a superior analytical perspective for understanding the adaptive processes of organizations. Selznick develops a theory of organizations based upon the analogy of the biological organism rather than the Paretian mechanical equilibrium model, which had characterized earlier theories (see below, pp. 33–8). His analysis turns on how the organization must satisfy the organic needs of stability and goal-attainment and how this is effected through defensive action. Like other functionalist writers, Selznick sees organizations as attempting to adjust constantly to their environment, and thus to be in organic equilibrium with it. He notes, however, that there may be both functional and dysfunctional results from such action. In particular, there will be functional alternatives in situations where needs cannot be met in accordance with the organization's central values.

Merton and Selznick compared In our examination of the work of Merton and Selznick we have seen that while these writers develop systems analyses, they are less concerned with explaining the interdependence of social systems than forms of disequilibrium. Merton focuses upon the dysfunctional effects of rules as a means of bureaucratic control and Selznick upon the dysfunctional consequences of delegation and specialization.

From this point on, however, their analyses diverge. Selznick suggests an organic model of organization based on the pervasiveness of needs and the process of adapting to the external environment. The problem for the organization is to find ways of limiting the potentially destructive influence of bureaucratic dysfunctions, which Selznick suggests can be achieved through 'ideology' and 'cooption' (Burrell and Morgan 1979). In focusing on issues of needs, adaptation and survival, Selznick, far more than Merton, offers a structural-functional analysis of organizations.

The generic systems approach

While in a direct sense the impact of structural-functionalism on organizational analysis was relatively short-lived, the classic example being the TVA study, it influenced centrally an emerging generic systems perspective, especially through the development of organic or 'open' systems analogies.

In the late 1950s, many functionalist models appeared in new, organizational guises, with several structural-functional scholars writing as 'open systems' analysts of organization (Burrell and Morgan 1979). Writers who had developed equilibrium models in sociology recast their analyses within an open systems approach to administration. Mayntz (1964) argues that this transference of mainstream social systems theory to the field of organizations proved decisive for the development of an administrative science orthodoxy.

The generic systems perspective on organizations emerged from the joining of concepts from structural-functionalism with those of another popular movement, general-systems theory, the origins of which lie in biology and physics. Structural-functionalism, on the one hand, stresses the similarity between biological and social structures. Social institutions, like living organisms, are assumed to have needs for survival and adaptation which they satisfy by means of a particular pattern of interdependence between parts. Presented as 'natural systems', formal organizations comprise an interrelated series of processes. It is upon these interrelation-ships and processes, rather than constituent sub-systems, that the focus of study should rest.

On the other hand, general-systems theory stresses the similarity of systems processes occurring in many different forms of relationship. Whether we are analysing a machine, an organism or an organization, it is argued that we should document relationships between the supply of resources (input), the conversion process (throughput), and the production of an object or objects (output). It is the manner in which the parts are shaped by the process as a whole that should be the central concern of study.

The image of a system that emerges from this conflation is of a group of phenomena that is inter-dependent in such a way that it strives to accomplish a common goal. Advanced systems contain sub-systems which operate in an independent way but again tend to be inter-dependent and oriented toward the overall goal of the wider system. In fulfilling this goal a system always interacts with and exists within a specific environment. The nature of this interaction means that a system can both influence, and be influenced by, its environment. This quality of interaction allows us to discuss the exchange of inputs and outputs, which in turn enables us to determine the system boundary. On recognizing the different forms of system boundary, we are able to talk of organizations displaying closed, partially open or open systems behaviour (see Silverman 1970, Clegg and Dunkerley 1980).

Organizations as closed systems

When conceived of as closed systems, organizations are viewed as self-sufficient entities. The emphasis in this approach is upon the internal operation of the organization and the adoption of rationalistic approaches taken from physical science models. The organization is considered as sufficiently independent that its problems can be analysed in terms of internal structure, tasks and formal relationships. In organization theory, the closed system perspective is frequently one where analysis is directed toward general laws of sociology or psychology and thus where the variables being researched are assumed to be unaffected by environmental forces. At the heart of this perspective is the positivist assumption that objective forces, detected by controlled scientific observation, can exert a direct influence on human activity. This is typically the case in experimental or laboratory approaches to organizational analysis, where there is a conscious attempt to exclude environmental forces by the random assembly of experimental conditions. Here behaviour is explained according to the pure laws of social or psychological forces, laws which are unaffected by external exigencies.[1]

In organization theory, however, the development of a sociological orthodoxy around the open systems perspective has often seen the closed system position portrayed as an aberration. The closed systems perspective is attacked from many quarters, with the basic criticism being that it fails to do justice to a 'true' systems perspective because it ignores relationships between higher and lower systems which interact both within and across organizational boundaries (Silverman 1970). Closed systems perspectives are associated with approaches which focus exclusively on maximizing the internal efficiency of the organization. The emphasis is upon finding optimal functional relationships between internal sub-systems, as, for example, in Taylorist efficiency studies of production processes, or in 'classical' prescriptions for administrative structures or procedures (see Sofer 1975).[2]

Organizations as partially open systems

In the partially open perspective, while the role of the environment is recognized, in order to limit the scope of study prior attention is given to organizational variables. External influences, such as social background or cultural traditions, are most often used as controls to explain *ex post facto* difficulties in the patterning of the data.

Silverman (1970) has argued that this perspective contains a major flaw. If we develop hypotheses exclusively in terms of internal variables, and then only introduce external variables as a means of reducing inconsistencies in the data, we prevent rather than assist an understanding of the processes through which the two are systematically related. This understanding can only come, he feels, from theories and hypotheses which begin from both.[3] Therefore, although partially open systems research designs appear sophisticated – because they account for the organization's environment – they are in fact simple and disappointing, because they deal with it only in the final stages of analysis.

Organizations as open systems

Finally, in the open systems perspective the organization is in a dynamic relationship with its environment: it receives various inputs, transforms these inputs in some way and exports outputs. The organization is 'open' not only in relation to its environment, but also in relation to itself; it is open 'internally' in that interactions between components affect the system as a whole. The open system adapts to its environment by adjusting the structures and processes of its internal components.

In being in constant interaction with its environment, the system attempts to achieve dynamic equilibrium, or a 'steady state', while still retaining its capacity for work or energy transformation. The system would simply not survive without continuous inflow, transformation and outflow, which in the biological or social system represents a continuous recycling process. Systems must receive sufficient input of resources to maintain operations and to export the transformed resources to the environment in sufficient quantities to continue the cyclical process.[4]

From this perspective, organizational analysis should focus on the boundary exchanges of resources betweeen the focal system and the sub-systems of the environment, as organizations depend for their survival on an efficient exchange of goods and services with the environment. This provides them with a goal and with resources to achieve this goal; for example, land, labour and capital (input). At the same time, each sub-system must react by making adequate use of the resources it receives and by solving the problems created by the form of these resources (through-put).[5] In attempting to solve such problems, the organization is able to provide resources for other sub-systems and also to generate problems that they must resolve (output). This produces a changed environment with which the system must deal once again (feedback) (Silverman 1970). Organizational stability and change is thus explained by positing a tendency towards homeostasis, which governs the relationships between sub-systems.

Systems theory and organizational analysis

To explain the influence of social systems thinking on organizational theory, we can document the development of a closed system, mechanical equilibrium approach in 'classical' studies of administration and show how this was superseded, in later research, by a generic open-systems model, notably in socio-technical and contingency theory work. In so doing, we will begin where for many the systems approach to organizational analysis begins, with the report by Roethlisberger and Dickson (1939) of industrial research at the Hawthorne Works of the Western Electric Company, Chicago, between 1924 and 1932, the investigations commonly referred to as the Hawthorne studies.[6]

The Hawthorne studies

In contrast to the accepted wisdom of many modern management texts, the significance of the Hawthorne studies lies not only in the discovery of 'social man', but also in the formation of an early systems-based approach to organizational analysis.[7] For the development of schools of thought in organizational theory, one of the most important, yet neglected features of the Hawthorne investigations is that the explanatory model presented in *Management and the Worker* (Roethlisberger and Dickson 1939) moves away from the narrowly behavioural and deterministic approach of Taylorism and 'classical' administrative management and towards a mechanical equilibrium systems model based upon the ideas of Pareto (Burrell and Morgan 1979). Put briefly, we see in the Hawthorne Studies the beginnings of a social systems approach to organizational analysis, and also an anticipation of the later socio-technical approach to organizational design.

It is, indeed, the development of a mechanical equilibrium model that represents the most enduring contribution of the Hawthorne investigations to formal organizational theory. While organizational analysts have long criticized the methodology of the Hawthorne studies (see Rose 1988 on this point), a great many continue to base their work upon the theoretical model. It has been argued that despite the methodological shortcomings of the Hawthorne investigations, mainstream organizational analysis has not progressed far beyond the basic model employed to explain the findings of Elton Mayo and his colleagues. We will, therefore, describe the Hawthorne equilibrium model prior to explaining its centrality in the development of a systems orthodoxy in modern organizational analysis.

The research perspective

In origin, the Hawthorne studies represent a set of ergonomical investigations into the relationships between conditions of work and levels of fatigue and monotony. In the tradition of inter-war industrial psychology, it was argued that laws for such relationships could be established through experimenting with variables such as temperature, lighting levels and hours of sleep. The initial aim of the studies was thus a simple one: to identify cause and effect relationships between elements of the physical work environment and levels of employee efficiency.

When we refer to the report by Roethlisberger and Dickson, however, we not only find details of the experimental research, but also of the way the research perspective changed as the initial hypotheses failed to gain support. The authors describe how the results of the investigations were confusing, and how they seemed to contradict the logic of experimentation. The authors outline, in fact, how the controlled experimental approach was replaced by an attempt to understand the social nature of the workplace as a 'system of interdependent elements' (p. 183). Roethlisberger and Dickson describe how the focus of attention changed from an appreciation of the physical characteristics of the work environment to factors such as

POSSIBLE SOURCES OF INTERFERENCE   RESPONSES

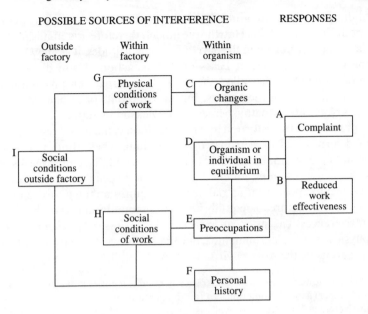

Figure 1 Mechanical equilibrium model

leadership, supervision, and the attitudes and values of employees. In order to investigate these latter factors the nature of the research design changed from emphasis on experimentation to a lengthy programme of employee interviews, this being conducted as 'action research' aimed at improving supervisory training. The authors note how the interview programme marked a turning-point for the research, and that for a long period this overshadowed all other aspects of the work. Indeed, it is only after describing at some length the details of the interview programme that Roethlisberger and Dickson delineate the systems model which forms the basis for the second half of their analysis.

A mechanical equilibrium approach

Based on the early parts of the research, and directing the form of analysis in the latter stages (especially Part 3, pp. 255–376), the Hawthorne systems model (Figure 1) is essentially a conceptual scheme for understanding processes of employee dissatisfaction. The model demonstrates the way in which an individual can attain a state of equilibrium in the work situation. The basic premise is that if this can be achieved, the employee will contribute to the overall effectiveness of the organization.

Roethlisberger and Dickson report how in attempting to fit the interview findings into a meaningful 'whole', they had to evolve a new way of thinking about the worker. The Hawthorne model, therefore, distinguishes between 'fact' and 'sentiment' in the development of attitudes: it acknowledges both the manifest and latent bases of dissatisfaction. These distinctions are important in that they allow the researchers to treat certain complaints not simply as facts in themselves, but as symptoms of implicit problems of workplace life. Roethlisberger and Dickson describe how complaints characterized by distortion and exaggeration came to be seen as indicators of deeper states of personal disequilibrium. They argue that employee complaints cannot be confined to one cause, and that employee dissatisfaction is, in most cases, an effect of a complex social situation. Given such complexity, proper industrial analysis requires an integrated understanding of the nature of equilibrium or disequilibrium and the nature of interferences. The latter can in fact stem from a variety of sources: from the physical work environment, from the social work environment, or even from outside the work environment. As Roethlisberger and Dickson note,

to cloak industrial problems under such general categories as 'fatigue', 'monotony', and 'supervision' is sometimes to fail to discriminate among the different kinds of interferences involved, as well as among the different kinds of equilibrium. (Roethlisberger and Dickson 1939, p. 3)

Roethlisberger and Dickson, indeed, acknowledge the advances a systems model of 'the interrelation of factors in mutual dependence' makes over the 'simple cause and effect analysis of human situations'. Only by developing such an equilibrium model, they suggest, can we appreciate the processes through which 'any major change in one of the factors (interference or constraint) brings about changes in the other factors, resulting in a temporary state of disequilibrium until either the former equilibrium is restored or a new equilibrium is established' (1939, p. 326).

The advances made by the development of this model are in fact considerable. In contrast to the quasi-causality of classical theory and early industrial psychology, the Hawthorne model emphasizes how work behaviour can only properly be understood in terms of a complex network of interacting elements. These elements interact within and outside the work situation and also within the individual. The model therefore anticipates the open systems perspective in that it acknowledges the influence of environmental forces, especially upon the personal history of the individual. To quote Roethlisberger and Dickson,

the relation of the individual employee to the company is not a closed system. All the values of the individual cannot be accounted for by the social organization of the company ... The ultimate significance of his work is not defined so much by his relation to the company as by his relation to the wider social reality. (1939, p. 376)

Hawthorne and systems orthodoxy

As a contribution to a systems orthodoxy, the Hawthorne model can be seen as fusing aspects of the sociologies of Durkheim, Spencer and Pareto. The impact of Pareto on the Harvard group of sociologists in the 1920s and 1930s sees his notion of the social system in equilibrium become central to the Hawthorne model (Burrell and Morgan 1979). Added to this is the Paretian interest in 'non-logical' forms of behaviour. The emphasis the Hawthorne researchers place on the notion of 'sentiments' – to denote attitudes which are not based on 'facts' – is derived directly from Paretian theory.

On the other hand, the emphasis on 'social facts' is derived from Durkheim, and Roethlisberger and Dickson duly acknowledge his influence on their work. The emphasis Durkheim places on relations between the individual and society finds subtle expression in the analysis of *Management and the Worker*, especially the linking of the individual personality to social solidarity, a theme developed more thoroughly by Parsons. Although it is Pareto's notion of a system in equilibrium which provides the organizing framework for the report, it is Durkheim's concept of anomie – the disjuncture between individuals and their work – which provides the metaphysical direction (Burrell and Morgan 1979).

In *Management and the Worker*, however, the Durkheimian strands of analysis are not elaborated on to their full extent. It is in a parallel thesis by the principal investigator of the Hawthorne investigations, Elton Mayo, where justice to this influence is done. In *The Human Problems of an Industrial Civilisation* (1933) Mayo's analysis turns on a Durkheimian approach, especially in his proposal that human problems must be understood in relation to the erosion of social values brought about through the demands of economic and technical change. In commenting upon the Hawthorne results, the influence of Durkheim on Mayo's thinking is clear, notably in his remark that

human collaboration in work, in primitive and developed countries, has always depended for its perpetuation upon the evolution of a non-logical social code which regulates the relations between persons and their attitudes to one another. Insistence upon a merely economic logic of production ... interferes with the development of such a code and consequently gives rise to a sense of human defeat. (1933, p. 120: quoted in Burrell and Morgan 1979, p. 139)

Put simply, Mayo suggests that society should be conceived of as a system tending towards equilibrium; if the social equilibrium is disturbed then forces are set in motion to restore it. This analysis is transferred almost wholesale to the study of organizations, Mayo suggesting that work behaviour can be conceptualized as the attempt to maintain or restore equilibrium. As economic and technological forces dominate workplaces, social organization represents one of the principal means for restoring industrial equilibrium.

Socio-technical systems

By the late 1940s, a mechanical equilibrium model was also developed by researchers in Britain. Early work into organizational design by the Tavistock Institute, London, saw an equilibrium model of industrial behaviour developed within a General Systems Theory framework. The use of this model in a study of technical change in the British coalfields gave rise to a new style of organizational analysis, the socio-technical systems approach (see Trist and Bamforth 1951; Trist *et al.* 1963).

The Durham mines study

The concept of the socio-technical system originates specifically from an analysis of the introduction of 'long-wall' mining technology in the North-West Durham coalfield, England. This study focused upon how a mechanized, mass production method of coal mining had replaced the traditional 'hand-got' method, and how this involved a revolution in the forms of work and social systems within the mines. Being informed heavily by psychoanalysis and Gestalt theory – and particularly by Bion's (1950) work on small group relations and Lewin's (1951) work on task closure – the researchers came to perceive work situations in terms of relations between countervailing social and technical forces. As Trist and Bamforth suggest,

these interactive technological and sociological patterns will be assumed to exist as forces having psychological effects in the life-space of the face-worker, who must either take a role and perform a task in the system they compose or abandon his attempt to work at the coal face. (1951, p. 11)

In this view, the working group should not be regarded as either exclusively a technical group or a social group but as an interdependent socio-technical system. The work system of the colliery should be interpreted in terms of 'fields' (Lewin 1951) of social and psychological forces, the balance being influenced by the relationship between technical and human factors. It is argued that

inherent in the socio-technical approach is the notion that the attainment of optimum conditions in any one dimension does not necessarily result in a set of conditions optimum for the system as a whole. If the structures of the various dimensions are not consistent, interference will occur, leading to a state of disequilibrium, so that achievement of the overall goal will to some degree be endangered and in the limit made impossible. The optimization of the whole tends to require a less than optimum state for each separate dimension. (Trist *et al.* 1963, p. 7)

This early Tavistock perspective, like the Hawthorne model, is thus underpinned by the assumptions of a mechanical equilibrium model. In this case, however, it is one which owes debt to gestalt theory as much as to Paretian mechanics. In the Durham mines study, the technical change brought about by the long-wall method is perceived as disturbing the social and technical equilibrium of the hand-got system, with the reactions of the colliers being taken as evidence of this disturbance.

Open socio-technical systems

Although making advances for a systems appreciation of work relationships, this early Tavistock approach, like the Hawthorne studies, was subsequently criticized for adopting a closed system model that denied access to environmental influences.

In response, Tavistock studies from the mid-1950s saw the socio-technical concept developed in terms of an 'open rather than closed system theory' (Trist *et al.* 1963, p. 6). The new goal was to determine 'the enterprise–environment relation' and notably 'the elucidation of the conditions under which a steady state may be attained' (Trist *et al.* 1963, p. 6). From this point onwards, the doctrine of an open-systems theory was to dominate the Tavistock perspective. A clear example of this policy is contained in a passage from Emery and Trist (1960), who suggest that

considering enterprises as 'open socio-technical systems' helps to provide a more realistic picture of how they are both influenced by and able to act back on their environment. It points in particular to the various ways in which enterprises are enabled by their structural and functional characteristics ('system constraints') to cope with the 'lacks' and 'gluts' in their available environment. Unlike mechanical and other inanimate systems they possess the property of 'equi-finality'; they may achieve a steady state from differing initial conditions and in differing ways. Thus in coping by internal changes they are not limited to simple quantitative change and increased uniformity but may, and usually do, elaborate new structures and take on new functions. (p. 94)

By the mid-1950s, therefore, and having drawn heavily upon the systems theory of Ludwig von Bertalanffy (1950), the Tavistock researchers had incorporated the socio-technical concept into a generic open systems approach. This perspective advanced organic rather than mechanical analogies. As with Tavistock work in general, the new open-systems approach would influence practice through sponsored research and consultancy. Nowhere was this more evident than in the study by A.K. Rice into organizational change at the Jubilee Calico Mills, Ahmedabad, India.

The Calico Mills study

Rice's study of work design in the Jubilee Mills was based explicitly on the model of the firm as a living organism. The firm is seen as 'open' to its environment: it maintains itself by exchanging materials and goods with its environment, importing capital, raw materials and equipment, and exporting finished goods, dividends, pollution and so forth. If the organization does not engage in such commerce it is assumed not to be adapting to the environment and thus to be in danger of extinction.

Rice's research is driven by the notion of the 'primary task'. Each system or sub-system has a primary duty to perform the task for which it, as a system or sub-system, was created. It is the primary task which unites the organization as a whole. As Rice suggests,

the performance of the primary task is supported by powerful social and psychological forces which ensure that a considerable capacity for cooperation is evoked among the members of the organization created to perform it, and that, as a direct corollary, the effective performance of a primary task can provide an important source of satisfaction for those engaged upon it. (Rice 1958, p. 33)

In Rice's analysis, the organic, open systems analogy is combined with the view of the organization as a unitary social system in order to form a conservative functionalist analysis (Burrell and Morgan 1979). For Rice, the social system is a positive force contributing to the accomplishment of the primary task. Technology, on the other hand, is a force which imposes constraints upon the range of possible organizational arrangements, but within which choice is possible. The crucial variable is organizational design, or more correctly the design of a mode of work organization which meets the demands of technology and the needs of individuals: a design which produces a consensual and productive organization. The relationships between the various sub-systems which make up the textile mill gain their significance from this basic perspective on the function of the industrial organization. This is a systems view which is based upon a philosophy of social engineering and which seeks to ameliorate the problems created by technological change.

Boundary management

The open systems perspective was developed further in Tavistock work which took the management of the interaction between the enterprise and the environment as the specific focus of study. The best example of this is Rice's work *The Enterprise and its Environment* (1963), in which he suggests the primary task of the leader is 'to manage the relations between an enterprise and its environment so as to permit optimal performance of the primary task of the enterprise' (p. 15).

In this work, rather than the open systems perspective simply drawing attention to the importance of events at the system boundary, it is now these boundary events and relationships which are crucial to the organization's well-being. Increasingly it is the notion of boundary regulation and management which is the chief concern for both the practising manager and professional organizational analyst.

These concerns were expressed forcefully in a book of sectoral studies written by Rice in partnership with E. J. Miller, *Systems of Organization: the Control of Task and Sentient Boundaries* (1967). In this volume, boundary regulation is depicted as the basic managerial control function of the organization. Miller and Rice focus attention on the problems of boundary definition both within the organization and between organizations and their environments. The organization is perceived as a tool for task performance in which human needs are regarded as potential constraints upon the level of effectiveness.

Miller and Rice define technical and social sub-systems in terms of task and sentient groups respectively. The task group is that which comprises the individuals employed in a work activity (technical) system. This is essentially the formal work group because it is prescribed by management to achieve part of the organization's primary task. In contrast, the sentient group is 'the group to which individuals are prepared to commit themselves and on which they depend for emotional support' (Miller and Rice 1967, p. 253). This group is more of an informal work group, whose relationships are based on human needs for security and social support.

Miller and Rice consider the prime responsibility of management to be the regulation of the boundaries between task and sentient groups. They describe how, according to the demands of the work situation, the boundaries between task and sentient systems may range from virtual coincidence to almost no overlap. It is management's job to regulate these boundaries in a manner consistent with the demands of the larger context. Miller and Rice believe that virtual coincidence is required for the performance of tasks devoid of intrinsic motivating potential and where the larger context is stable. In contrast, for routine, unchallenging tasks, the sentient group can perform a compensatory role: it can provide outlets for need satisfaction not otherwise available from the task grouping. However, Miller and Rice caution that during an era of increasing environmental change, coincidence in task and sentient boundaries may actually constitute a liability for the organization. In this case, management must expend considerable resources in attempting to manage – to 'regulate' – the boundaries between technical and social systems. The authors attempt to offer solutions to the problem that sub-systems make demands at various points in time and space (see also Miller 1959).

The causal texture of environments

The Tavistock concern with the nature of organizational environments reached its highpoint in a treatise by Emery and Trist (1965) called 'The Causal Texture of Organizational Environments'. In this work, the focus shifts from analysis of the specific task environment of the organization towards a recognition of the environment as a 'quasi-independent domain'. Emery and Trist are concerned to document the turbulent nature of the world environment as a whole and to denote its contextual implications for organizational activities.

The 'causal texture' of environments refers to sets of relationships that exist outside the realm of any organizational monitoring or boundary spanning. In contrast to normal enterprise–environment relations these are extremely dangerous because they are indirect relationships. These relations represent the area of interdependencies that belongs to the environment itself but that can potentially determine the ultimate survival of the organization. Because the causal texture is made up of relations between components of the external environment, changes in the causal texture are not likely to be detected and monitored very effectively. Consequently, the organization's reactions to changes in the causal texture tend to lack the speed and confidence associated with changes in direct transactional linkages. Put briefly, because these causal texture linkages are not under the direct control of the organization, they can contribute considerably to the uncertainty facing the organization. They represent a quasi-independent domain and may be regarded as the most critical attribute of the environment in terms of potential impact on organizational survival.

In a later book influenced by the causal texture thesis, *Toward a Social Ecology* (1972), Emery and Trist's concern with the context of environmental turbulence, and the attempt to understand organizations as open socio-technical systems, led to an analysis of the patterns of life associated with the post-industrial society (Burrell and Morgan 1979). The focus here was upon the way social patterns are changing, and in particular how these changes influence the operation of organizations as complex adaptive systems. Here we see the beginnings of an analytical fusion between socio-technical systems and theories of post-industrialism, a fusion which leads Emery and Trist away from narrowly based concerns with the theorizing of organization and toward broader concerns of social structure and social change.

Contingency theory

Whereas from the 1950s the socio-technical approach was one of the major contributions to organizational analysis, it was gradually encompassed within a perspective which claimed to reconcile open systems concepts at a number of organization levels. This style of analysis is known as contingency theory.

Contingency theory asserts that to be effective, an organization needs to develop appropriate matches between its internal organization and the demands of its environment. In developing a set of propositions for achieving appropriate matches, contingency theory draws upon empirical research into, for example, leadership style, work motivation, job satisfaction, technology and organization structure.

While elements of the contingency approach are found in open socio-technical theory, and whereas many studies developed in the 1950s anticipated a formal contingency analysis (see Woodward 1958; Burns and Stalker 1961), it is in work on organizational structure by Lawrence and Lorsch, reported in their book *Organization and Environment* (1967), that we find the purest statement of this position.

Lawrence and Lorsch

Lawrence and Lorsch attempt a systematic analysis of relationships between contingency variables of internal organization structure and the nature of the external environment. The first stage of this research focuses on an empirical study of ten organizations operating in a range of business sectors. The research aims to discover the forms of organization best suited to dealing with various market and economic conditions. Basing the analysis on the organic metaphor of organization, the research adopts an explicit open systems framework and views an organization as a set of interrelated parts influenced by the wider environment. As Lawrence and Lorsch state,

we find it useful to view an organization as an open system in which the behaviours of members of an organization are also interdependent with the formal organization, the tasks to be accomplished, the personalities of other individuals, and the unwritten rules about appropriate behaviour for a member. Under this concept of system, the behaviour of any one manager can be seen as determined not only by his own personality needs and motives, but also by the way his personality interacts with those of his colleagues. Further, this relationship among organization members is also influenced by the nature of the task being performed, by the formal relationships, rewards, and controls, and by the existing ideas within the organization ... It is important to emphasize that all these determinants of behaviour are themselves interrelated. (p. 6)

The thrust of Lawrence and Lorsch's work is to identify regular structural patterns associated with the functioning of particular organizational systems in differing environments. To this end, their analysis turns on the implications of two particular aspects of systems functioning. The first is the principle that as systems become larger we find demands for the greater differentiation and integration of parts. The second is the view that a central function of any system is its adaptation to the demands of the wider environment.

Lawrence and Lorsch argue that the complex organization, as a system which is internally differentiated, must attain a satisfactory level of integration if it is to adapt to the demands of its wider environment. Their research suggests that effective organizations are those which achieve levels of integration and differentiation commensurate with environmental demands. In diverse and dynamic sectors such as the plastics industry, effective organizations are those whose structures are highly differentiated and highly integrated. In environments which are more stable and less diverse, like the container industry, effective organizations are those which are less differentiated but which still achieve a high degree of integration. In order to attain ideal structural patterns, organizations in differing sectors operate differing procedures for conflict resolution in order to maintain the required levels of differentiation and integration.

The importance of the Lawrence and Lorsch work on contingency analysis rests on the fact that it, more than any other contemporary work, provides an empirical model for systems research in organizations; an approach which can subsume the premises of previous approaches. Contingency theory suggests that while the traditions stemming from scientific management and human relations psychology appear contradictory, they can in fact be reconciled. While scientific management and human relations approaches offer alternative 'universal' solutions to organization problems, Lawrence and Lorsch suggest that a range of organizational principles are appropriate to the various environmental circumstances which twentieth-century organizations face. They are even able to show how, under certain conditions, success can be achieved through adopting an highly structured, authoritarian and bureaucratic style of management.

Contingency theory and systems orthodoxy

Contingency theory represents the most influential of modern open systems perspectives on organizational analysis. In contrast to universalism, it emphasizes that management strategy is context-dependent: management principles must be concordant with the type of situation being encountered. The work by Lawrence and Lorsch represents the most eloquent expression of a form of systems analysis which has its origins in works by Woodward (1958), who demonstrates how successful companies are those whose structures are compatible with their technology, and Burns and Stalker (1961), who show how effective firms adopt organization styles which are consistent with the demands placed upon them by their environment. Later research by, for example, the Aston group in Britain (see Pugh and Hickson 1976) and Richard Hall (1972) in the USA, also reflects this approach, and similarly illustrates the diversity of structural forms found in large organizations. All of these studies echo Burns and Stalker's advice that 'the beginning of administrative wisdom is the awareness that there is no one optimum type of management system' (Burns and Stalker 1961, p. 125).

Systems theory and management texts

Finally, the hegemony of systems theory is also evident in the contents of best-selling textbooks on management. In the 1960s and 1970s, in particular, many organizational behaviour texts suggested the power of open systems theory for solving business and management problems. In Katz and Kahn (1966), Kast and Rosenweig (1970), and Koontz and O'Donnell (1974), for example, systems theory is accorded 'paradigm' status; it is portrayed as the only viable approach for organizational analysis.

Katz and Kahn

Of these volumes, Katz and Kahn's (1966) *The Social Psychology of Organizations* has been the most influential. It remains one of the most widely read texts on organizational behaviour. Katz and Kahn develop a perspective in which the systems metaphor is used to mediate approaches as diverse as Marxism, human relations and event-structure theory. In the spirit of structural-functionalism, Katz and Kahn depict modern society as having 'no structure apart from its functioning' (p. 32). They feel that the open systems model represents a powerful tool for analysing the context within which social action is created, enacted and transformed.

In synthesizing structural-functionalism with principles of general-systems theory, Katz and Kahn develop a process model for interpreting organizational actions in terms of input, throughput and output. Their thesis revolves around the notion that formal social systems are homoeostatic, possessing qualities of negative entropy, feedback, differentiation and equifinality. Katz and Kahn argue that there are five generic types of sub-system to consider in organizational analysis: production or technical sub-systems (concerned with organizational throughput), supportive sub-systems (which attain input or dispose of output), maintenance sub-systems (which retain people in functional roles), adaptive sub-systems (which deal with organizational change) and managerial sub-systems (which direct the activities of all other sub-systems).

Their framework is akin to Parsons' AGIL model, being directed, like his, at the motive forces behind the creation and maintenance of stable systems. In the functionalist vein, their goal is to explain how social systems persist through time and adapt to changing circumstances. The mechanical model is rejected as a valid explanation of social affairs on the grounds that it neglects the concept of environmental exchange in respect of production and maintenance inputs and ignores the significance of the maintenance input for the social system. Instead Katz and Kahn adopt the biological analogy in which they recognize the complexity of maintenance requirements for the social system as a whole.

In sum, Katz and Kahn's work reflects two main theoretical influences: the structural-functionalism of Parsons and the general-systems theory of von Bertalanffy. We find a structural analysis based on principles of sociological functionalism joined by a process analysis based on principles of systems dynamics. More than any other text, Katz and Kahn (1966) represents an exemplar of the generic social systems approach to organizational analysis.

The McKinsey 7-S Model

The use of the systems approach as a basis for texts on organization has also continued through the 1980s and into the 1990s. Particularly influential during this period has been a very basic form of systems framework, the '7-S' model of the American consultancy firm McKinsey and Co. The seven Ss of the model stand for:

Strategy: systematic action and allocation of resources to achieve company goals;

Structure: organization structure and authority relationships;

Systems: procedures and processes such as information systems, manufacturing processes, budgeting and control processes;

Style: the way the management behaves and collectively spends its time to achieve organizational goals;

Staff: the people in the organization and their socialization into the corporate culture;

Skills: the distinctive capabilities of the organization; and

Shared Values: the values and philosophies shared by members of the organization.

Graphically, the McKinsey model is presented in the form of a six-pointed star with a central locus. The star points are all linearly interconnected with the locus and with each other, forming seven reference points for the 'S' variables. The first six Ss thus form satellites around the seventh, 'shared values', the linchpin of the model. By using the term 'shared values' – sometimes called 'superordinate goals' – the McKinsey writers emphasize the integrating role of culture in modern work organizations. Indeed, special attention is given to the relationship between personal and organizational values in the management of corporate systems.

The 7-S model is best known for providing the analytical basis of three best-selling books on management, *The Art of Japanese Management* (Pascale and Athos 1982), *In Search of Excellence* (Peters and Waterman 1982) and *Managing on the Edge* (Pascale 1990). In these books, the framework is used to identify key variables of the internal management system and to show how these relate to elements of the modern business environment. One assumption which underpins these works is that the modern business environment is extremely turbulent, and that flexible boundary management is the key to business success, especially given the 'chaotic' nature of contemporary corporate life (see Peters 1988).

Conclusions: the hegemony of systems

In this chapter, we have attempted to describe some of the main ways in which a social systems theory hegemony has been established in organizational analysis. We have documented the rise of structural-functionalism as the dominant paradigm of sociology and shown how its underlying biological metaphors are translated into the study of organizations. The influence of Talcott Parsons has been noted and especially his view that the central task of sociology is to analyse society as a system of functionally interdependent parts. It is Parsons who suggests that the study of any social process is the study of boundary maintenance.

Indeed, when Clegg and Dunkerley (1975) talk of the 'hegemony' of organizational analysis, and particularly of 'that style of research whose hegemony is maintained by the pages of *The Administrative Science Quarterly*' (p. 2), they are referring to an image of organization which emanates from the acceptance of a conservative biological metaphor. As this metaphor becomes 'sedimented' (Clegg and Dunkerley 1980), it is taken for granted that organizations are purposive and rational in character and have 'needs' which must be satisfied if the organization is to survive. An organization must possess functional unity, with failure to achieve this signalling that there are dysfunctions in its adaptation processes. The dynamic of organization is presented as a goal-setting process, and one which accepts the notion of the 'primary task'. The actions of sub-units are evaluated in relation to the organization's ability to achieve its primary task.

Social systems thinking, therefore, has played the major role in establishing a generic paradigm for contemporary organizational analysis. This paradigm is directed at clarification of the imperatives which make human systems survive, continue and change. The dominant method of modern organizational analysis, contingency theory, suggests that social, technical and environmental imperatives must be reconciled if the system is to operate optimally. Factors such as capital, technology and human resources are all inputs to a functionally rational process whose goals are survival, adaptation and profitability.

3   From functionalism to fragmentation

> The unity of the discipline is nothing other than the debate between the competing lines of analysis which takes the organization as their common object. It is the absence of debate that would really threaten the discipline.
>
> (Karpik 1988, p. 28)

Introduction

The aim of this chapter is to discuss the 'crisis' model of social science and to show how it is used to explain intellectual divisions in both sociology and organization theory.

We argue that the power of systems analysis has diminished as new paradigms for sociology and organization theory have emerged. To support this, we describe the conceptual and methodological limitations of structural-functionalism and social systems theory. These limitations both explain the decline of functionalism as a dominant paradigm and provide analytical openings for the development of new sociological methods.

Elaborating upon this argument, we suggest that a Kuhnian (Kuhn 1962, 1970a) revolution swept across Western sociology in the late 1960s and early 1970s and that this found expression in organization theory during the late 1970s and early 1980s. As a result, the development of new schemes for analysing society was replicated in the study of organizations, this trend representing a move towards paradigm heterodoxy. We document the growth of crisis theory and paradigmism in organization theory and discuss specific instances of use. In particular, we analyse a range of attempts to define the theory communities of social and organization theory as paradigm structures.

Finally, we argue that writers are unsure whether analytical fragmentation represents a threat or an opportunity. While on the one hand an eclectic approach finds support amongst those who advocate new, often radical perspectives, on the other hand it meets with criticism from those who support established systems theory positions. We highlight one recent debate in which the fragmentation thesis is rejected by writers who defend structural-functionalism as a dominant paradigm of social analysis, the debate between contingency theorists and the so-called 'critics' of organization theory.

Paradigm lost: the decline of sociological functionalism

Two positions confront the writer wishing to decipher the epistemological status of social and organizational theory. On the one hand, we note the considerable influence of sociological functionalism on the development of organization theory. It is argued that success in joining principles of sociological functionalism with those of general-systems theory made for a robust and enduring method for organizational analysis. We have described how the systems perspective came to attain an intellectual hegemony over organization studies for half a century and how it still influences teaching and research today.

On the other hand, organizational sociologists find shortcomings in the systems approach. Functionalism is criticized for being a static theory which is ill-suited to the analysis of complex and dynamic social and organizational environments. The emergence of intellectual alternatives to social systems theory, and subsequently of radical paradigms in organization theory, is attributed to functionalism's failure to deal with changing social conditions. The debate over the current community structure of social and organizational analysis revolves around differing interpretations of the health of functionalism, with social systems theory in particular being the subject of careful scrutiny by those who would establish an alternative model to that which suggests the continuing hegemony of equilibrium theory.

In order, therefore, to understand the community structure of social and organizational analysis we will explain the strengths and weaknesses of the major intellectual positions. The starting-point for this analysis is again located in the writings of structural-functionalist sociology and, in particular, in the works of Talcott Parsons.

The limitations of functionalism in social and organizational analysis

Functionalism is commonly deconstructed by reference to the weaknesses inherent in its substantive and ideological foundations.[1] Substantive limitations question the sociological adequacy of functionalism. The main substantive criticism is that, in emphasizing equilibrium, integration and interdependence, functionalism fails to take account of two basic elements of social action – change and conflict. This criticism is attributed specifically to Parsons' (1951, 1965) works that separate equilibrium analysis – assuming systems as given – from structural change, which does not. Parsons argues that change must be pictured against a wider appreciation of equilibrium, and that it is nearly always necessary to assume

some structural elements to be *given*, while analysing processes of change in others, particularly changes in the structure of sub-systems to the more extensive system. (Parsons 1965, p. 31, quoted in Silverman 1970, p. 57)

Parsons argues that change stems from two sets of processes – from the demands of the environment and from within systems (or organizations) themselves (see Chapter 2, pp. 21–6, above). The former is exogenous change and reflects movements in the central value system. It is the central value system which defines the goal of an organization as well as the basis for the forms of legitimate authority exercised within it. In contrast, endogenous change stems from tensions or strains in the system itself, these being tendencies to 'disequilibrium in the input–output balance between two or more units of the system' (Parsons 1967, p. 196, quoted in Silverman 1970, p. 57). This situation occurs when too much focus is placed on either efficiency (adaptation and goal-attainment) or stability (integration and latency). From this analysis, Parsons concludes that the natural response of a system or organization to exogenous and endogenous tension is to adapt by moving toward a new form of stability. This law of the dynamic equilibrium of social systems is one of the basic principles of functionalist theory.

This leaves us, however, with a major problem for organizational analysis. Even if we accept that systems can be said to take action, we cannot argue that their reactions to external or internal forces are necessarily adaptive (Van den Berge 1963). If we take, for example, instances of perceived conflicts of interest, the ruling assumptions within an organization may be questioned, with any subsequent change to them not necessarily being in the form of props to stability. Change may be driven by conflict and contradiction rather than by the incorporation of expressions of dissent.

This inadequate treatment of change and conflict results from Parsons' prior orientation towards the consequences of action rather than its causes, tensions that can be noted in his analysis of the relations between organizations and society (Silverman 1970). In portraying an organization as an open system, he defines it and the environment as two distinct and given domains. Parsons offers an analysis of the ways in which the former simply adapts to conditions dictated by the latter (Whyte 1964). We are not told, for example, why particular organizations, directed as they are towards certain goals, arise at particular times and in particular places;

instead, organizations are portrayed as established and going concerns (see Parsons 1960, p. 23ff.). Also, we are not told why organizations must have a goal consistent with the central value system of the wider society or, if this is universal, how deviant organizations emerge and develop. It is difficult for Parsons to explain, for example, the origins of revolutionary movements without taking recourse to tautological statements about inconsistencies in the central value system (Silverman 1970). As an analysis of those conditions which make for stability, Parsonian functionalism fails to recognize how organizations can survive and even flourish without a common value-orientation among their members. As Van den Berge (1963) suggests, the substantive problems of functionalism arise from a failure to acknowledge that

reaction to extra-systemic change is not always adjustive ... [that] social systems can, for long periods, go through a vicious circle of ever deepening malintegration ... [that] change can be revolutionary ... [and that] the social structure itself generates change through internal conflicts and contradictions. (p. 698)

As a substantive sociological paradigm, functionalism, therefore, is found wanting. It overstresses the normative aspects of social life, undervalues the importance of social conflict at the expense of social harmony, and fails to accommodate social change, and indeed treats this as abnormal. Functionalism gives scant attention to what goes on within organizations, and it is difficult to obtain data that would either support or refute its concepts of organization.

Functionalism and ideology

Functionalism has also been evaluated as a socio-political ideology. The chief criticism here is that it possesses an inherent conservative bias, which is often attributed to the influence of Durkheim's theory of social stratification. In emphasizing the harmonious relations between system parts, functionalism appears to treat each system as a positive social state (Cohen 1968). Stratification, for example, is portrayed as an inevitable fact of complex societies. In this view, where tasks are specialized, certain roles require abilities which are scarce, or which are found more readily in some individuals than others. To fulfil a society's functional requirements it is necessary that the more talented be attracted to roles that employ their skills optimally, such roles as a consequence receiving higher material and prestige rewards and the possibility of the exercise of greater power. Eventually the possession of greater wealth, prestige and power differentiates certain members of society as a class (Cohen 1968).

During the 1950s and 1960s, however, there emerged several critiques of this conservative stratification theory. Buckley (1958), for example, suggested that social differentiation must eventually hinder the efficient operation of a social system by preventing those with natural abilities from effecting roles which have become the preserve of a privileged and exclusive stratum. Similarly, Cohen (1968) challenged the view that some tasks are more crucial to society than others, by arguing that in complex productive systems the superordinate is no more vital than the subordinate, for the one cannot operate without the other. He questioned the assumption that reward differentials will and do reflect real differences in the skills required for particular roles.[2] Finally, Tumin (1953) claimed that the class structures of industrial societies are more the consequence of existing stratifications than of the logic of complex systems, with the inheritance of privilege, or systems of privilege, ensuring its own continuity.

Criticisms of generic social systems theory

Functionalism and systems theory are often conflated in critical commentaries on the discipline structure of social science. Problems with the one are often regarded as synonymous with problems with the other. Examples of this are found in works which deconstruct the models, methods and definitions of the generic social systems approach.

We see a simultaneous critique of natural-systems models and functionalist theories of organization in Gouldner's (1959) paper on 'rational' organizational analysis. Gouldner suggests that a major shortcoming with the natural-systems model is its concentration on the organic response-structuring of formal organizations to the neglect of the more purposive and planned aspects of organizations, such as strategic decision-making and corporate structuring. Gouldner describes how 'purposive rationality' is a prime force in the maintenance and development of organizations. He argues that the natural-systems model is problematic in its unreflective acceptance of the functionalist theory of differentiation, especially in taking for granted the organic reproduction of divisions of labour, professional elites and rational bureaucratic structures.

Gouldner also notes the limitations arising from the model's presentation of sub-system interdependence. As the organization is the prime level of analysis, sub-system relations are treated homogeneously. Consequently, variation in the degree of interdependence between sub-systems is a topic which is not systematically addressed. In developing the concept of 'functional autonomy', Gouldner not only highlights variations in degrees of interdependence, but also the fact that some sub-systems can survive even if separated from others. He thus moves away from the notion that interdependence necessarily implies functional symmetry. Gouldner argues that the main consequence of emphasis on integration is a neglect of the forces of functional autonomy. As an example of this, he points to the emphasis on goal orientation in Parsons' (1956) definition of an organization. Gouldner suggests that what Parsons takes for the goal-directedness of the organization is really the goal-directedness of a particular professional stratum. Gouldner feels that a proper understanding of goal-orientation requires specification of the various goals of the individuals, sub-groups and strata that comprise the organization. He argues that such a specification would indicate how ends 'may vary, are not necessarily identical, and may in fact be contradictory' (1959, p. 420). Because the natural-system/open-system model ignores this fact, due to its neglect of functional autonomy, the concept of organization which emerges is a reification. In Parsons (1956), for example, we see the tendency to treat the organization's goal as a thing-in-itself rather than as a consensus which is generated and reproduced by the members of an influential group and which is then imposed on other less influential members of the organization.

The methodological shortcomings of the generic systems approach are discussed by Allen (1975), who focuses on the underlying notion of causality in organizational research, a notion which fosters 'the dogma of empiricism'. He argues that methodological problems become evident when we consider the common research focus for generic systems analysis, the organizational case study (cf. Jaques 1951, Trist and Bamforth 1951, Rice 1958, Trist et al. 1963). Despite claims to the contrary, the typical systems case study focuses attention on the internal relations involved in the problem under investigation. It assumes that it is meaningful to study these relationships in relative isolation. It is as if a boundary isolated and insulated those relationships from any causal link with others.

Allen argues that when system analysts study organizational problems we witness an empiricism in which problems are treated in a fragmented way. The methodology of applied systems research suggests that 'if each problem has its own analytical existence it follows that the social relationships involved in them can be divided into problem areas, each of which can be treated as an independent system' (1975, p. 79). Allen suggests that there is no logic in such an arbitary division: such divisions he feels are made by 'others' according to their own criteria. The argument is that a problem can be broken down into a number of lesser problems, each of which can be analysed separately according to the whims of the investigator. While the empirically oriented systems sociologist might trace a causal relationship between the components associated with particular problems, such detection would depend entirely upon the empirical investigation; it would not be given a priori. The systems case study is thus founded on a belief in a plurality of causes, a belief that in refusing to give an a priori causal rank the analysis is escaping from charges of dogmatism.[3]

For Allen, however, this refusal to give an a priori rank to factors means that empiricist systems analysis takes a theoretical stance which is as 'dogmatic' as any other course of action. It acts as a fixed determinant of the form of empirical studies. The retreat from causal explanations is not a fortuitous happening but a direct consequence of the theoretical basis of empiricism. We can only sustain the epistemological consistency of organizational systems analysis by accepting that society is devoid of any structural contradictions which influence behaviour. It is only possible to justify the separate analytical treatment of segments of society, without reference to the whole, if the structure of the whole is assumed to be irrelevant for the behaviour of its parts. It is a view of society which assumes a basic organic unity. The systems case study method rests on the assumption that societies contain no class conflict and are harmonious systems with common internalized values and generally accepted aims. The systems case study method is thus static in conception in that

the integrity of each problem can only be protected if it is assumed that there is no change, or that change is never sufficient to penetrate the boundaries, or that each little system of social relationships possesses some kind of internal mechanism which continually restores the status quo. (1975, p. 81)

Thus, for Allen, organization theorists who have used the tools of systems analysis have been attempting the impossible task of explaining the reality of change with static concepts.

Finally, linked to these methodological issues are ones concerning problem orientation and definition.[4] When conducting organizational analysis, systems theorists are criticized for addressing the problems of corporate practice rather than those of social science. The goal is to increase company efficiency and profits rather than to further scientific knowledge. Rose (1988), for example, argues that in socio-technical systems analysis the research questions arise not so much from the problems of social science but from those of management consultancy. This stems from the authors of the approach, mainly psychologists from the Tavistock Institute, playing two contradictory roles simultaneously, those of academic researcher and paid consultant. The first is a public role while the second is a private one.

Likewise, Allen (1975) has argued that although applied systems research is 'problem-centred', the problems addressed are of a type that require solution by managers, bureaucrats or other senior policy makers (cf. Trist and Bamforth 1951; Rice 1958; Trist et al. 1963). Such problems are not thrown forth by nature to science, but are 'identified when difficulties occur in the reality of the dominant ideology' (1975, p. 74). The issues tackled by applied systems researchers are defined for them by those for whom the problem was a reality, that is by administrators and employers.

Applied systems research is similarly an example of what Gouldner (1965) calls 'engineering' sociology. The engineering approach is less reflective than the alternative, 'clinical' approach in that it does not question the definition of the problem which is given to the sociologist. Instead, from the engineering standpoint

the problems as formulated by the client are usually taken at face value; the engineer tends to assume that his client is willing to reveal the problems which actually beset him. The clinical sociologist, however . . . assumes that the problems as formulated by the client may often have a defensive significance and may obscure, rather than reveal, the client's tensions. (1965, p. 17)

Emphasis on the engineering approach has meant that certain organizational problems have been treated as sociological when they have not been so. At the heart of applied systems work are problems defined in relation to the interests of particular clients whom sociologists are serving.[5] Although social scientists who obtain funds for applied research may consider it an affront to be described as 'servants of power' (Baritz 1960), the critics suggest their protests are hollow because implicit in this form of problem-centred research is a consultant–client relationship.

Paradigmism and fragmentation in social and organization theory

These criticisms are representative of the kind levelled at functionalism and social systems theory throughout the 1960s and 1970s. As a sociological perspective, the generic social systems approach is denounced because its methodology is static and its ideology conservative. In emphasizing equilibrium and integration, it fails to account for change and conflict. In emphasizing harmonious relations between system parts, it overlooks the dysfunctional elements of social differentiation.

During the 1970s, these criticisms were contextualized by reference to Kuhn's (1962, 1970a) work in the philosophy of science. Although Kuhn (1962, 1970a) spoke primarily to natural scientists, his ideas were accepted readily by social scientists. In offering a structural explanation for the rise and fall of scientific perspectives, Kuhn's work was employed to explain the developmental status of social science traditions, or to use his primary term, 'paradigms'.

Nowhere was this interest in the developmental status and discipline structure of social science more excited than in the area of analysis known as the 'sociology of sociology'. Here numerous writers attempted to plot paradigm schemes for social science and to predict trends in theory development. In the early 1970s, several works appeared which used a Kuhnian interpretation to account for analytical fission in social theory.

The sociology of sociology

In this tradition, Gouldner's *The Coming Crisis in Western Sociology* (1970) was the most celebrated description of intellectual perspectives in transition. Gouldner described the paradigmatic dominance of structural-functionalism in the post-World War II period and its decline during the early to mid-1960s. He explained how, as a result of the decline of functionalism, a range of new perspectives and theories emerged, the most notable being Goffman's dramaturgy, Garfinkel's ethnomethodology, Homans and Blau's exchange theory, and (especially in Europe) various expressions of Marxist analysis.

Another explanation of the crisis phase was by Atkinson (1972) in *Orthodox Consensus and Radical Alternative*, a book which specified alternatives to the 'orthodox consensus' of which Parsons' work was the dominant post-war element. Atkinson based his analysis on principles from the sociology of knowledge and in so doing rejected what he saw as the determinism evident in Parsons, Weber and the mature Marx. Although Atkinson differed from Gouldner in suggesting that the sociology of the late 1960s and early 1970s was not so much polarized as convergent, his alternatives were found in much of the same literature. Atkinson stressed the need for a more adequate theory of the subject (actor), and offered as exemplars the works of 'Gouldner, Garfinkel, Douglas, Laing, Gross, Goffman and Matza' (p. 287). He argued that this 'micro' approach, which stressed voluntarism and situational analysis, should be complemented with an alternative 'macro' approach, and that we must develop concepts such as 'action classes' and 'social kaleidoscopes' to replace the static, and essentially bourgeois, notions of social structure which modern sociologists peddle. Atkinson suggested that this radical, alternative sociology would develop from a dynamic and humanistic interpretation of symbolic interactionism.

The most direct attempt at a Kuhnian interpretation, however, was found in Friedrichs' (1970) book *A Sociology of Sociology*, which defines the structure of sociology as a multiple paradigm science. Friedrichs set the tone for many later contributions by describing the rise and fall of functionalism in terms of a Kuhnian 'science in crisis' thesis. Like Gouldner (1970), he described the theoretical and analytical hegemony of structural-functionalism in the post-World War II period, this approach taking the form of full-blown Kuhnian paradigm during the 1950s and early 1960s. Friedrichs, however, developed this analysis to document the gradual erosion of the hegemony of functionalism from the mid-1960s onwards, with American sociology thereafter being in a state of 'revolutionary crisis'.

To support his thesis, Friedrichs drew upon arguments similar to those of Gouldner (1970). He suggested that the problems which beset functionalism and systems theory stemmed from the failure of consensus-based equilibrium models to explain the rise in political activism and social tension during the 1960s. Consequently sociology witnessed renewed interest in so-called radical approaches, and notably in the humanism of the young Marx. It was the failure of the systems paradigm to provide answers to problems of change and conflict which led to the emergence of a Kuhnian 'anomaly'. In documenting this scenario, Friedrichs outlined how conflict theory emerged as the main paradigm contender to functionalism. Friedrichs suggested that by the mid-1960s the conflict paradigm held as much sway with sociologists as did the systems paradigm, with sociology being subsequently locked in a revolutionary struggle between these two rival theory communities.

To explain this struggle, Friedrichs produced an ideal-type model based on the division between 'first- and second-order' paradigms. First-order paradigms referred to the images sociologists held of themselves as academics and scientists. Second-order paradigms concerned the image they held of the subject-matter. Of these, Friedrichs eleborated upon two forms of first-order paradigms to which sociologists subscribe, the 'priestly' and the 'prophetic'. The 'sociologist-as-priest' is committed to value-free analysis of social phenomena, whereas the 'sociologist-as-prophet' sees him- or herself as a social critic and agent of social change. For the former, the primary role of the sociologist is the scientific development of the discipline. For the latter it is the resolution of social problems. Friedrichs argued that both paradigms have at various times ruled the discipline, with sociology's second-order shifts being dependent upon which self-image was dominant. Friedrichs suggested that while the prophetic mode was dominant prior to World War II, it still remained 'pre-paradigmatic' at the second-order level. After World War II, however, when the priestly paradigm was dominant, sociology began to achieve paradigmatic status at the second order level, with the systems paradigm.

Friedrichs argued, therefore, that sociology has a history which can be explained in Kuhnian terms. This is a history based on three discontinuous periods. Before World War II, although governed by the prophetic mode, sociology was pre-paradigmatic. Subsequently, between World War II and the early to mid-1960s (Friedrichs specifies 1963 as the terminal year), sociology was dominated by the image of the sociologist-as-priest. During this period the systems approach proliferated to the extent that it achieved hegemonic control and became sociology's first paradigm. Finally, from around 1964, the discipline entered a period of 'revolutionary science' or 'science in crisis'. During this phase, conflict theory emerged as a strong candidate for paradigm status.

Paradigm models in sociology

In the sociology of sociology we find the themes, issues and problems of concern to analysts wishing to develop Kuhnian interpretations of social and organizational theory. While the importance of structural-functionalism, and of Parsonianism in particular, is accepted, the question of whether the social systems approach ever achieves full paradigmatic status remains moot. Similarly, while the relative decline of functionalism during the early to mid-1960s is suggested, there is less agreement over the list of possible paradigm replacements.

Uncertainty over these questions led to numerous attempts to define the paradigmatic status of sociology. Indeed, for the 1970s, it was argued that there were 'almost as many views of the paradigmatic status of sociology as there [were] sociologists attempting such analyses' (Eckburg and Hill 1979, p. 925). During this decade, debate centred on how literally the history of sociology should be interpreted in Kuhnian terms. While, for example, Friedrichs (1970) and Lehmann and Young (1974) argued that in Parsonian functionalism post-World War II sociology witnessed a full-blown Kuhnian paradigm, other commentators, such as Effrat (1973) and Denisoff et al. (1974), contested that this did not accord with Kuhn's (1962) view that sociology was an 'immature' science, and thus 'pre-paradigmatic'.

When we examine works which have attempted to specify the parameters of sociological paradigms we find ourselves in a virtual Tower of Babel. In Denisoff et al. (1974) we find the argument that sociology has never held a paradigm, and that instead there are merely paradigmatic assumptions which underpin the sociological enterprise. In an account based on a very broad definition of paradigm, as a belief matrix, Denisoff et al. suggest that the five main paradigm rivals in sociology are functionalism, conflict theory, micro-sociology, nominalism–voluntarism and social evolutionism.

Other interpretations have been more complex. Effrat (1973), for example, although professing a Kuhnian interpretation, strays widely from Kuhn's first principles, notably on interchanging the terms 'theory', 'perspective' and 'paradigm' almost at will. Effrat decides to employ a 'looser and more generous use of [Kuhn's] criteria' (1973, p. 11), arguing that we should go beyond Kuhn, for his thesis is 'still too rational, his revolutions still too bloodless' (p. 11). The end result is a typology in which to situate competing elements of the sociological enterprise. Based on the intersection of two dimensions – 'level of analysis' (micro–macro level paradigms) and 'substantive component emphasized' (the substantive factors that the paradigm treats as the principal independent variables or explanatory agents, i.e. 'material, affective, interactional and ideal/ symbolic') – Effrat uses this typology to define eight major competing paradigms for academic sociology, namely: Marxists; exchange theorists and utilitarians; culture and personality school; Freudians; Durkheimians or French collectivists; symbolic interactionists and activity theorists; Weberians and German idealists, Parsonians, cyberneticists; and phenomenologists and ethnomethodologists. Despite this long list, Effrat maintains there are still other paradigms he has not analysed.

More conservative in scope was the semi-historical inventory of Bottomore (1975). Like Friedrichs (1970), Bottomore stressed the relative dominance of functionalism during the post-World War II period and its decline from the early to mid-1960s. However, he suggests that we should not exaggerate the significance of these developments, for sociology has always been a multiple paradigm science. Indeed, Bottomore insists that crises similar to that of the late 1960s and early 1970s took place during the nineteenth century. Elaborating upon this theme, he argues for greater sophistication in the way we treat the fragmentation of the discipline, noting that although functionalism was the dominant creed of American sociology during the 1950s, its influence was never matched in either Eastern or Western Europe.

Bottomore qualifies this view, however, to argue that increased international academic communication has left a situation whereby from the mid-1960s a set of well-articulated and established paradigms have emerged. Like Friedrichs (1970) and Gouldner (1970), he attributes the relative decline of the functionalist paradigm to an overconcentration upon the static aspects of society and upon social equilibrium, which served to posit an unreal degree of functional unity and to display indifference to historical processes and historical explanations. Bottomore feels that this largely accounts for the revival of historical sociology, and especially of the earlier humanist works of Marx and an emphasis on consciousness. Notable in this revival were the works of Lukács, Gramsci and the critical theory of the Frankfurt School. Bottomore argues that in its assault upon sociological positivism, critical theory holds much affinity with modern philosophy of language and with phenomenology. Similarly, critical theory, in being an attempt to develop a 'radical' sociology, has certain affinities with an action-centred Marxian structuralism, although the latter could in many ways be accused of being ahistorical, with the main link being in the mode of structuralism advocated in the works of Althusser (1969, 1972). The historical inventory is complete when Bottomore outlines the paradigm advances made by phenomenological sociology, citing the growth of interest in the Weberian method of *verstehen*, the impact of Schutz's application of Husserl's ideas and, more recently, the emergence of ethnomethodology from phenomenology.

The most celebrated attempt to develop a paradigm model during this period, however, was that by Ritzer (1975) in *Sociology: a Multiple Paradigm Science*. Another to suggest that sociology has never been dominated either completely or relatively by any single theory community, he argues that since the 1940s it has witnessed three competing belief systems, which he terms the 'social facts', 'social definition' and 'social behaviour' paradigms. Advancing a Kuhnian thesis, Ritzer's work revolves around discussion of the four constituents which underpin the formation of these paradigms, namely 'exemplars', 'theories', 'methods' and, above all, 'images of the subject-matter'.

To define the paradigms, Ritzer attempts to make logical connections between these components. For the social facts paradigm, he describes how advocates of structural-functionalism, conflict theory, and systems analysis conduct their research using questionnaire and interview methods, view the subject-matter in terms of macroscopic social structure, and share an exemplar in the work of Durkheim. For the social definitionist paradigm, advocates of symbolic interactionism, action theory and phenomenology employ observation research (particularly participant observation), define the subject-matter in terms of micro-level intra- and inter-subjective phenomena and take as an exemplar Weber's work on social action and *verstehen*. Finally, for the social behaviour paradigm, advocates of behaviourism and exchange theory conduct field and laboratory experiments, define human behaviour in terms of responses controlled by external stimuli or reinforcement and take Skinnerian psychology as their exemplar.

For the developmental progress of sociology, Ritzer maintains that a dominant paradigm is unlikely to emerge in the short or medium term. Instead, he moots the possibility of paradigm reconciliation and discusses the notion of paradigm 'bridges'. Ritzer argues that 'all of the great sociological theorists were able to bridge paradigms. They were capable of moving ... between two or more of the paradigms discussed' (pp. 212–13). However, whereas Durkheim, Weber and Marx are all cited as 'bridgers', only Parsons is credited with reconciling all three paradigms successfully.[6]

Because Ritzer's work has made more impact than most, his paradigms have been scrutinized more closely, especially for internal consistency. There have been, thus far, assessments of the theoretical, empirical and historical accuracy of his paradigm propositions. For theory, the logic of Ritzer's analysis has been questioned in that it subsumes, under the 'social facts' paradigm, structural-functionalism and conflict theory, two approaches often cited as sociological rivals. Similarly, his choice of

Skinner's work as an exemplar for social behaviour paradigm has been questioned because it violates the sociological frame of reference (Hassard 1985).

When Ritzer's paradigms have been subject to empirical scrutiny, for example, by Snizek (1976) and Friedheim (1979), the results have failed to support the paradigm differentiation proposed. Instead of paradigms being empirically distinct,

> factists, behaviourists and definitionists merge with each other; individual theorists often bear more resemblence to theorists from outside their group than to fellow perspective members. (Friedheim 1979, p. 64)

Similarly, for Ritzer's two central paradigm components, 'images of the subject matter' and 'methods', 'there appears to be little in the way of empirical support for each of the intra paradigm linkages proposed' (Snizek 1976, p. 219). Finally, Wells and Picou (1981), who focus on the issue of paradigm evolution, criticize Ritzer for developing an ahistorical account, one in which the issue of paradigm maturity, and in particular the relationship between paradigms and normal science, is inadequately addressed. As Ritzer gives the impression that all paradigms are at the same developmental stage, 'the question of whether a multiple paradigm field is paradigmatic remains moot' (p. 74).

Paradigm models in organization theory

Although from the early 1970s the Kuhnian crisis model became a dominant framework in theoretical sociology, it was some years before it was employed extensively in organization theory. Although elements of crisis theory are found in David Silverman's *The Theory of Organizations* (1970), it is not until the late 1970s and early 1980s that such analysis becomes common in organization studies (see Driggers 1977, Benson 1977a, Burrell and Morgan 1979, Benson 1983, Morgan 1983, Clark 1985, Guba 1985, Lincoln 1985). When they do appear, works again vary markedly in their correspondence to Kuhnian theory. Like sociologists, organization theorists adhere only loosely to Kuhn's first principles. Rather than being the 'classic laws' of sociological theory (Kuhn 1962) paradigms are defined in less tangible ways, characteristically as the theoretical spaces produced when we contrast methodological and philosophical traditions.

Review and critique

In organization theory, examples of such practice during this period are found in works by Pondy and Boje (1981), Evered and Louis (1981), and

Burrell and Morgan (1979). Pondy and Boje (1981) define their paradigm spaces by way of a community structure model of organization theory. Rather than develop a new model, however, they simply take Ritzer's (1975) framework for sociology and input names, concepts and networks from organization analysis. In so doing, Pondy and Boje argue that while Ritzer's social behaviourist and social factist paradigms have historically dominated organization theory, this has been to the neglect of the third paradigm, the social definitionist. To provide 'fresh insight' into the discipline the social definitionist paradigm must be developed into 'parity with the other two reigning paradigms' (p. 82).

This assertion heralds an argument for conducting multiple paradigm research in organizations. Pondy and Boje suggest that if we reject a truth-value function of theory, where only one theory can be most nearly true, and accept the explanatory power of multiple embedding paradigms, we find 'the function of theory shifts from that of truth providing to insight seeking' (p. 84). When theories are no longer struggling for the prize of sole explanation, the acceptance of several incompatible theories is no longer problematic. Instead, the criterion becomes one of discovering 'how much insight and understanding can be extracted from the entire constellation of theories generated from the several paradigms in use' (p. 84).

On exploring these spaces, we find in the social facts paradigm work on structural differentiation, contingency theory, organizational role sets, interorganizational relations, socio-technical systems, power structures and organizational design. Social factists include Charles Perrow, Richard Hall, Amatai Etzioni, (post-exchange theory) Peter Blau, Derek Pugh and the Aston School, Paul Lawrence and Jay Lorsch, Joan Woodward, Jerry Hage and more recently Howard Aldrich and Jeffrey Pfeffer.

In contrast, the social behaviourist paradigm reflects work on industrial psychology more than sociology. The major research areas are management or leadership style, job design, group pressures, incentive schemes and organizational climate. Prominent figures are Victor Vroom, Ed Lawler, Lyman Porter, Fred Fiedler, Robert Hulin and Richard Hackman.

Finally, for the less developed social definition paradigm, theorists and researchers are more difficult to locate. Indeed, only three works are cited, with the 'exemplar' of March and Simon's *Organizations* (1958) being joined by Weick's (1969, 1974) works on the processes of organizing and Silverman's (1970) treatment of action theory.

As with Ritzer (1975), however, questions arise over the internal consistency of these paradigms. Although Pondy and Boje (1981) admit to having 'possibly offended people by omission or improper classification' (p. 86), a closer examination reveals that their groupings are problematic in relation to each of the four paradigm components. Regarding 'methods', for example, one of the leading factists, Derek Pugh, based his Aston studies work on techniques of factor analysis, a methodology characteristic of the social behaviour paradigm. This work saw methods from the psychology of personality used to research organization structure, an approach which owed its origins to Pugh's training as a psychologist in Edinburgh.[7]

For the second component, 'theories', it can be argued that Pondy and Boje fail to differentiate adequately between scholars and their perspectives. Proponents of contingency theory, for example, such as Fiedler, Lawrence and Lorsch, Woodward and others, are found in both the social facts and social behaviour paradigms. Similarly, systems theory forms the basis for research located in both these paradigms, for example, sociotechnical systems, interorganizational relations, and management and leadership functions.

For the third component, 'exemplars', March and Simon's *Organizations* (1958) is the model cited for the social definitionist paradigm. This work, however, is commonly held to be a modified form of behaviourism. Although March and Simon allow for an element of subjective rationality arising from an individual's personal frame of reference, they generally portray human behaviour as being shaped by stimuli in the environment. Such stimuli provide the influences to which humans respond in the somewhat mechanistic manner of 'administrative man', adapted by March and Simon from the earlier work of Simon (1947).

Finally, for the 'images of the subject-matter', there seem to be as many substantive similarities as differences. By invoking standard sociological dimensions it can be argued that both factists and behaviourists reflect an objectivist and positivist orientation to the study of organizations. In Friedrichs' (1970) terms, they reflect the priestly approach of value-neutrality rather than the conflict orientation of the prophets. Further, whereas most commentators point to the rise of conflict theory during the crisis phase, no such development is acknowledged by Pondy and Boje, even though Ritzer (1975) highlighted this when defining the factist paradigm.

Qualitative vs. quantitative

A second method for defining paradigm spaces in organizational analysis has been through taking methodological positions and suggesting that these equate with differing belief systems or world views. Writers who attempt this often suggest that new insights into the subject-matter can be gained through developing variations on the theme of qualitative versus quantitative data gathering techniques.

This approach is found in Evered and Louis (1981), who cite the second edition of Kuhn's *Structure of Scientific Revolutions* (1970a) in defining a paradigm as a 'disciplinary matrix', rather than as an 'exemplar' (see postscript to Kuhn 1970a). This discussion sees two methodological paradigms defined for organizational research, 'inquiry from the outside' and 'inquiry from the inside'. Evered and Louis argue that by defining these methodological spaces we 'increase the understanding and appreciation of epistemological issues in organizational inquiry' (p. 386). On filling their spaces, Evered and Louis argue that inquiry from the outside represents the orthodox approach to organization studies. It is the positivist model for organizational research, which calls for detachment on the part of the researcher who gathers data according to a priori analytical categories. The aim of inquiry from the outside is to uncover knowledge that can be generalized to many situations. In contrast, inquiry from the inside involves the experiential involvement of the researcher, the absence of a priori analytical categories and an intent to understand a particular situation. Systematic methods for this paradigm are found in ethnomethodology, anthropology and clinical methods.

As methods for organizational research, however, these paradigms differ in their developmental status. At present, according to Evered and Louis, insider strategies should be used only in the exploration of initial research projects. This methodology is useful for 'generating tentative categories . . . [which] . . . may subsequently be used as the a priori categories guiding the more deductive hypotheses-testing from the outside' (p. 390). Although other possibilities exist for combining the paradigms, only this approach is considered feasible because developing a new social science that can synthesize the paradigms, 'human action science', seems distant, while the aggregation of paradigm results within a single research report runs up against problems of 'acceptability' for journal publication due to the 'strong bias toward inquiry from the outside' (p. 392). Orthodox professional practice suggests that inquiry from the inside 'may appear to be so foggy that its findings often have dubious precision, rigour or credibility', although 'these shortcomings can be overcome by inquiry from the outside' (p. 392).[8]

Metatheory

Finally, of works that have attempted to define paradigm spaces in organization theory, Burrell and Morgan's (1979) *Sociological Paradigms and Organizational Analysis* has attracted the most attention (see Salaman 1981, Griffiths 1983, Louis 1983, White 1983, Hopper and Powell 1985, Clark 1985, Holland 1990). Burrell and Morgan specify four paradigms for

THE SOCIOLOGY OF RADICAL CHANGE

'Radical humanist'

'Radical structuralist'

SUBJECTIVE

OBJECTIVE

'Interpretive'

'Functionalist'

THE SOCIOLOGY OF REGULATION

Figure 2 Four-paradigm model of social theory

organizational analysis by intersecting subject–object debates in the theory of social science with consensus–conflict debates in the theory of society. The four paradigms produced are the functionalist, the interpretive, the radical humanist and the radical structuralist (Figure 2).

Burrell and Morgan dissect social science by reference to the philosopher's toolkit of ontology and epistemology. They concentrate upon the metatheoretical assumptions which underpin theoretical statements. Having identified such assumptions, they plot various theoretical positions on their four-paradigm model.

For analysing the nature of social science, they suggest it is useful to conceptualize 'four sets of assumptions related to ontology, epistemology, human nature and methodology' (p. 1: see Figure 3). Burrell and Morgan argue that all social scientists, implicitly or explicitly, approach their disciplines via assumptions about the nature of the social world and how it should be researched. Assumptions are made about 'the very essence of the phenomena under study' (ontology), 'the grounds of knowledge' (epistemology), 'the relationships between human beings' (human nature) and 'the way in which one attempts to investigate and obtain 'knowledge' about the 'real world' (methodology).

For assumptions about the nature of society, Burrell and Morgan draw upon attempts by earlier social theorists (e.g. Lockwood 1956, Dahrendorf 1959) to distinguish between 'those approaches to sociology which concentrate on explaining the nature of social order and equilibrium . . . and those . . . concerned with the problems of change, conflict and coercion' (p. 10). However, instead of invoking the usual terms of order–conflict or consensus–conflict debates, Burrell and Morgan talk of differences between

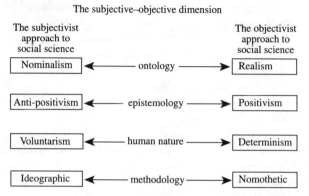

Figure 3 Scheme for analysing assumptions about social science

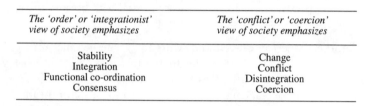

Figure 4 Sociology of regulation and the sociology of radical change

the sociology of regulation and the sociology of radical change (Figure 4).

Through polarizing these dimensions, the 'conservative' functionalist and interpretive paradigms are contrasted with the 'radical' humanist and structuralist paradigms. Conversely, with regard to the nature of social science, the functionalist and radical humanist paradigms, which adopt an objectivist and scientific stance, are contrasted with the subjectivist emphases of the interpretive and radical humanist paradigms. In presenting the model the authors argue that these paradigms should be considered 'contiguous but separate – contiguous because of the shared characteristics, but separate because the differentiation is ... of sufficient importance to warrant treatment of the paradigms as four distinct entities' (p. 23). As such, the four paradigms 'define fundamentally different perspectives for the analysis of social phenomena. They approach this endeavour from contrasting standpoints and generate quite different concepts and analytical tools' (p. 23).

Although the Burrell and Morgan model has been well received within organization theory (so much so that it has formed the basis for conferences on both sides of the Atlantic), those borrowing it have often done so with little regard to its internal validity. As a result many problems have been overlooked. Pinder and Bourgeois (1982), for example, note how Burrell and Morgan's application of ontology is misplaced. In a paper on cross-discipline borrowing, in this case organization theory borrowing from philosophy, they argue that Burrell and Morgan adopt the non-standard use of ontology that has been popular during the last thirty years. Pinder and Bourgeois explain that this use refers not to ontology *per se* but to the set of 'existential pre-suppositions' of a theory, or the set of assumptions that must be made if one is to accept a theory as valid. Pinder and Bourgeois argue that for the past three centuries ontology has had a relatively stable meaning as 'the study of being *qua* being, i.e. the study of existence in general, independent of any particular existing things' (p. 13). In the strict sense of the term, therefore,

it is not a question of ontology to ask whether organizations exist ... whether organizations exist is a matter for science to deal with because it concerns the existence of particular things, not the nature of existence. (p. 13)

Another issue for Burrell and Morgan is whether the intra-paradigm networks specified in their model adhere to common, or at least similar, images of the subject matter. In the same way as Friedheim (1979) criticized Ritzer (1975) for placing conflict theory and structural-functionalism within the same paradigm, it can be argued that their location of Silverman's (1970) action theory in the same paradigm as Skinnerian behaviourism (Skinner 1953) is problematic. Silverman's (1970) work on the action frame of reference could be better located within the interpretive paradigm, despite the arguments Burrell and Morgan make for the metatheoretical assumptions being characteristic of the subjectivist region of the functionalist paradigm.

Also of concern are the debates Burrell and Morgan use to separate their theoretical spaces. Notable here is the way they divorce Marxian humanism from Marxian structuralism by advancing Althusser's (1969) thesis of the epistemological break, which suggests that in Marx's work there is a cleavage between his earlier philosophical and humanistic works and his later, or 'mature', scientific and economic writings. In social theory, this thesis is far from uncontested. For many writers there is an underlying unity in Marx's work, not a gestalt switch from idealism to materialism.

Of importance to our later work (see Chapters 4 and 5), however, is the fact that because the four paradigms are exclusive entities, we are left with problems concerning the justification for paradigm incommensurability, the relativism to which this seems to lead, and ultimately of how inter-paradigm understanding can be achieved. In Burrell and Morgan, as in the majority of neo-Kuhnian models, we are given no indication as to how progress is to be signalled or standards met. Instead, we are left in a relativist vacuum, where theory communities operate in hermetic isolation, researchers talk past their professional enemies, and paradigms explain the world with equal status and power. Although Burrell and Morgan offer examples of paradigm transitions through gestalt-like leaps of faith (e.g. by Marx and, in organization theory, David Silverman), the explanation of the change process is never developed beyond a rather superficial acceptance of the instant-paradigm thesis (see Watkins 1970 and Maruyama 1974 on this issue). This means that in Burrell and Morgan references to inter-paradigm understanding are confusing. While initially there is the assertion that 'the four paradigms are mutually exclusive ... they offer different ways of seeing' (1979, p. 25), later there is oscillation between Giddens' argument that 'some inter-paradigm debate is also possible' and their own, rather equivocal, view that 'relations between paradigms are better described in terms of 'disinterested hostility rather than "debate"' (1979, p. 36). This equivocation invites Friedheim's (1979) censure about sociologists arguing for paradigm blindness and paradigm bridges simultaneously.

A defence of functionalism in organization theory

We have, thus far, deconstructed many of the analytical pillars of the functionalism paradigm and described some approaches presented as rivals to it. We must note, however, that the debate over the paradigm status of functionalism continues. This debate has, in fact, become particularly heated in recent years, with discussion of the incommensurability of paradigms leading to highly polarized positions.

In organization theory, the Burrell and Morgan model has been at the centre of this debate (see Donaldson 1985 and 1991, Reed 1985, Ackroyd 1989 and 1992, Willmott 1990). As the model's basic premise is that rival paradigms are incommensurable, it appears to adopt a very extreme form of Kuhnism. Burrell and Morgan advance a very pure and hermetic form of sociological relativism, one which brings into question the very basis for scientific communication and progress. They are apparently not alone in this, however, for similar criticisms have been levelled against Silverman (1970), Mouzelis (1975), Benson (1977a, 1977b, 1983), Perry (1977), Clegg and Dunkerley (1980) and Morgan (1986, 1990). It is claimed that such writers advocate paradigm closure, a situation where researchers develop their approach only by reference to the ideas of like-minded colleagues. The corollary is that only a limited number of accounts of organizations are possible, these being determined by metatheory. As Ackroyd (1992) argues 'the discovery of the relevance of metatheory to organization ... is made by these writers only to be strictly and intentionally limited to a specific range of alternatives' (p. 12). In this view, suggests Ackroyd, the act of choosing between theories involves reference to criteria which are external to the meaning of ideas about the organization.

Concern with paradigm closure has been expressed most forcefully in Donaldson's book *In Defence of Organization Theory* (1985), which attempts to refute the Burrell and Morgan (1979) thesis and also the arguments of Silverman (1970), Benson (1977a), Heydebrand (1977), Goldman and Van Houten (1977), and Clegg and Dunkerley (1980), the 'critics' as he calls them (see also Donaldson 1991). Above all, Donaldson denies the claim that for the last twenty-five years social research has been in a state of conceptual crisis, with the credibility of structural-functionalism having been undermined by schools that advance subjective theories and political interpretations of social structures and processes. He also denies the associated claims that social science is now characterized by the proliferation of competing paradigms; the failure of functionalism to account for voluntarism and social conflict has promoted rival perspectives based on principles of phenomenology and Marxism; those who promote subjectivist or conflict-based approaches are located within two paradigms which challenge the systems theory orthodoxy, namely social action theory and radical structuralism.

In his 'reply to the critics', Donaldson defends functionalist concepts such as goals and needs, and argues that the concepts, theories and explanations of the social systems approach are both meaningful and philosophically sound.[9] He rebuts, in particular, the twin charges that structural-functionalism is unable to explain social change and that it advocates an exclusively consensus-based orientation to values. Donaldson turns defence into attack when he suggests that the paradigms which are supposed to explain change and conflict – social action theory and radical structuralism – can, in fact, be incorporated within functionalism.

Indeed, these arguments culminate when Donaldson examines, critically, the four main 'alternative' paradigms adopted by the critics. He argues that social action theory overstates individual volition, understates socio-economic determinations and displays a tendency towards psychological reductionism and low-level, unconnected generalizations. The sociology of organizations approach is analytically 'fruitful', although it will never assimilate organization theory with general sociology. Marxian organization theory is caught between the subject-matter of organization and the Marxist concern with societal change, and has an unfortunate predilection to dissolve organization into sites of class conflict. And the strategic choice thesis represents an inconsistent amalgam of systems theory, social action theory and radical structuralism; it takes recourse to political determinism and consequently neglects important design contingencies. Overall,

Donaldson suggests that, in comparison with functionalist organizational research, and principally contingency theory, the critics' work is partial and their arguments superficial.[10]

Attack and defence

Concern over Donaldson's analysis has been sufficient to see an edition of a leading academic journal devoted to the issues it raises. The editors of *Organization Studies* (1988) invited a panel of researchers – Howard Aldrich, John Child, Stewart Clegg, Bob Hinings and Lucien Karpik – to contribute to a symposium based on Donaldson's defence of functionalism, under the banner 'Offence and Defence'.

A central concern for the panel was the relationship between sociology and organization theory. One panelist, Hinings (1988), suggested that the organization theory Donaldson defends has moved away from sociology and developed in its own right. Hinings argues that although, initially, sociology and the study of organizations were synonymous, this is no longer the case. Instead, one of the major changes of the past twenty-five years has been the shift of those studying organizations at the macro-level from sociology departments to business schools.[11] Although Hinings originally felt this represented simply a displacement of people from the one to the other, he now thinks an institutionalized split has developed, with the business schools producing their own particular form of intellectual product. Rather than discuss, therefore, paradigm switches from functionalism to action theory, or from structuralism to humanism, Hinings suggests we should devote our attentions to that from sociology to organization theory. This disciplinary separation has to be accepted because, although organization theory has epistemological, theoretical and methodological issues to face, these are not necessarily the same as those of the sociology of organizations. Instead, organization theory 'legitimately follows a *different* drummer to sociology' (p. 3, emphasis in original). This situation leads us to consider the whole set of issues about the legitimacy of a discipline, issues which sociology itself faced when separating itself from philosophy and anthropology.

In contrast, another panelist, Clegg (1988) denounced the idea of discipline separation and argued that this belittles the power implicit in a more critical sociology of organizations. He suggests that Donaldson is exceptionally partial in his use of the term 'organization theory', which is in fact inconsistent with the way it is routinely applied by members of the organization theory community. Donaldson constructs a theoretical space called 'organization theory' in terms which accord with its use in a particular context, that of North American business and management schools. Indeed, during the course of *In Defence of Organization Theory*, and notably in the latter stages 'this space has suffered erosion down to an essential centre: that of the "contingency-design approach"' (p. 7).[12]

Redirections

The discipline structure of organization theory is also the main concern of Reed's (1985) book *Redirections in Organizational Analysis*. This work represents a partial endorsement of the critics' views rather than those of Donaldson. Reed is another to assess developments in organization theory over the past twenty-five years. Initially he analyses the systems theory perspective of the 1950s and 1960s, which he links to managerialism and technocracy. He then documents the challenge to functionalism and the rise of new perspectives of action theory, negotiated order theory and ethnomethodology. Although supporting the need for organization analysis to account for subjective perceptions and social interaction, he notes the neglect of larger social structures in these approaches. This leads Reed to document the next redirection for organizational analysis, which sees the rise of critical theory and radical structuralism.[13]

In predicting future directions for organizational analysis, the merits of the 'social practice' framework are discussed. This perspective links the concept of organization as 'coordinated bureaucracy' to those of an 'institutional web of social norms' and a 'stratum of production controlled by an administrative cadre responsive to the interests of a dominant class'. The practice framework involves the simultaneous pursuit of four modes of analysis: cognitive mapping, interpretive understanding, structural analysis and historical reconstruction.

The analysis finally sees Reed outline four possible future programmatics within which this framework could develop: 'integrationism' – which is for eclectic reconciliation; 'isolationism' – which is for separate development of paradigms; 'imperialism' – which is for take-over by Marxian theory; 'pluralism' – which is for a discourse between partial perspectives that reflects ambiguities and rejects premature closure by any one integrated explanation. Of these, Reed champions pluralism, which is a dialogue between perspectives in which ambiguity and tension are retained rather than resolved, and in which the scientific method is abandoned in favour of alternative metatheories.

In Reed's book we find historical interpretations similar to those of Burrell and Morgan (1979) and Clegg and Dunkerley (1980), but coupled with an eschewing of paradigm apartheid and incommensurable positions. Reed differs from both Donaldson and the critics in attempting to produce a balanced appreciation of theory developments rather than interpreting events from a Marxian, interpretive, or functionalist standpoint. This balanced commentary is indeed the main strength of the book for, rather than being pure thesis, it offers a detailed sociological overview, albeit largely at the level of metatheory. Instead of discussion of individual theories of organization, we find epistemological positions and sociological pespectives described, contrasted and criticized. One result, however, is that the book contains relatively little direct analysis of organizations, since instead organization theory is portrayed as a field beset by internal debate.

Reed has recently engaged in a dialogue with Donaldson over the competing interpretations of organization theory found in their books (see Donaldson 1989; Reed 1989). Donaldson (1989) feels that Reed's work is flawed, because 'numerous writers on organizations come in for the quick chop, not backed by any real explanation of where their work is defective' (p. 247). The Aston group's work, for example, is apparently dismissed by Reed in this way. Donaldson states that one cannot reasonably evaluate the past or future of organizational analysis without a consideration of the details of the subject. He feels that Reed's 'light touch' leads to the familiar misrepresentation of the structural contingency approach.[14]

Donaldson argues further that an underdeveloped view of the past leads Reed to a similarly underdeveloped view of the future. In particular, Reed's practice framework is problematic, for it develops no theoretical propositions beyond the generally thematic, and there are no chains of deductive inference. The vague nature of the practice framework is evident when it is employed on three case studies: Selznick's (1949) work on the Tennessee Valley Authority, Gouldner's (1954) analysis of the gypsum plant and Crozier's (1964) work on French bureaucracy. The reworking of these cases represents, for Donaldson, nothing more than the same highly general commentary about the status of organization theory, one which repeats the same broad critical themes.[15]

Donaldson suggests finally that although Reed rejects the notion that organization theory must develop in each paradigm separately, he nevertheless retains in his pluralist model 'an image of separate theoretical camps which intercommunicate but which retain their separation to guarantee the continuing "tension"' (Donaldson 1989, p. 249). Donaldson finds this nihilistic, for there seems little prospect of developing an internally coherent body of valid, objective knowledge in this way. Although Reed claims to eschew the worst excesses of paradigmism, Donaldson feels he is still 'under the influence of epistemologicalism à la Burrell and Morgan (1979)' (p. 249).[16]

In response, Reed (1989), like Clegg (1988), has suggested that the context in which Donaldson places his remarks is of organization theory as a specialist sub-discipline with its own theoretical frameworks, research strategies and objects of study.[17] Donaldson locates organization theory within the project of legitimizing positivism as the basis for conducting social research and champions a policy of intellectual closure associated with the development of a profession. Donaldson's assessment of *Redirections in Organizational Analysis* is thus predicated on assumptions in direct opposition to those informing Reed's own work. Rather than define the *modus operandi* of a professional discipline, Reed's own objective is 'the recovery and retrieval of organizational analysis as a constituent element within the Western tradition of socio-political theory' (Reed 1989, p. 257). Unlike *In Defence of Organization Theory*, which aims to differentiate organizational analysis as a specialized branch of applied social science, *Redirections* advocates the intellectual openness and diversity which, Reed feels, has blossomed in the wake of the breakdown of the systems theory orthodoxy.

Reed argues, therefore, that it is not surprising that Donaldson finds the historical interpretations of *Redirections* erroneous, for they directly challenge his view of the recent past as a brief and wasteful interruption to the progress of organization theory as a policy science. What is interesting is that Donaldson offers no historical analysis to support his own interpretation. Instead, Donaldson presents

a decontextualised and ahistorical account of contemporary organizational analysis that is shaped in such a way that it automatically supports the universal truth of an intellectual orthodoxy which has been violated in various ways by heretical counter-movements. (p. 258)

Conclusions

In earlier chapters we have documented the origins and effects of intellectual orthodoxy in social and organizational analysis. In this chapter we have attempted to deconstruct some of the principles on which that orthodoxy rests. We have discussed the thesis that organization theory is currently in a state of conceptual crisis in which the hegemony of social systems analysis is threatened by a series of alternative intellectual perspectives. This situation represents a 'crisis' in that there is no obvious successor to systems theory. Writers either radically defend the principles of systems theory or advocate a range of alternatives to it. There is little consistency between their proposals. The organizational cake is sliced in various ways according to differences in method, philosophy, image of the subject-matter and level of analysis.

The crisis is deepened by the fact that the notion of paradigm heterodoxy is often joined by one of paradigm closure. Writers who specify a range of paradigm candidates often add that these various communities are incommensurable with one another. Professional practice in different traditions is based on philosophies which are antithetical: scientists from different paradigms do not debate, they talk through one another. This is a problem in that paradigm incommensurability seems to infer an extreme form of sociological relativism. If scientists cannot debate how can progress be signalled? In place of the linear accretion of facts we appear to possess different traditions offering different interpretations, with none nearer the truth than any other.

Finally, as a 'live' example of the kinds of problem which beset the analyst of organization theory, we have presented details from a continuing debate on the discipline structure of the subject. In the works of Donaldson, Reed and the 'critics', we see how polarized the views about the current nature of organization theory can become, as the various parties appear to pursue an internecine form of debate. There is no agreement on what the paradigm structure of organization theory is, or on whether paradigm plurality represents a threat or an opportunity. Instead we witness a failure to agree on even the most basic of questions which concern the community structure.

In the next two chapters, therefore, we will attempt to 'go beyond' the crisis debate in organization theory. Specifically, we will seek to breach the hermetic logic of the paradigm incommensurability thesis (Chapter 4) and, thereafter, develop a methodology for multiple paradigm research (Chapter 5).

4 Closed paradigms and analytical openings

The critics from Silverman (1970) to Burrell and Morgan (1979) have used as a cornerstone of their critique the concept of incommensurable paradigms in organization theory.   (Donaldson 1988, p. 31)

Introduction

In the last chapter we noted how the literature of organization theory has been replete with assessments of its paradigmatic status. We have seen numerous works analysing the study of organizations by reference to alternatives to the dominant 'functionalist' paradigm. The identification of new paradigm candidates has for many signalled a state of crisis, the orthodoxy being undermined by 'critics' who claim to solve problems which proponents of a generic systems approach are incapable of solving, mainly concerning change and conflict. These developments, in what may be termed the 'sociology of organization theory', have been predicated on Thomas Kuhn's history of science, with elements from *The Structure of Scientific Revolutions* thesis being used to justify descriptions of community structure. Kuhn's seminal concept of 'paradigm' has been the medium for depicting the development progress of organizational theory as 'poly-paradigmatic' (Lammers 1974).

However, despite the wealth of material generated by this process, the philosophy on which this style of analysis is based, 'conventionalism' (see Kuhn 1962, Hanson 1958, Feyerabend 1970a), has all too frequently been used in a superficial way. Kuhnian theory, in particular, has been used as the basis for works demonstrating scant awareness of primary principles. Concepts from conventionalist philosophy have been used in ways inappropriate to standard debate. In organization theory, for example, few concepts have been employed as inconsistently as that of paradigm. This concept, originally the centrepiece of Kuhn's argument, has become progressively devalued, so much so that a once powerful notion – similar, in many ways, to a *Weltanschauung* – is now employed at all levels of analysis, being substituted freely for terms such as perspective, theory, discipline, school, or method. Indeed, commentators' talk of an 'individual's paradigm' (Parkes 1976) illustrates the lack of discrimination.

We will, therefore, now address issues central to this paradigms debate. We will assess some logical problems emerging from commentaries depicting paradigms as incommensurable, and discuss the questions this raises for the communication of ideas in organization theory. The chapter will assess the correspondence between paradigm models and the philosophical principles upon which they are founded. It is argued that only by returning to the original philosophies of science on which these ideas are based can we discover whether original principles have been interpreted correctly and whether they have provided a sound basis for mapping the intellectual terrain of organizational theory. Analysis will show that current paradigm schemes in organizational sociology are not only based on a truncated reading of Kuhn, but also that their logic is ambiguous when confronting issues of scientific communication.

To tackle these problems, we will first return to basics. We will discuss Kuhn's philosophy of science and centrally his concept of paradigm.

Elements of Kuhnism

The widespread reputation of *The Structure of Scientific Revolutions* (1962, 1970a) results from Kuhn's claim that traditional wisdom in the philosophy of science did not equate with the historical evidence. Kuhn's suggestion is that dominant theories of scientific practice, whether inductivist or falsificationist, are incompatible with the facts of how science has actually progressed. Falsificationists, however 'sophisticated' (Lakatos 1970), are methodologists whose ideals are never met. Scientific practice is never realized in Popperian terms and, as such,

no process yet discovered by the historical study of scientific development at all resembles the methodological stereotype of falsification by direct comparison with nature. (Kuhn 1962, p. 77)

For Kuhn, the everyday reality of science is more akin to the life cycle of the political community than to the dictates of formal logic. Theories which portray science as the linear accretion of verified hypotheses are completely rejected, as instead Kuhn speaks of discontinuous periods of normative and revolutionary activity. Kuhn claims that the history of science has witnessed numerous upheavals in which accepted wisdom is replaced by a new way of seeing, this process serving to change fundamentally the basis of a science's reality concept. Indeed, the degree of change is such that the standards, concepts and procedures of the post-revolutionary approach are totally incompatible with those of the pre-revolutionary consensus. For scientists, this change experience is akin to the appreciation of a new gestalt, the process being similar to religious conversion. When science changes, a new approach emerges based upon the fresh dictates of an alternative community structure, the new tradition, like the old, being what Kuhn terms a 'paradigm'.

For us, it is Kuhn's likening of paradigm change to the instant transformation of the gestalt-switch which is important, for this argument seems to deny any possibility of communication between paradigms. As Kuhn states, during periods of revolutionary science, 'scientists do not see something as something else; instead, they simply see it' (1970a, p. 85). Kuhn argues that a change of paradigm allegiance cannot be based on open debate as there are no logical arguments to demonstrate the superiority of one paradigm over another. As the new paradigm is incommensurate with the old, there is no recourse to an independent arbiter or mediating third party. Indeed, there can be no logical demarcation of the supremacy of one paradigm over another, for their advocates hold fast to separate sets of standards and metaphysical beliefs. Being a proponent of a particular paradigm means one can never concede to the premises of another. The findings of a rival paradigm are not acceptable. Kuhn argues that 'when paradigms enter ... into a battle about paradigm choice, their role is necessarily circular. Each group uses its own paradigm to argue in that paradigm's defence' (1970a, p. 94). Rival paradigms cut up the world with different standards, different assumptions, different language. The result is that 'the normal-scientific tradition that emerges from a scientific revolution is not only incompatible but often actually incommensurable with that which has gone before' (1970a, p. 103).

This analysis has made a considerable impact upon organization theory. As most commentators argue that the social and organizational sciences are poly-paradigmatic, this suggests that communication and debate is impossible. Paradigms are based on assumptions which are in fundamental opposition to those of their rivals (Burrell and Morgan 1979; Jackson and Carter 1991). This, however, has led to a contradiction. For while analysts argue that paradigms are exclusive, and that scientists tend to remain locked within their paradigm-learned perceptions, many also claim that we need people who are specialists in more than one paradigm (Pondy and Boje 1981; Martin 1990). This has meant that in virtually all paradigm models there is confusion over the issue of incommensurability. We have seen that in the best-known scheme, by Burrell and Morgan (1979), references to inter-paradigm communication are confusing – they assert that paradigms are mutually exclusive, but imply that inter-paradigm understanding is possible (see above, p. 69). We know also that Burrell and Morgan are not alone in this. Similar accusations have been made by Friedheim (1979) about Ritzer's (1975) work, and by Eckburg and Hill (1979) regarding descriptions of paradigm relations in theoretical sociology.

To accomplish progress on paradigm mediation we need to resolve many of these contradictions. To establish a basis for discourse we require a thesis with which to confront the relativism of paradigm incommensurability. Initially we must go beyond a basic, second-hand reading of Kuhn and explore deeper to expose some of the logical inconsistencies in his writings.

The main problems: incommensurability and relativism

Kuhn's original position, in attacking the proposition of theory-independent 'facts', seems to deny the possibility of objective choice between paradigms. There can be no 'good reasons' for prefering a new paradigm as such reasons will always be paradigm-dependent. As Kuhn states, 'the competition between paradigms is not the sort of battle that can be resolved by proof' (1962, p. 47).

In Kuhnian theory the two traditional pillars of science, objectivity and progress, are seemingly removed. We are denied any external means for rationally evaluating competing paradigms; our evaluations are instead based on principles which reflect our own belief system. We see a unique world from whichever paradigm we are situated in. This position appears a relativist one in that while scientific theories may change this can never signal progress. As Kuhn said, 'Like the choice between competing political institutions, that between competing paradigms proves to be a choice between incompatible modes of community life' (1970a, p. 94).

These problems of relativism were central to the contributions collected by Lakatos and Musgrave (1970), or the literature commonly known as the 'Kuhn–Popper debate'. For our purposes, the central issue is Popper's attack on Kuhn's use of irrationalist symbols, that is Kuhn's descriptions of dogmatic scientific activity. While Popper's well-known suggestion in *Logik der Forschung* (1968) is that there is a necessary place for dogma – because we must not reject theories too easily or their power will never be realized – he later qualified this (Popper 1970) by suggesting that his was a totally different conception of dogma to that presented in *The Structure of Scientific Revolutions* (1962). In Kuhn's work, science is characterized by the existence of a ruling dogma which exercises hegemonic control for lengthy periods. In periods of so-called 'normal' science the Popperian tenets of real debate are inaccessible. Popper argues that Kuhn's images of 'puzzle' solutions within a common framework, while appealing, do not match up with fundamental, rational principles. He suggests that 'the relativistic thesis that the framework cannot be critically discussed is a thesis which can be critically discussed' (p. 56). Kuhn's restrictiveness is seen as misplaced because alternative frameworks are not inconceivable. In Popper's famous statement,

I do admit that at any moment we are prisoners caught in the framework of our theories; our expectations; our past experiences; our language. But we are prisoners in a Pickwickian sense; if we try we can break out of our frameworks at any time. Admittedly, we shall find ourselves again in a framework, but it will be a better and roomier one; and we can at any moment break out of it again. (1970, p. 86)

In Popper's view, a comparison of frameworks, and thus critical discussion, always remains possible. What in Kuhn is regarded as an impossibility should better be regarded as a difficulty.

A major watershed in this debate was the withdrawal of the 'later' Kuhn (1970a and 1970b, 1977) from the 'exclusivist' incommensurability thesis and his tentative adoption of the possibility of communication. While rarely acknowledged in organization theory, this 'later' Kuhn finds it increasingly difficult to hold on to the full-blown incommensurability thesis. Indeed when distancing himself from Feyerabend (1970a), he insists, 'where he [Feyerabend] talks of incommensurability tout court, I have regularly spoken also of partial communication' (1970b, p. 232). Whereas Popper (1970) vigorously argued that even the most incongruous languages can be translated, Kuhn takes refuge in the argument that, ultimately, there are crucial differences in meaning which are beyond access. We can only translate up to a point before we are forced to compromise between incompatible objectives. As Kuhn notes:

Translation . . . always involves compromises which alter communication . . . what the existence of translation suggests is that recourse is available to scientists who hold incommensurable theories. That recourse need not, however, be to full restatement in a neutral language of even the theories' consequences. (1970b, p. 268)

While this position does not suggest that paradigm mediation is possible through liberal translation, it does reflect the fact that Kuhn is now far removed from the grand isolation of the instant-paradigm thesis. This new position does attempt to offer a way out of hermeticism. Kuhn (1970b) argues that there is an objective sense in which a new paradigm is better than the one it replaces. The crucial factor is the role he finds for nature. While Kuhn originally documented how, for example, Einstein's paradigm replaced Newton's because it was able to solve any problem equally well or better, he also maintained that this paradigm change did not signal a closer approximation to reality. This led to cries of relativism, as the whole question of progress was brought into question. In 'Reflections on My Critics' (1970b), however, Kuhn attempts to remedy this situation by suggesting that for the linear paradigm changes of the natural sciences, scientific problems are not exclusively determined by paradigm forces, but that nature exerts a paradigm-independent, factual world which brings forth problems for solution. Kuhn suggests:

no part of my argument . . . implies that scientists may choose any theory they like so long as they agree in their choice and thereafter enforce it. Most of the puzzles of normal science are directly presented by nature, and all involve nature indirectly. Though different solutions have been received as valid at different times, nature cannot be forced into an arbitrary set of conceptual boxes. (1970b, p. 263)

By only applying Kuhn's original thesis, organization theorists have failed to acknowledge the important qualifications made to this argument. These later reversals signal, as Shapere (1971) has said, 'for better or for worse, a long step towards a more conventional position' (p. 708). Kuhn's later articles herald almost a *volte face* over this central question of incommensurability. Instead of arguing for exclusive paradigm determination of meaning, he advocates not only the seemingly progressive influence of nature, but more concretely, certain overlaps of paradigm meaning. Kuhn talks of 'shared everyday vocabularies' which serve to isolate 'areas of difficulty in scientific communication', and which subsequently illustrate 'what the other would see and say when presented with a stimulus to which his own verbal response would be different' (1977, p. 202). This process indeed leads to a position whereby competing scientists

may in time become very good predictors of each other's behaviour. Each will have learned to translate the other's theory and its consequences into his own language and simultaneously to describe in his language the world to which that theory applies. (p. 202)

For our purposes, however, these more orthodox statements do not offer a deep enough explanation of how we may retain a sense of relativity whilst also allowing for inter-paradigm understanding. Although in his later works Kuhn argues for 'partial' communication, he oscillates between 'persuasion' and 'conversion', 'translation' and 'isolation' (1970b). For the goal of paradigm mediation, Kuhn fails to go far enough toward a form of analysis which would retain the uniqueness of paradigm identity whilst offering an alternative to hermeticism, that is a form that would allow a dissected world to be explored. Such a position, what Giddens (1976) calls 'sustain[ing] a principle of relativity while rejecting relativism' (p. 18), would present analytical openings for those who argue that organization theory holds a plurality of exclusive paradigms. As the majority of commentators, including Kuhn, take the social sciences to be pluri-paradigmatic, this would offer a rationale for those who advocate advantages from conducting multiple paradigm research in organizations (e.g. Pondy and Boje 1981; Steinle 1983; Morgan 1986). In seeking such a position, we will move away from Kuhn (1962, 1970a) and toward Wittgenstein (1953), and signally his concept of 'language-game'.

Analytical openings: the 'later' Wittgenstein

We have noted how Kuhn's attack on traditional positions stresses the failure of positivism to recognize that what we choose to regard as knowledge is inseparable from the time and space within which it is produced. Kuhn argues that the purest forms of positivism fail to grasp their own relativity and dependence on cultural values. Each position gains its identity through learning its own language, or alternatively the way in which it beholds the 'world'. Just as Hampshire (1959) suggests, 'we cannot step outside the language we use, and judge it from some ulterior and superior vantage point' (p. 192), so for Kuhn, 'the proponents of different theories are like the members of different language-culture communities' (1970a, p. 205).

For Kuhn then, as for the later Wittgenstein, there is considerable recognition of the ways that language can cut up the world, and thus of Wittgenstein's notion that the meaning of words is dependent upon the given 'form of life'. In Kuhn, the scientific community is largely bound by the pre-suppositions it holds, such premises in turn providing the rules discerning the perceptual limits of problems and solutions. Language erects the boundary encircling what scientists think and therefore do. Although this position may seem deterministic, we will argue that Wittgenstein's thesis is less so. Indeed, we will suggest that it approaches a middle ground between the extremes of relativism and absolutism which can alleviate many difficulties arising out of Kuhn's (1962) strong incommensurability thesis.

Fundamental to Wittgenstein's 'later' arguments is this notion of the impossibility of separating language from the human milieu of its location (Kenny 1973). The *Philosophical Investigations* (1953) are for many levelled against his thesis in the *Tractatus Logico-Philosophicus* (1922) that words in an utterance are in some way mutually related to the objects for which they stand. In the later works, language is a social activity expressive of human needs, a means of communication within the world and not merely a reflection of the order of the world. As Wittgenstein suggests, 'the term "language game" is meant to bring into prominence the fact that speaking of language is part of an activity, or of a form of life' (1953, p. 23).

The concepts of 'language-game' and 'form of life' are, however, like paradigm, rather elusive. In *The Blue and Brown Books* Wittgenstein states,

I shall in the future again and again draw your attention to what I call language games. These are ways of using signs simpler than those in which we use the signs of our highly complicated everyday language. Language games are forms of language with which a child begins to make use of words. The study of language games is the study of primitive forms of language or primitive languages. (1958, p. 17)

Word language is activity, and not merely a static and abstract sign structure. As Disco (1976) puts it, 'when language is spoken there is a speaker and, usually, a listener . . . here we have a language game, language in use, the production of meaning'. Any other conception of language therefore, 'must accede to the charge that it has de-contextualised the symbol system. It has removed from the semiotic structure the behaviour in which it is, *ab origine*, embedded' (Disco, p. 270).

The middle ground we mentioned is forged through Wittgenstein's thesis that language is both a product of human activity and a producer of meaning, and thus of new forms of human action (Phillips 1977). We witness a dialectic between language as a producer of new meanings and as itself dependent on conditional 'facts of nature'. Wittgenstein does not wish to advocate that facts of nature wholly prescribe language, nor on the other hand that facts of nature are entirely the products of our language. Instead, as Phillips (1977) notes,

while he [Wittgenstein] gives many examples of imaginary peoples with forms of life different to that of our own and, therefore, with such basically different conceptions of the way things are that they can be said to live in a 'different world'; this is not the case for the world in which we live. Of course, there are different language-games among us, but there are certain facts of nature which have a priority over all language games. In other words, nature has something to say, but it does not determine what we can say. (p. 84)

Wittgenstein seeks to infer an infrastructure of species-specific possibilities delimiting the conceptions that can emerge: a form of life expressing both the grounds for language and the limits of its possibilities. Nature itself, however, is not limited to our form of life. There remains another domain of elements with which we interact and which thus delimits our language. This concerns the unanalysed ways in which 'the world is'. Such a world is made sensible because the language within which its thought is cast offers no grounds to question its material basis. Any such rejection would hold recourse to a solipsist position.

By drawing upon Giddens' (1976) proposal of the conceptual correspondence between language-games and paradigms, this analysis can accommodate our questions of incommensurability and relativism. These problems can be addressed by way of the dialectic of language and nature, or the argument through which Wittgenstein seeks to undermine deterministic explanations whereby either one causes us to act. By illuminating such a tension, Wittgenstein avoids adherence to the relativism evident in Kuhn's work and in fact in much of the sociology of organizations.

The language-game of everyday life

The central element in this relationship is Wittgenstein's chief distinction in the field of language-games: that between what he terms the 'everyday language-game' and other technical and special language-games. The everyday language-game is our basic language, the first language we accommodate. Our early years of life are characterized by the quest for assimilating the natural structures of the everyday language-game. We learn to speak, to ask questions, to discriminate between waking and dreaming. This elementary framework forms the foundation for our later linguistic acquisition and for the accommodation of special language-games. It is the basis for language, and thus of what we can possibly think (Disco 1976). As the everyday language-game is the basis of thought it needs no justification. Justification is but a special language-game. Wittgenstein, however, cautions that

what we have ... to do is to accept the everyday language-game; and to note false accounts of the matter as false. The primitive language game which children are taught needs no justification, attempts at justification need to be rejected. (1953, p. 200)

Phillips (1977) notes similarly that

the everyday language-game constitutes the very rock bottom of our knowledge and experience. It would simply make no sense to ask whether it is true (or false), for there is no transcendental criterion – which would have to stand beyond or outside language – by which such a judgement could be made. (p. 88)

We are therefore left in a position where

the everyday language-game has ... an epistemological and ontological primacy. It interpenetrates and shapes as well as contextualizing all other language-games played in a society. (Disco 1976, p. 277)

It is this interpenetration of the everyday language-game into all other language games that is important for us. Technical language games can be seen as discrete and bounded but for differing purposes. While we have a language-game of science, we also have other language-games which mediate science, like physics, biology, and sociology, with further interpenetrations coming from games such as theorizing, calculating and testing. None of the latter is discipline specific. On the contrary, all overlap with other technical language-games in seeking to make sense of some bounded portion of everyday life, thereby constructing language-games applicable to this particular form of understanding (Phillips 1977). Although such special language-games can develop, there is always basic interpenetration, that is the necessary recourse to the language-game of everyday life as the foundation of all special languages. We can therefore only learn the language-game of organization through use of ordinary language. This practice is beyond justification, although what we say within a special language-game is not.

While metaphysical models, and especially the 'shared models' of Kuhn's (1970a) 'disciplinary matrix', can be equated with community bound language-games, we have also noted how other language-games, such as calculation and testing, while themselves bounded, nevertheless overlap with other technical language-games in making sense of the world. Although the language-game of 'truth' may be ascribed through intra-paradigm and intersubjective consensus, the 'consensus theory of truth', the language-games employed in its justification do not necessarily exist in such a relativist vacuum. Language is employed by humans while partly dependent on certain 'facts of nature' and as such rests on constraints that are prior to the conventions of Kuhn (1962, 1970a), Hanson (1958) and Feyerabend (1970a).

We have noted how technical language-games have ultimate recourse to the metalanguage which underlies them – the everyday language-game. The everyday language-game establishes not only the possibilities of what we can think, but, with regard to perception, similarly what we can see. Although the limits of what we can see are set according to the metalanguage of our form of life, within such bounds there may be almost an infinite set of possibilities, the natural limits. Such a line of analysis underlies the solutions to paradigm mediation advocated by Maruyama (1974) and Phillips (1977), who both reject the grand isolation of Kuhn (1962, 1970a) and Feyerabend (1970a and 1970b), whilst similarly objecting to arguments such as Popper's (1970) for breaking out of our frameworks at any time.

Such an account can be removed from charges of pure relativism. It can suggest ways of undermining the strong incommensurability thesis through recourse to the dialectic of nature and the everyday language-game. It offers analytical openings for retaining relativity whilst rejecting relativism. This analysis, in stressing the interpenetration of technical language-games, begins to breach the hermeticism which characterizes the use of paradigm in organization theory. It thus offers analytical openings toward paradigm mediation.

Toward paradigm mediation

This reading of Wittgenstein argues that as our perceptual limitations are empirically established, the rules and conventions of our 'metalanguage in use' allow us to deal, not only with a present language-game, but also with a new language-game into which we may be trained. The emphasis is not on a sudden gestalt-switch which allows us to see the light, but rather, as

Watkins (1970) argues, of established perceptual arrangements which facilitate a transfer of allegiance. Phillips (1977) cites Kohler's faces and goblet drawing to explain the impossibility of appreciating the goblet if one only has knowledge of faces. As Phillips rightly states, 'unorganized experience cannot order perception' (p. 111).

It is therefore mistaken to talk in an unqualified way of instant switches of allegiance. To help us to mediate paradigms, Phillips has argued for a concept of 'seeing as' – the ability to reflect between seeing 'this' and seeing 'that'. The Kohler drawing, for example, is commonly cited as support for the theory-dependence of observation, notably by reference to Hanson's (1958) work. However, as Phillips stresses, it represents not so much an argument for incommensurability *per se*, as an example of how two language-games can be straddled at once. The learning of what faces or goblets are allows not simply a transference from the goblet to the faces – it permits us to see faces, see the goblet, or even see the Kohler drawing. These are experiential states which are transferable and capable of being reflected upon.

For Kuhn (1962) a scientist working under one paradigm cannot entertain another, that is until the conversion experience which changes his whole world view. Watkins (1970), Shapere (1971) and Phillips (1977), however, all question the logic of this instant-paradigm thesis, because unorganized experience is incapable of ordering perception. If we can be trained so as to straddle two paradigms, then as Giddens (1976) suggests it should not be too difficult to apply the logic to paradigms, especially as scientists sharing a paradigm are, as Kuhn (1962) states, sharing 'language'. As the rules and conventions of our 'metalanguage in use' serve to explain each special language-game, then in turn the interpenetration of language-games such as theorizing and testing can be used as the basis for the explanation and learning of other special languages. Practitioners in differing paradigms not only share ordinary language, they also experience the common overlap of intersecting technical languages. Although this process is never complete, it is the basis for being trained into future possibilities and realizing 'seeing as', that is the understanding of two language-games or paradigms. This, however, is through recourse not to a theory-neutral observation language, but to the everyday language-game which holds ontological and epistemological primacy – the dialectic of nature and language.

Conclusions

This chapter has discussed a major logical problem in recent organizational analysis, the assumption that while paradigms are incommensurable, movement between them is non-problematic. Writers argue that paradigms are exclusive but advocate inter-paradigm research (e.g. Ritzer 1975, Burrell and Morgan 1979, Pondy and Boje 1981, Morgan 1986, Holland 1990).

To make sense of this, and to establish an argument for paradigm mediation, we returned to the origins of the paradigms debate in Kuhn's philosophy of science. In finding much equivocation in Kuhn, and especially in his debate with Popper, we drew upon the 'later' Wittgenstein to facilitate Giddens' (1976) notion of 'relatively without relativism'. This analysis rejected both Kuhn's (1962) 'strong' thesis of incommensurability and Popper's (1970) notion of liberal transitions, in favour of a middle ground position – Wittgenstein's (1953) 'language-game of everyday life'. For organizational analysis, we have argued for being 'trained into' new paradigms, given the premise that 'unorganized experience cannot order perception' (Phillips 1977).

This form of analysis offers analytical openings for those who wish to address issues of paradigm incommensurability in organizational analysis. In particular it points to a more robust thesis for dealing with the problem of paradigm mediation. Although many writers have outlined advantages from conducting multiple paradigm research, none has offered a theory for breaching the intellectual hermeticism which results from paradigm incommensurability. This reading of Wittgenstein offers a way forward.

In the social philosophy of, for example, Giddens (1976), Phillips (1977), Watkins (1970) and Winch (1958), organization theory has a range of analytical tools for tackling questions of paradigm hermeticism. By taking recourse to the 'later' Wittgenstein in particular, we can address the middle ground between the paradigm relativism and absolutism. This argument forms the basis for the exploration of multiple paradigms which constitutes the next chapter.

5   Multiple paradigm research

> To translate a theory of worldview into one's own language is not to make it one's own. For that one must go native, discover that one is thinking in, not merely translating out of, a language that was previously foreign.
>
> (Kuhn 1970a, p. 204)

Introduction

Pondy and Boje (1981) suggested that 'organization theory is faced with a frontier problem ... how to conduct inquiry based on several paradigms' (p. 84). A few years later, Donaldson commented 'it is easy to write of the virtues of multi-level analysis ... It is quite another thing to do this in practice' (1985, pp. 284–5). In this chapter, we take up the challenge of employing a range of paradigms within one research investigation. Specifically, we develop a multiple paradigm study of work organization.

The chapter outlines a research programme in which the multiple paradigm model of Burrell and Morgan (1979) was used to conduct an empirical analysis of work behaviour in the British Fire Service. Insight into the organization was gained through using the four Burrell and Morgan paradigms as empirical frames of reference. Results were obtained through using a theory and method from each paradigm as the basis for research. Details of the fieldwork are given, research findings are presented, and the validity of the method is discussed.

The aim is to produce a methodology that is compatible with the view that organization theory comprises a plurality of competing perspectives. We argue that multiple paradigm research (MPR) offers great potential for understanding organizational problems because, unlike simple 'mono-method' approaches (see Martin 1990), it has several lenses for its analytical camera. As the truth claims of positivist sociology are increasingly under scrutiny, MPR offers a methodology in tune with the spirit of the times. It particular, MPR offers a more democratic method than those based on the absolute 'scientific' principles of positivism.

Mutiple paradigms

The Burrell and Morgan model

In Chapter 3, we noted that of models which define paradigms in organizational theory, that of Burrell and Morgan (1979) has received the most attention. Burrell and Morgan define four paradigms for organizational analysis by intersecting subject–object debates in the 'theory of social science' with consensus–conflict debates in the 'theory of society'. The four paradigms produced are the functionalist, the interpretive, the radical humanist and the radical structuralist (see Figure 2, p. 66, above). The four paradigms can be described as follows:

The functionalist paradigm rests upon the premises that society has a real, concrete existence and a systematic character and is directed toward the production of order and regulation. The social science enterprise is believed to be objective and value free. The paradigm advocates a research process in which the scientist is distanced from the subject-matter by the rigour of the scientific method. It possesses a pragmatic orientation, being concerned with analysing society in a way which produces useful knowledge.

In the interpretive paradigm, the social world possesses a 'precarious ontological status'. From this perspective, social reality, although possessing order and regulation, does not possess an external concrete form. Instead, it is the product of intersubjective experience. For the interpretive analyst, the social world is best understood from the viewpoint of the participant-in-action. The interpretive researcher seeks to deconstruct the phenomenological processes through which shared realities are created, sustained and changed. Researchers in this paradigm consider attempts to develop a purely 'objective' social science as specious.

The radical humanist paradigm shares with the interpretive paradigm the assumption that everyday reality is socially constructed. However, for the radical humanist, this social construction is tied to a 'pathology of consciousness', a situation in which actors find themselves the prisoners of the (social) world they create. The radical humanist critique highlights the alienating modes of thought which characterize life in modern industrial societies. Capitalism in particular is subject to attack in the humanist's concern to link thought and action as a means of transcending alienation.

In the final paradigm, the radical structuralist, we also find a radical social critique, yet one at odds with that of the radical humanist paradigm in being tied to a materialist conception of the social world. In this paradigm, social reality is considered a 'fact'. It possesses a hard external existence of its own and takes a form which is independent of the way it is socially constructed. The paradigm views the social world as characterized by intrinsic tensions and contradictions. These forces serve to bring about radical change in the social system as a whole.

A methodology

This attempt to operationalize multiple paradigm research involves a study of work behaviour in a division of the British Fire Service. In the study theories and methods characteristic of the four Burrell and Morgan paradigms were used to generate a range of empirical data sets. An understanding of the meta-theoretical principles of the Burrell and Morgan model enabled the researcher to become familiar with the four paradigm cultures. The approach to paradigm assimilation was one whereby specific social philosophies were accepted as the basis for immersion into the literature and methods of a theory community. Familiarization with a paradigm was accomplished by seeking to 'bracket' phenomenologically the assumptions of other paradigms. The object was to produce authentic paradigm accounts from first-hand experience. The result of the exercise was a social anthropological method for organizational research.

The research process saw three major positions adopted as methodological alternatives to the (systems theory) 'orthodoxy' of the functionalist paradigm. These were phenomenology (interpretive paradigm), critical theory (radical humanist paradigm) and Marxian structuralism (radical structuralist paradigm). In terms of the Burrell and Morgan framework, the investigations started in the functionalist paradigm and moved in a clockwise direction (Figure 5). The research programme began with a traditional functionalist investigation, in the form of a questionnaire survey. Investigations representative of each of the three remaining paradigms were undertaken thereafter.

Topics

Before the fieldwork commenced one question remained – should we study a single aspect of work organization or a number of aspects? One could either focus on a single issue of work organization and examine this from the four paradigm perspectives or else specify four separate research issues with each paradigm addressing a particular topic.

While at first the former method was favoured because it would have allowed the researcher to make straightforward paradigm comparisons,

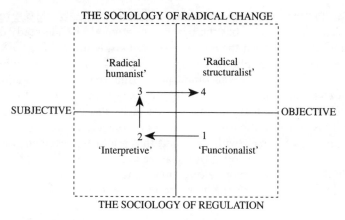

THE SOCIOLOGY OF RADICAL CHANGE

'Radical humanist'

'Radical structuralist'

3 ────► 4

SUBJECTIVE ──────────────────────── OBJECTIVE

2 ◄──── 1

'Interpretive'

'Functionalist'

THE SOCIOLOGY OF REGULATION

Figure 5 Route of the research investigation

this was later found to raise both logical and practical difficulties. An initial difficulty concerned problem definition. Whereas a particular research problem may be considered legitimate for one paradigm community, this may not be so for another. This invoked the epistemological debate about whether it is possible to translate the meaning of one technical language into that of another, given that the four Burrell and Morgan paradigms are apparently incommensurable (see Chapter 4). A second problem was that an iterative approach of this kind would not cover much research ground. While as a methodological exercise it would be interesting – producing four different accounts of the same topic – as an empirical exercise it would offer only marginal insight into the organization as a whole.

Given these considerations, it was decided to analyse a separate issue of work organization for each paradigm. Put briefly, the four main subjects of work organization studied were: job motivation (functionalist paradigm), work routines (interpretive paradigm), management training (radical humanist paradigm) and employment relations (radical structuralist paradigm).

The choice of topics and their pairing with particular paradigms was based upon pragmatic considerations as much as principles of logical research design. A particular worry that it might be difficult to conduct research from the so-called 'critical' (Donaldson 1985) paradigms – interpretive, radical humanist and radical structuralist – was overcome by the fact that there already existed examples of organizational analysis from these perspectives, notably work on task routines by ethnomethodologists, management education by critical theorists, and employment relations by labour process sociologists. While the research topics chosen were important for organizational analysis, the existence of these examples, coupled with the fact that the organization could provide ready data on such issues, influenced the design process considerably.

Pragmatism also played a part in deciding the order in which the investigations should be accomplished. While the decision to commence research in the functionalist paradigm was based primarily on the fact that Burrell and Morgan (1979) had started there, it was recognized that this would also offer political advantages. In particular, if a functionalist study was undertaken first – with the result that senior management was given some free consultancy – this would assist the researcher in establishing his credibility prior to undertaking investigations which might seem less relevant in the host organization's terms.

A multiple paradigm study

The Fire Service case

As each of the four studies was a fairly substantial project, only a series of introductions will be given (see Hassard 1991a). We will explain the decision processes involved in developing the methodology, give brief introductions to the fieldwork and present some examples from the data. To situate each study in terms of the methodology, a case review is presented for each paradigm. These reviews offer comparative analyses as the research progresses. Finally, comments on the research process and the methods employed are found in the conclusion.

The functionalist paradigm

For all the studies the first concern was to choose a theory and a method consistent with the work of the paradigm. In the Burrell and Morgan model the main approaches listed as representative of the functionalist paradigm are social system theory and objectivism, theories of bureaucratic dysfunctions, the action frame of reference and pluralism. Of these, social system theory is the approach they place at the heart of the paradigm. It represents work characteristic of what, in earlier chapters, we have termed the 'systems orthodoxy' in organizational analysis. By far the majority of work cited in the functionalist paradigm falls under this heading. This is material taught on organizational behaviour courses in business schools and university management departments. It encompasses classical management theory, human relations psychology, socio-technical systems analysis and contingency theories of organization structure. The aim is to define law-like relationships between, for example, organization structure, work

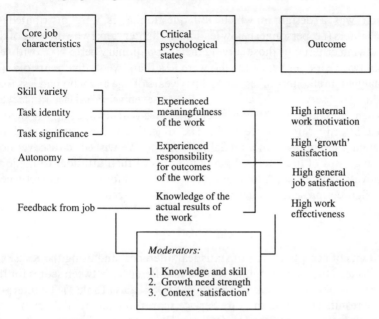

Figure 6 Job characteristics model

motivation and industrial performance. As an agreement was reached with the host organization to study work motivation as part of the research, it was decided – for political as well as pragmatic reasons – to complete this as part of the functionalist investigation.

The research

The functionalist research began with a review of the current theories and techniques available to researchers who wish to study work motivation. This review suggested that job characteristics theory (Hackman and Oldham 1976), a development of expectancy theory, was the most prominent research approach and that a questionnaire survey, the job diagnostic survey (JDS) (Hackman and Oldham 1975, 1980), was the most reliable research instrument. Consequently, the job characteristics approach (Figure 6) was chosen as the theoretical basis for the functionalist study, with the JDS as the main data collection instrument.

The research process was as follows. The aim was to assess how full-time firefighters evaluate job characteristics in terms of motivational potential. Coupled to this, the host organization requested attitudinal data for three specific groups of firefighters differentiated by age and length of service. The result was a design in which 110 questionnaires were distributed to firefighters (i.e. personnel below leading firefighter rank) who met one of the following criteria: (i) those serving their probationary period (i.e. with less than two years' service) and who were less than twenty-five years old, (ii) 'qualified' firefighters of less than thirty years of age and who had less than eight years' service (subjects from a five to seven years' service range were chosen) and (iii) firefighters of over thirty-five years of age and who had at least fifteen years' service each. The objective was to understand the changing orientations in a firefighter's career. We wished to discover how these groups of firefighters differed in terms of their attitudes to the job's motivating potential. A total of ninety-three questionnaires were returned, this figure representing a response rate of 85 per cent.

Examples from the data

In terms of accepted levels of statistical inference, and using the Kruskal–Wallis test, the analysis found significant differences between scores for the three Fire Service groups on 8 of the 20 JDS scales (Table 1). To interpret these results (Table 2), the Fire Service scores were compared against the normative scores published by Oldham, Hackman and Stepina (1979) for a range of jobs in the United States (data for these norms were obtained from 6,930 employees on 876 jobs in fifty-six organizations). US norms were used because of the lack of a database for British jobs.

From Table 2 we see that for the Fire Service sample overall, whereas high scores on the core job characteristics section were recorded for the skill variety and task significance scales, scores well below the US norms were found for task identity and autonomy, where the mean for the job feedback scale was marginally below the US norm. For the critical psychological states section, the Fire Service sample recorded a high mean on the experienced meaningfulness scale, but scores for knowledge of results and experienced responsibility were, respectively, slightly above and slightly below the US norm. For the affective outcomes section, which measures general satisfaction, growth satisfaction, and internal work motivation, on each scale the sample mean for the Fire Service was higher than the US norm. The score for general satisfaction was particularly high. Finally, for the moderator variables, the Fire Service sample recorded scores higher than the US norms on each of the four 'context' satisfaction scales – job security, pay satisfaction, social satisfaction and supervisory satisfaction. Particularly high scores were recorded for the job security, social satisfaction and supervisory satisfaction scales. Scores for the growth need strength scales, however, fell well short of the US norms.

On contrasting the results for the three Fire Service groups, the first thing

Table 1 *Analysis of variance*

	Mean Ranks			X^2	Significance	
	0–2 years	5–7 years	15–25 years			
Skill variety	43.4	46.0	36.2	2.977	0.2257	(N.S.)
Task identity	50.8	46.1	33.5	6.483	0.399	(0.05)
Task responsibility	46.0	45.3	36.2	2.846	0.2410	(N.S.)
Autonomy	37.5	48.5	35.0	5.998	0.498	(0.05)
Feedback from job	59.4	46.9	29.4	15.906	0.0004	(0.001)
Feedback from agents	52.5	47.0	31.7	9.493	0.0087	(0.01)
Dealing with others	50.5	47.0	31.7	9.493	0.0087	(N.S.)
Experienced responsibility	46.5	40.8	42.1	0.485	0.7846	(N.S.)
Experienced meaningfulness	58.4	42.8	35.2	7.582	0.0223	(0.05)
Knowledge of results	38.2	42.5	42.7	0.320	0.8523	(N.S.)
General satisfaction	44.5	45.9	35.9	3.120	0.2022	(N.S.)
Growth satisfaction	57.2	42.4	36.0	6.267	0.0436	(0.05)
Internal motivation	46.7	43.2	38.8	1.061	0.5882	(N.S.)
Pay satisfaction	59.2	37.4	41.9	7.095	0.0288	(0.05)
Security satisfaction	36.7	42.0	43.8	0.704	0.7034	(N.S.)
Social satisfaction	46.2	44.3	37.5	1.794	0.4079	(N.S.)
Supervisory satisfaction	42.9	44.6	38.2	1.267	0.5306	(N.S.)
'Would like' growth need strength	36.4	46.1	38.6	2.372	0.3055	(N.S.)
Job choice growth need strength	41.9	49.5	32.3	9.079	0.0107	(0.05)
Total growth need strength	39.1	48.4	34.6	5.963	0.0507	(N.S.)

Table 2 *Means and standard deviations*

	0–2 years x	S.D.	5–7 years x	S.D.	15–25 years x	S.D.	All fire groups x	S.D.	US norm x
Skill variety	6.0	0.69	6.0	0.95	5.5	1.34	5.9	1.08	4.7
Task identity	4.4	1.09	4.1	1.09	3.5	1.10	3.9	1.16	4.7
Task significance	6.6	0.41	6.5	0.70	6.2	0.97	6.4	0.78	5.5
Autonomy	4.0	0.86	4.4	1.05	3.7	1.21	4.0	1.10	4.9
Feedback from job	5.5	1.00	5.0	0.86	4.2	1.14	4.8	1.09	4.9
Dealing with others	6.5	0.82	6.4	0.57	6.0	0.99	6.3	0.78	5.6
Motivation potential score additive	26.6	2.86	26.0	2.89	23.0	3.86	25.1	3.44	n/a
Motivation potential score multiplicative	128.0	49.9	123.0	41.3	84.0	47.8	109.0	47.0	128.0
Experienced meaningfulness	6.2	0.80	5.7	0.90	5.5	0.88	5.7	0.87	5.2
Experienced responsibility	5.5	0.65	5.2	0.79	5.2	0.96	5.3	0.81	5.5
Knowledge of results	5.3	0.67	5.3	0.86	5.3	1.21	5.3	0.94	5.0
General satisfaction	5.8	0.96	6.0	0.58	5.4	1.18	5.8	0.90	4.7
Internal motivation	5.9	0.58	5.8	0.59	5.7	0.75	5.8	0.65	5.6
Growth satisfaction	5.9	0.50	5.5	0.86	5.2	1.07	5.5	0.91	4.8
Job security	5.3	1.05	5.6	0.89	5.5	1.21	5.5	1.02	4.8
Pay satisfaction	5.7	0.40	4.3	1.49	4.4	1.87	4.6	1.57	4.3
Social satisfaction	6.1	0.48	6.0	0.64	5.7	0.89	6.0	0.73	5.3
Supervisory satisfaction	5.7	0.54	5.5	1.21	5.2	1.42	5.4	1.19	4.8
'Would like' growth need strength	5.2	0.93	5.6	1.14	5.3	1.06	5.5	1.04	5.7
Job choice growth need strength	3.8	0.63	3.9	0.52	3.5	0.56	3.8	0.60	4.4
Total growth need strength	4.5	0.67	4.7	0.68	4.4	0.61	4.6	0.66	5.1

which strikes us is the consistent and related way in which the groups score the various scales. With the exception of scores for growth need strength, the rule is that for each scale the probationers' group records the highest mean and the fifteen to twenty-five years' group the lowest, with the five to seven years' group recording a mean somewhere between these two. If we analyse the results in terms of the three main sections of the Hackman and Oldham model, we find that for core job characteristics the probationers' group and the five to seven years' group record substantially higher normative scores than the fifteen to twenty-five years' group on all scales. When the between-group differences in mean values are computed using the Kruskal–Wallis test, the comparison results in levels of statistical significance being recorded for the scales measuring task identity ($p > .05$), autonomy ($p > .05$), feedback from job ($p > .001$), and an additional feedback scale, feedback from agents ($p > .01$). Similarly, the scores for the critical psychological states also reflect this pattern, with a statistically significant between-group difference computed for the experienced meaningfulness scale ($p > .05$). The pattern is again visible for the affective outcomes section, with a significant between-group difference recorded for the growth satisfaction scale ($p > .05$). Only for the growth need strength scales does the pattern change, with probationers scoring lowest for 'would like' growth need strength and again below the five to seven years' group for 'job choice' growth need strength. All the Fire Service groups scored below the US norms on the growth need strength dimensions.

The evidence from this research suggests that although the firefighter's job possesses relatively modest levels of motivation potential, this is not in fact a problem for employees whose needs for psychological growth at work are also modest. We discover that whereas the overall motivation potential score (MPS) for the job is low (109 compared with the US norm of 128), the scores for the job satisfaction scales are generally high. There are, of course, reasons for this. The way the motivation potential score is computed (see Hackman and Oldham 1980) makes for a rather distorted picture of the firefighter's job. In particular the low scores for task identity and autonomy – which represent two of the four main dimensions on which MPS is calculated – serve to reduce significantly the overall motivation score. However, whereas in industry a job possessing low task identity and low autonomy would be viewed negatively, in the Fire Service the absence of these characteristics is not a matter of great concern. In the Fire Service, low task identity stems mainly from firemen being called out to emergencies, and low autonomy from working in a paramilitary organization. More important to the fireman in terms of motivation is that his job offers task significance and skill variety.

The research also examined both the intercorrelations between the model's predicted relationships and the internal consistency reliabilities of the JDS scales. Intercorrelations were computed using both Pearson product-moment and Spearman rank-order methods. For the relationship between core job characteristics and their corresponding critical psychological states, no major correlational differences were found between the findings of this research and the results cited by Oldham *et al.* (1979). However, the internal consistency reliabilities revealed that several scales contained questions with low, and in some cases negative, correlations with other items measuring the same construct.

Case review

In terms of the Burrell and Morgan model the functionalist study sees an account which is realist, positivist, determinist and nomothetic. The research develops a methodology in which psychometric techniques and computer-based analysis are used to provide a sophisticated understanding of the factual nature of the organization. The research process draws inspiration from the scientific method, with statistical tests being used to discern those relationships we can consider 'significant' for future organizational success. The study obtains generalizable knowledge of a form which claims to be valid and reliable. Explanations are couched in a form promising practical success, especially through defining the concept of organization as a practical activity. This approach is one which attempts to divorce the role of social values from social research. The study epitomizes the classical quasi-experimental approach to organizational analysis.

The interpretive paradigm

The interpretive paradigm involved an ethnomethodological analysis of Fire Service work routines. The study examined the main activities of the working day and in particular how firefighters take recourse to context-linked typifications in order to make sense of their activities. The research asked firefighters to describe and explain their daily tasks, the ethnography being produced from a database of unstructured conversational materials collected during a three-month period of non-participant observation. In conducting the analysis we accepted the premise that it is only through the speech, gestures and actions of competent participants that we can understand the essence of their work. The aim was to let the participants themselves structure their conversations, descriptions and analyses. An inductive approach was developed in which the knowledge of the participants was treated as 'strange' to the researcher. During the observation period, the researcher employed the phenomenological suspension method of *epoche* in order to 'bracket' existing personal beliefs, preconceptions and assumptions (Husserl 1931, pp. 108ff.).

The research

In practice the research used the methodology developed by Silverman and Jones (1976), in which subjects are required to explain activities in terms of how they are worked through. The fieldwork involved accompanying firefighters during the working day and asking them to explain their activities before, during and after each event. The aim was to appreciate the 'stocks of knowledge' and 'recipes' firefighters employ in making sense of their work (Schutz 1967). The ethnography was presented as a description of the routine events which occur during a normal working day.

Examples from the data

The analysis highlighted how in the Fire Service routine events are accomplished within a context of uncertainty. An absence of firm personal control over immediate future events, which stems primarily from the threat of emergency calls, is accepted within a general cultural framework of instability. While there exists an official task schedule to direct non-operational periods, the factual nature of this schedule is established through the constant interpretation of its usefulness by the station officer and the watch (team of firefighters). The main reason for such interpretation is that events within the shift must be assembled so as to make the day run smoothly, without any temporal gaps. The official work schedule is rarely congruent with the actual process of events. As many events in the schedule routine are considered 'low priority', firefighters are frequently transferred to activities deemed more appropriate to maintaining a smooth flow of activity:

FIREFIGHTER A: We were supposed to go for a divisional drill this morning and we've got this station efficiency [exercise] here as well. But the machine [fire engine] I'm on has got this water leak on the radiator so we knocked it off the run. The drill went out the window. [And] the station efficiency for me went out the window. I went back and got another machine from another station and brought it back, and everybody knocked off drill then to put it back. They're still working on it now. Whether we'll carry on with drill after I don't know . . .

One of the main reasons for this lack of fixity is the strategic relationship between the station officer and the divisional officer. A major concern of station officers is to be able to account for the deployment of watch personnel during periods laid down for routine work (for example, equipment tests, cleaning, building inspections). This is prompted by the uncertainty as to whether a divisional officer will visit the station without warning and question the validity of the tasks being undertaken. With this in mind, Station Officers attempt to make the day 'acceptable' by either including, or excluding, tasks as necessary. This 'safeguarding' process is most notable in the late afternoon when, although work may be in progress, the 'real work' may have been finished much earlier. When the real work has been finished 'fill-in' work will be prescribed in order to 'keep the day going'. Fill-in work can take the form of work of a peripheral nature or the repetition of work completed earlier:

FIREFIGHTER B: The favourite of the Fire Service is 'inside gear'. That's the favourite one. They can get you on that any time of the day, any day. You've possibly used a ladder and a standpipe and two lengths of hose this morning on drill. So you've used them, wiped them off and put them back. Now for all intents and purposes they're clean because you've done them and you've put them back on. But probably if they've run out of work at 4 o'clock [they will say] 'er well carry on with the inside gear until 5 o'clock'. And you know you've done it, but you've got to do it again ...

FIREFIGHTER C: Now yesterday's a typical example. Now I leathered off that machine [fire engine] four times, me, God Almighty. But they wanted it done. Now the last time I'd leathered it off, put it [the fire engine] away, the lot, finished, it was half past four. Now Larry [the sub-officer] says 'you can't go yet it's not five o'clock. Don't go sloping off doing anything you shouldn't be' ...

A recurrent theme was that behaviour is indexed to group-wide knowledge of strategies for personal advancement in the organization. Instances of such processes are probationer firefighters enacting tasks 'differently' to qualified personnel, and 'promotion-minded' firefighters displaying different behaviour patterns to their less promotion-minded (and commonly older) colleagues. To this end the watch becomes stratified as to whether tasks are completed 'properly' in terms of the 'code of context' (Weider 1974).

As an example, the first main task of the shift is the 'machine check', or inspecting the fire engine to make sure that it, and the equipment stored on it, is ready for operational duty. Although 'officially' this task should be completed by firefighters checking the various pieces of equipment against an inventory board, in practice they adopt various strategies for its completion. While probationers will suggest that they do complete the job by checking off the items, other firefighters either 'make a show' by simply carrying the inventory board around with them or, as in the case of other, frequently older, firefighters, check the fittings by just lifting up the lockers and noting whether the contents seem intact. Firefighters take recourse to a criterion of 'knowing what's expected of you' in assessing the 'proper' actions to be taken.

FIREFIGHTER D: You make short cuts when you get to know what's expected of you. It comes with experience really. You know a bloke in his probationary period wouldn't dream of doing some of the things you do when you've finished it. He thinks, well I've got to do that properly, you know, I must do that. But when you've done it and you're sort of out of your probation you think well I can relax a bit now ...

FIREFIGHTER E: If you're youngish and still keen on the promotion side, then you're going to put a little more effort, well not effort so much as the way you go about it is going to be a little bit happier. Because if you're seen to be doing things properly then hopefully this will come out in any report that the boss puts in for you ...

Coda

These are some examples of themes explored in the interpretive ethnography. The research overall portrays the everyday work of a fire station in terms of how firefighters make sense of and enact the task system. The cement which binds the analysis is a concern for the social construction of task routines and for the phenomenology of work organization.

Case review

In the interpretive study the form of evaluation has changed markedly from that of the functionalist paradigm. We now find explanations which in Burrell and Morgan's terms are nominalist, anti-positivist, voluntarist and ideographic. Whereas in the functionalist study we found an 'organized' world characterized by certainty and self-regulation, in this second study we discover a 'life-world' of social construction (Schutz 1967). Instead of statistical correlations, we see a web of human relationships. The analysis outlines how participants create rules for 'bringing-off' the daily work routine, with personal actions being indexed to a contextual system of meanings (Garfinkel 1967). The research de-concretizes the view of organizational reality created in the first paradigm; it suggests that (Fire Service) organization is a cultural phenomenon which is subject to a continuous process of enactment.

The radical humanist paradigm

In terms of research contributions, the radical humanist is the least developed of Burrell and Morgan's four paradigms. For social theory, it includes French existentialism, the anarchistic individualism of Stirner, and the critical theory of Gramsci, Lukács and the Frankfurt School. For organizational analysis, some steps 'towards an anti-organization theory' are outlined. Burrell and Morgan cite Beynon's (1973) *Working for Ford* and Clegg's (1975) *Power, Rule and Domination* as characteristic of a nascent 'critical theory' approach to organizational analysis.

The research

The third study was conducted from the perspective of critical theory. In this research the links with social and political theory were made more explicit than in the works of Beynon, Clegg and others, with Gramsci's concept of ideological hegemony being used to derive interpretations of workplace culture. In line with Gramsci's thesis on 'Americanism and Fordism', the research highlighted the role played by administrative science in reproducing organizational 'common sense' (Gramsci 1977, Adler 1977). The study describes how administrative science is used to train firefighters to cross what Goodrich (1920) calls the 'frontier of control'.

In producing this analysis two arguments were developed. The first was that the cohesion between administrative science and capitalist ideology should be described as a symbiotic relationship (Baritz 1960, Fleron and Fleron 1972, Nord 1974, Allen 1975, Clegg and Dunkerley 1980). The second was that this symbiosis is fostered by the growth of management training in both the public and private sectors. In line with Clegg and Dunkerley's (1980) view that a function of management education is the 'reproduc[tion] [of] ideology as well as middle class careers' (p. 578) and that this ideology is produced through learning 'modern management techniques' at training institutions, the radical humanist research explained how such processes are accomplished in the Fire Service.

Examples from the data

The fieldwork involved an analysis of training practices on courses designed to prepare firefighters for promotion to first line supervision. The objective was to discover, first-hand, the impact of training at this important level. To achieve this, the researcher enrolled on a 'cadre leading firefighters'' training course (four weeks), a course designed to teach promotion candidates the techniques of managerial work. The research described not only the formal processes of presentation but also the personal experiences of participants. Data were gleaned from tape recordings of class sessions, especially of discussions between the instructors (Fire Service training officers) and the cadre leading firefighters (CLFs).

The analysis, which again took the form of an ethnography, described how the use of supportive educational materials on in-house training programmes allows the organization to keep tight control over both the medium and the message. Although course members are removed from their immediate working environments (fire stations) in staying within the bounds of the organization's influence (Fire Service training school) they remain subject to normal constraints and conditions.

TRAINING OFFICER 1 (on the use of Maslow's 'ladder of needs'): What is 'esteem' nowadays? What does that word mean? You know, you can have a dustman driving a Rolls Royce now, and an executive managing director redundant. So where is 'esteem' nowadays? We've found a terrific comparison in terms of Maslow's ladder. That [Maslow's ladder] needs updating. So we do our own ...

The research described how senior training officers were able to select materials which reinforced the logic of the authority structure. An example from the research was the synergism between Adair's (1968, 1973, 1983, 1984) work on leadership and the reproduction of loyalty in military and paramilitary organizations. As Adair's ideas have been well received in the Army, so has his Sandhurst Package, to quote one senior training officer, become 'the gospel' for an organization with a similar command structure, the British Fire Service. Adair's 'theory' has become a key ingredient of the organization's recipes for maintaining commitment.

For this theme the ethnography outlined how a main objective of CLF training is to establish the view that a leading firefighter's loyalties must lie with the command structure of the Fire Service rather than with the rank and file. Senior officers feel that on promotion to leading firefighter a major problem facing the role incumbent is a sense of ambiguity over the direction his loyalties should take. A major function of training at this level is therefore to establish the logic of the leading firefighter's allegiance to the command structure of the organization.

TRAINING OFFICER 2 (de-brief to CLFs for the film *A Question of Loyalties*): Well there you are. There's the situation. Now can anyone tell me it wouldn't happen in the Fire Service? One day a fireman, your best mucker, all night at the bar with him, best snooker player on the watch. The next day he's the leading fireman on the watch. No doubt about it, he's there, he's got it, all the badges of office ... [And conversely] there's a bloke [negative character on film] – a temporary LF if you like, twenty year fireman – all of a sudden its swiped off him and given to the youngster on the watch. You can see the problems. You can identify the problems ...

Throughout the course the dominant theme was of instructors seeking to settle the CLFs' doubts over this question of loyalties. Training officers attempted to establish a climate conducive to performing simulations of 'effective' management practice. This was a climate in which the roles of the 'transmitters' of authority were portrayed as qualitatively different to those of the 'receivers'. Stages of the training programme saw various media deployed to accomplish this objective – lectures, videos, role plays. The instructions which accompanied these media ranged from philosophical discussions of the division of authority and non-authority positions to basic messages about career enhancement.

TRAINING OFFICER 2 (from class discussion following the de-brief): I can tell you that the only loyalty you should consider above all else is loyalty to the command structure. That's got to be your prime consideration and any other loyalties you have should come second to that.

CLF 1: For argument's sake say you are a Leading Fireman on a particular watch and you've got a cracking bunch of blokes and the two blokes above you (station officer, sub-officer) are, you know, a right bunch of wankers. Any problem that you get as a result from your blokes has directly arisen because of these two. Then where's your loyalties then?

TRAINING OFFICER 2: Well first of all think realistically about the situation. Out and out wankers or not who's going to give you your next rank, the firemen or the SO and Sub-O? Who's going to recommend you as showing the potential to hold any further rank?

CLF 2: M'm I think that what's being said though is that there are some situations where your loyalties will be reversed because of your superiors. If you like, your loyalties will have to be to the watch.

TRAINING OFFICER 2: These are problems you can't sort out until they manifest themselves, and the best way of dealing with the problem is your way. But you've been given the guidelines haven't you. What you've done you've sat there for two days now and all of a sudden this morning you've broadened your horizons. When you're made up to Leading Fireman you'll have the ammunition. But I make no bones about it, I can't deal with specifics. I can't do it. It would be wrong of me to do it. And I'm sure you're intelligent enough people to appreciate that ...

Coda

The research for the radical humanist paradigm demonstrates how Fire Service training instructors use administrative science to solve a set of recurrent problems about the authority structure, problems whose solutions are pre-determined in the hegemony of the organization. The analysis illustrates the ways in which the dominant culture of the organization is reproduced with the help of 'acceptable' theories of management.

Case review

In the radical humanist study, we find a different mode of explanation again. Although this paradigm, like the interpretive paradigm, views the social world from a perspective which is nominalist, anti-positivist, voluntarist and ideographic, it is committed to defining the limitations of existing social arrangements. A central notion is that human consciousness is corrupted by tacit ideological influences. The common sense accorded to hegemonic practices such as management training is felt to drive a wedge of false consciousness between the known self and the true self. The fieldwork for the radical humanist study shows how firefighters not only create social arrangements but also how they come in turn to experience them as alien, especially in respect to the power dimension which underpins the construction process. The research notes how the hegemony of the organization is dependent upon the reproduction of social arrangements which serve to constrain human expression.

The radical structuralist paradigm

Having analysed the work organization from the functionalist, interpretive, and radical humanist paradigms, the research programme moved finally to the radical structuralist paradigm and to a study of the labour process in firefighting.

For contributions to this paradigm, Burrell and Morgan cite the Mediterranean Marxism of Althusser and Colletti, the conflict theory of Dahrendorf and Rex, and the historical materialism of Bukharin. Burrell and Morgan develop a duality of traditions to show the influence of Marx's work on political economy and the more radical implications of Weber's work on bureaucracy. This duality is later developed into a formal framework for assessing contributions to a 'radical organization theory'. For radical Weberian approaches Burrell and Morgan list works such as Eldridge and Crombie's (1974) *A Sociology of Organizations*, Mouzelis' (1975) *Organizations and Bureaucracy*, and Miliband's (1977) *The State in Capitalist Society*. For Marxian structuralism Burrell and Morgan cite Marx's *Capital* as an exemplar for the analysis of economic systems. In this tradition Baran and Sweezy's (1968) *Monopoly Capital* and Braverman's (1974) *Labor and Monopoly Capital* are referenced as two important works for labour process theory.

Following Braverman's (1974) seminal work the major thrust of research in this paradigm has been a revival of labour process analysis. In the wake of *Labor and Monopoly Capital* we have seen a wealth of case study work linked to Braverman's original de-skilling thesis (see Zimbalist 1979, Nichols 1980, Wood 1982, Knights, Willmott and Collinson 1985). Subsequently, the scope of this research has widened to incorporate issues such as flexible specialization, post-Fordism, gender and time (see Piore and Sabel 1984, Hirst and Zeitlin 1991, Knights and Willmott 1986, and

Nyland 1989, respectively). Much work in this area has concerned longitudinal studies and especially craft histories. Following criticisms that Braverman's analysis peddles 'managerial determinism', writers have stressed voluntarist initiatives by labour within a control-resistance dialectic (e.g. Gospel and Littler 1983, Storey 1983).

The research

Given these developments a labour process study of firefighting was chosen as the research topic for the radical structuralist paradigm. The focus was placed upon the development of employment relations in British firefighting, and especially 'the struggle for a normal working day' (Marx 1867).

Research into the history of British firefighting found working time to be the most contentious issue in contractual negotiations between the trade union, the employers and the state (Blackstone 1957, Fire Brigades Union 1968). The radical structuralist research subsequently documented changes in the duration of the working period from the start of full-time firefighting in Britain in 1833 to the last major change in the duty system, which followed the firefighters' strike of 1977–8. In explaining such changes the analysis took recourse to a sectoral assessment by way of fiscal crisis theory (O'Connor 1973). Contractual issues were pictured against the backcloth of rapid increases in militant state sector unionism during the 1970s. The research described how the experiences of firefighters were mirrored by workers in other state service sectors (see Cousins 1984 on this point). The study outlined the mechanisms devised to redress such expressions of conflict, which in the Fire Service meant the development of an 'upper quartile' agreement following the 1977–8 strike. This agreement provided a fixed payment level in relation to workers in other service and manufacturing sectors.

Examples from the data

The analysis suggests that as working hours for firefighters have approached the national average, questions of 'productivity' have increasingly come into focus, despite firefighting being a 'non-capitalist state apparatus' (Carchedi 1977). During the 1970s, when the length of the firefighters' working week came into line with other manual occupations, the emphasis was displaced from 'covering' to 'using' time. In suggesting that firefighters' pay should be assessed in relation to a normal working week, the Cunningham Report (1971) pointed to the scope for better manpower utilization within non-operational periods of the working day. The recommendations of the Cunningham Report were in line with those of the earlier Holroyd Report (1970) which recommended improving productivity by replacing 'unskilled' cleaning work with 'skilled' inspection work. In future many unskilled tasks would be carried out by auxiliary cleaners and porters, both employed on low incomes.

Moreover, the reduction to forty-two hours was contingent upon a move to greater 'professionalism', which would see stand-down periods reduced. Previous systems had allowed not only for statutory evening stand-down from 8.00 p.m. (with some variations) but also free time on weekend rotas from mid-day on Saturday and all day Sunday. With the forty-two hour system, weekend stand-down was officially pushed back to midnight. During the working day itself not only was inspection work to be increased but also training schedules made more sophisticated, with elaborate, itemized quota inventories devised for daily drills and a yearly training plan required for each firefighter. Since the 1978 agreement, station officers have been encouraged to cover three hours' drill on every day shift with usually one to two hours being allocated to practical training and the remainder for a technical session.

We see, therefore, that as firefighters' working hours are reduced to a figure approaching that of other manual occupations, measures have been taken which enhance management's control over the work process whilst yielding greater productivity from the working period. As a result of the first, we see an increased formalization of roles and more tightly controlled work, while, for the second, the upskilling of core workers plus the employment of unskilled peripheral groups.

Coda

The radical structuralist research has shown that as firefighting represents intensive yet 'unproductive' (Carchedi 1977) labour it has been in the interests of employers to maintain a long working week. It is only during the 1970s, with the development of a national duty system comparable in duration to that of other manual occupations, that questions of 'productivity' become important. The intensification of labour that was the result of this process was achieved through completing more highly skilled work within the time available.

Case review

In the radical structuralist study we return to a realist perspective, but one directed at fundamentally different ends to those of functionalism. In this paradigm, the focus is upon instances of structural conflict rather than functional integration. The study analyses the strategic relations between capital and labour, especially in regard to the development of the employment contract. The research highlights crisis points in the firefighting labour process, and describes the role of state agencies in seeking to mediate contradictory forces and restore system equilibrium. Instead of examining the reproduction of hegemony, the radical structuralist study illustrates the concrete actions of labour, capital and the state in the labour process.

Conclusions: reflections on the problems of practice

The Fire Service study represents a first attempt to develop a multiple paradigm analysis of work organization. The research has examined some of the empirical possibilities arising from models of paradigm heterodoxy in order to demonstrate how differing frameworks contribute to our understanding of organizational behaviour. We have illustrated how contrasting images of the subject-matter emerge when we base our investigations upon incompatible sets of theoretical assumptions. In the present case the result has been four studies yielding alternative 'images of organization' (Morgan 1986).

This research is not, however, without its shortcomings. Problems have been identified with both the theory and practice of multiple paradigm research. Five issues of particular concern are as follows.

A first problem was encountered during the access negotiations. The researcher was faced with the dilemma of being convinced of the validity of the research exercise yet fearing that the host organization might not see the virtue in some of the studies to be undertaken, especially those for the radical humanist and radical structuralist paradigms. Forsaking normal ethical considerations, only a partial explanation of the project was presented during these negotiations. The progamme was described in exclusively functionalist terms, with no mention being made of plans to conduct phenomenological, existential or Marxist investigations. Although the topic areas were discussed – motivation, work design, training and industrial relations – with the exception of the motivation study (functionalist paradigm) few theoretical details were presented. It could be claimed, therefore, that as the researcher engaged in a form of deception over the disclosure of objectives the ethics of the work undertaken can be questioned. This would suggest that for any future multiple paradigm research such disclosure issues are addressed in an ethical way from the outset.

A second methodological issue concerns the relationship between the subject-matter and the modes of analysis. It could be argued that despite the problems outlined earlier, a more powerful methodology would have seen a single topic investigated rather than, as in the present case, four discrete topics. Such a methodology may have yielded some fascinating cross-paradigm interpretations and, as a result, served to counteract the kind of absolutist analysis found within the pages of, for example, *The Administrative Science Quarterly*, *Omega* and *The Academy of Management Journal*. Although in theory such a methodology would contribute to the development of a more reflective organization theory, in practice it is unlikely that an empirical research programme can be accomplished.

A third problem relates to the degree of pragmatism employed in the research design process. With four studies to complete in a relatively short research period (of two years), and thus with pressure to start the fieldwork quickly, topics were allocated to paradigms on the basis that similar associations had proven successful in the past. Although reference to empirical exemplars seemed defensible on practical grounds, this denied an opportunity to explore the methodological limits of the four paradigms and to consider research issues other than those identified by Burrell and Morgan. We would suggest that any future multiple paradigm investigation adopt a less pragmatic approach to research design to that adopted here. This should allow for greater methodological freedom in research design.

A fourth issue concerns the direction the research journey has taken through the paradigms. The author feels that if a similar exercise were considered in the future it would be better to take a different route. Instead of replicating the clockwise progression of Burrell and Morgan, the whole range of paradigm routes should be considered. Above all, any future researcher should assess the specific needs of the investigation before deciding upon an empirical itinerary. The present programme, for example, would have benefited from starting in the interpretive paradigm rather than the functionalist. A more appropriate course would have been to examine the interpretive, the radical humanist, the functionalist and the radical structuralist paradigms in that order. This progression would have facilitated the systematic accumulation of data from micro to macro levels of analysis, whilst including opportunities to criticize and re-interpret the methods and findings. For any future investigation this methodology would help build a more generic organizational analysis. Such a methodology would avoid the mistake made in the present research of completing a psychometric analysis of work motivation (functionalist paradigm) before a qualitative understanding of the work organization (interpretive paradigm) had been obtained. The author's experience was of beginning to understand the meaning of work motivation in the Fire Service only after the psychometric analysis had been completed!

Finally, an issue related to the above but of more general concern is whether a paradigm is ideally suited to the analysis of a particular topic or whether it can assess any topic. While we have not addressed this issue formally, one may suggest that, in practice, the solution will lie in developing a typology which specifies appropriate combinations of topics, methods and paradigms. The research described here supports such a proposal, for it suggests that each of the Burrell and Morgan paradigms is limited in its methodological scope. Thus the author feels it is wrong to assert that any paradigm can or should be used to assess any issue. This argument should be discounted both on empirical grounds, because we cannot address certain topics from certain paradigms, and on methodological ones, because it draws us towards the black hole of pure relativism.

In conclusion, despite the methodological problems outlined above, paradigm heterodoxy holds many benefits for organizational analysis. Multiple paradigm research, if operationalized successfully, may allow us to learn the languages and practices of a wide range of academic communities and in turn to develop analytic skills representative of their forms of life. Through refining such a poly-paradigm methodology we may be able to realize epistemological variety in our studies of organization. Such a spirit of pluralism may indicate a move towards greater democracy in organizational analysis.

6 Postmodernism and organization

> The postmodernism debate poses in a very dramatic way the issue of competing paradigms for social theory and the need to choose paradigms that are most theoretically and practically applicable to social conditions in the present era.
> (Kellner 1988a, p. 276)

Introduction

In this final chapter, we introduce a new paradigm for social and organization theory – postmodernism. We start by contrasting modern and postmodern forms of explanation, and explore a family of terms derived from these two generic concepts. In so doing, we consider whether postmodernism is better described as an 'epoch' or an 'epistemology', a distinction which underpins much current debate.

We then go on to assess the chief theoretical positions of modernism. Here we analyse the differences between 'critical' and 'systemic' modernism, and outline Habermas' well known 'defence of modernity'. The section is completed by a review of different approaches to the modernist trajectory in organizational analysis.

Finally, through reference to the works of Jean Baudrillard, Jacques Derrida and Jean-François Lyotard, we produce an inventory of postmodern concepts for social theory. When coupled with the distinction between epoch and epistemology, this inventory provides a framework for a nascent postmodern theory of organizations. A case study of a deconstructionist approach to organizational power is described.[1]

What is postmodernism?

In its starkest sense, postmodernism stands for the 'death of reason' (Power 1990). It offers a frontal assault on methodological unity. Through the postmodern method of 'deconstruction' (Derrida 1978) a whole range of philosophical pillars are brought down, the most notable of which are the 'unities' of meaning, theory and the self.

Power (1990) suggests that as there is no absolute line to demarcate the modern from the postmodern, the latter comes to signify both the termination of the former and a differentiated continuation of it. This inherent ambiguity is accepted in order to offset the tendency of commentators to make simple categorizations. Power notes, for example, that while modernist trajectories in the visual arts have challenged the concept of autonomous representation, postmodernism appears in contrast to be more radical still. Postmodern visual art seems to represent

a continuation of this avant-garde aesthetic without a nostalgia for direct contact with a 'real world' ... the postmodern aesthetic of the sublime is precisely such a conscious withdrawal from traditional concepts of artistic reality. It seems to make visible the fact that there is something which may be thought but cannot in principle itself become visible or represented. (p. 110)

The first characteristic feature of postmodernism, therefore, is that it rejects the notion that reference is, or can be, a univocal relation between forms of representation (words, images etc.) and an objective, external world. At the postmodern level of analysis the focus is upon 'the rules grounded in practices which precede subjectivity' (p. 111), which is essentially the structuralist attack upon the philosophy of consciousness. There is no real space for the voluntary actor as, instead, the actor's space is found in the notion of action as 'play' rather than as 'agency' (see Lyotard and Thébaud 1986). For Power, postmodern analysis succeeds in distancing itself from the assumptions of unity implicit in the Enlightenment notion of reason. Unlike modernism, where there is faith in the recovery of a relationship with nature, postmodernism gives rise simultaneously to 'increasing liberation from the natural world and to the splintering of culture into discrete spheres' (p. 111). In postmodern thought, therefore, energies are released that demand reunification yet assert its impossibility.

Antinomies

Other writers define the modern or postmodern through contrasting associated sets of antinomies (cf. Featherstone 1988, Clegg 1990). Featherstone (1988), for example, expands upon a family of terms derived from these two generic concepts. Specifically he contrasts: 'modernity and postmodernity', 'modernization and postmodernization', and 'modernism and postmodernism'.

On deploying these terms, Featherstone notes how the prefix 'post' seems to signify 'that which comes after'. The postmodern appears to represent a break with the modern, which is defined in contrast to it. Like Power, however, he suggests that the situation is more complex than this, for the term 'postmodernism' is also used to denote not so much a rupture with, as a negation of, the modern. While in one sense the postmodern is what comes after the modern, in another it is an abandonment of the modern, with the emphasis being placed on a relational move away. On being faced with such an ill-defined term, Featherstone takes a closer look at the words used in its signification.

Modernity and postmodernity

The first distinction, modernity–postmodernity, suggests the epochal meaning of the terms. The idea is that 'modernity' came into being with the Renaissance and was defined in relation to antiquity, or the debate between the ancients and moderns. Alternatively, from the perspective of German sociology of the late nineteenth and early twentieth centuries – from which much of our understanding of modernity comes – the modern is contrasted with the 'traditional' order. It suggests the progressive differentiation of the social world as witnessed specifically in the development of the modern capitalist industrial state (see Weber 1947).

In contrast, to discuss 'postmodernity' is to assume an epochal break with modernity. The emergence of a new social totality with its own organizing principles is implied. This is of the order of change suggested in the writings of Jean Baudrillard and Jean-François Lyotard (see pp. 122–5 below). Baudrillard (1983a), for example, argues that new forms of technology and information have become central to the break from a productive to a reproductive order in which 'models' increasingly constitute the world, with the result that the distinction between the 'real' and the 'apparent' becomes blurred. Similarly, in Lyotard (1984), we have talk of the 'postmodern society', or postmodern age, which is founded on the clear shift to a post-industrial state.[2]

Modernization and postmodernization

Featherstone's second pair of terms, modernization–postmodernization, sits rather uncomfortably amidst discussion of modernity–postmodernity and modernism–postmodernism (Featherstone 1988). Modernization is commonly used in the sociology of development to denote the effects of economic 'progress' on traditional structures and cultures. Modernization theory is also used to denote stages of social development based upon 'industrialization, the growth of science and technology, the modern nation state, the capitalist world market, urbanization and other infrastructural elements' (p. 201). It is assumed that cultural changes based on increasing secularization and a spirit of self-development result from the modernization process.

When we turn to postmodernization, it is suggested that a similar definition of social processes and institutional changes remains to be achieved. At present we possess only the possibility of deriving the term from those uses of postmodernity which reference a new social order through epochal shift. Featherstone argues, however, that the postmodern simulation world described by Baudrillard (1983a) may represent a relevant example. In the simulation world the development of commodity production coupled with information technology leads to the 'triumph of signifying culture'. In this process the direction of determinism becomes reversed.[3]

Modernism and postmodernism

For the final coupling, modernism–postmodernism, although we are confronted with a range of meanings for these terms, common to them all is the centrality of culture (Featherstone 1988). Modernism relates to styles associated with artistic movements which originated around the turn of the century and have dominated the various arts until recently.[4] The distinctive features of modernism which emerge from these movements are

an aesthetic self-consciousness and reflexiveness; a rejection of narrative structure in favour of simultaneity and montage; an exploration of the paradoxical, ambiguous and uncertain open-ended nature of reality; and a rejection of the notion of an integrated personality in favour of an emphasis upon the destructured, dehumanized subject. (Featherstone 1988, p. 202; see also Lunn 1985, pp. 34ff.)

One of the main problems facing those wishing to comprehend this debate in the arts, however, is that many of these modernist characteristics are also encapsulated in definitions of postmodernism. For the origins of postmodernism, Featherstone (after Hassan 1985) suggests the term was first used by Frederico de Onis in the 1930s to denote a minor reaction to modernism. Later, in New York in the 1960s, the term became fashionable when used by young artists, writers and critics such as Burroughs, Barthelme, Cage, Fiedler, and Sontag to indicate a movement beyond 'high' modernism, which was rejected because of its institutionalization in the museum and the academy. In the 1970s and 1980s, the term became more widely used in architecture, music, and the visual and performing arts.

The term 'postmodernism' has thus been transmitted back and forth between Europe and the United States as the search for theoretical explanations of artistic postmodernism has included wider discussions of postmodernity. This process has generated interest in the works not only of Baudrillard and Lyotard, but also in those of other theorists, such as Bell, Derrida, Habermas and Jameson. Based on the various arguments of these writers, the central features associated with postmodernism and culture can be summarized as

> the effacement of the boundary between art and everyday life; the collapse of the hierarchical distinction between high and mass/popular culture; a stylistic promiscuity favouring eclecticism and the mixing of codes; parody, pastiche, irony, playfulness and the celebration of the surface 'depthlessness' of culture; the decline of the originality/genius of the artistic producer and the assumption that art can only be repetitious. (Featherstone 1988, p. 203)

Epoch or epistemology?

Reflecting many of the themes outlined above, but offering a simpler formulation, is the distinction between postmodernism as the signifier of an historical periodization, or as a theoretical perspective. This underpins both Bauman's (1988a and 1988b) demarcation of 'postmodern sociology' and a 'sociology of postmodernity' and Parker's (1990) splitting of post-modernism (with a hyphen) from postmodernism (without a hyphen). Both writers use their first term to signal a new epoch of sociological inquiry and the second to suggest a new form of epistemology.

In the first use, postmodernism as an epoch, the goal is to identify features of the external world that support the hypothesis that society is moving toward a new postmodern era. The practice is based on the realist notion that we simply need to find the right way of describing the world 'out there'. Parker (1990) notes how the 'post' prefix is related to a number of other concepts which reflect specific features of post-modern society. While the most common of these are post-Fordism, post-capitalism and post-industrialism (Bell 1973, Piore and Sabel 1984, Harvey 1989), he notes, following Callinicos (1989), how at least fifteen other 'post'-prefixed terms share this naming of a new historical period. A theme associated with many of these post-prefixed concepts is that the social and economic structures reproduced since the industrial revolution are now fragmenting into diverse networks held together by information technology and underpinned by what Lash and Urry (1987) call a 'postmodernist sensibility'. The emphasis is placed upon 'disorganization, untidiness and flexibility'. Writers who ride this bandwagon suggest that these 'New Times' (Hall and Jacques 1989) require explanation and codification. It is assumed that if we can understand them we may be able to control them.

In contrast to the notion of post-modernism as an historical epoch, postmodernism as an epistemology reflects developments in post-structuralist philosophy. Postmodern epistemology suggests that the world is constituted by our shared language and that we can only 'know the world' through the particular forms of discourse our language creates. It is argued, however, that as our language-games are continually in flux, meaning is constantly slipping beyond our grasp and can thus never be lodged within one term. The task of postmodern writing, therefore, is to recognize this elusive nature of language, but never with the aim of creating a meta-discourse to explain all language forms. We must beware of trying to explain formal structuring, for this is impossible. The 'myth of structure' is just one of the processes through which social action is reproduced. The postmodern theorist should instead seek to uncover 'the messy edges of mythical structure, the places where the [structuring] process becomes confused and defies definition by the discourses that are used within it' (Parker 1990, p. 13).[5]

Postmodernism and culture

Postmodernism is also of interest because it focuses our attention on another topic currently considered important for sociological analysis – culture. Although once of peripheral interest to sociologists, work on culture has now come to the fore. This is witnessed through the increase in the number of articles and books on the subject; in new academic journals with the term culture in the title; and in the development of professional associations whose goal it is to encourage theory and research on the topic, such as the Standing Conference on Organizational Symbolism (SCOS) and Group for Anthropological Policy and Practice (GAPP).[6] Above all, it is the way in which modern societies appear to be experiencing a number of major cultural transformations that has made postmodernism an import-ant issue for writers on social and organizational analysis.

Modernism: theory and analysis

To examine the possibilities for a postmodern paradigm in social and organizational analysis, we must first explore the characteristics of our other generic concept, modernism. To achieve this, we will define the main theoretical positions within the modernism debate, examine Habermas' (1981, 1987) well-known 'defence of modernity' and clarify what is meant by the modernist approach to organizational analysis.

According to Cooper and Burrell (1988), modernism is 'that moment when man invented himself; when he no longer saw himself as a reflection of God or Nature' (p. 94). Like Power (1990) and Featherstone (1988), Cooper and Burrell trace the origins of the modernist trajectory to the Enlightenment notion of 'reason', which is held to be the highest of human attributes. Similarly they point to the influence of Kant, and centrally his suggestion that we discover reason when we cease to depend on any external authority as the basis of belief. Kant's idea of 'dare to know' (*aude sapere*) offers a 'critical' posture in which we not only display powers of rational discrimination but also have the courage to express them.

Cooper and Burrell suggest that reason was also appropriated by writers on society. Notable were works by Saint-Simon and Comte on the particular problems of government and administration brought about by increasing industrialization. Indeed, in these writings we find elements of organizational thinking. Cooper and Burrell suggest that at this historical point reason was appropriated by 'an early form of systems thinking which subverts its critical edge to the functional demands of large systems' (pp. 94–5). While Saint-Simon's followers were drawing up a blueprint for the *système de la Mediterranée* (a projected association of peoples of Europe and the Orient through a network of railways, rivers and canals), Comte was, likewise, defining industrial organization as the foundation for community and progress. Modernization became represented by the organization of knowledge as expressed in the development of macro-level technological systems.

We find, therefore, two theories of modernism emerging here. On the one hand, we have a *systemic modernism*, which reflects 'the instrumentation of reason envisioned by Saint-Simon and Comte', and, on the other, a *critical modernism*, which offers 'a reanimation of Kant's programme of enlighten-ment' (Cooper and Burrell, p. 95). We will examine these in turn.

Systemic modernism

In contemporary writing it is systemic modernism which represents the dominant form of reason (Cooper and Burrell 1988). This is characterized by the notion of 'instrumental rationality', a significant expression of which is found in Bell's (1973) thesis that modern, or 'post-industrial', society differs from earlier societies in relying on knowledge that is predominantly theoretical. In Bell's notion of the post-industrial epoch we find theoretical knowledge of a kind that is both systematic and technocractic. The main purposes of knowledge are to facilitate social control and to direct innovation and change. Theoretical knowledge offers a rational methodo-logy for administering the large-scale systems which control patterns of activity in the modern world. The technologies developed to accomplish this include cybernetics, game theory and decision theory. The main function of these technologies is to define rational action and the means for achieving it. Rational action is that which will choose the best outcome when confronted with numerous competing alternatives. The main social achievement of systemic modernism, therefore, is to facilitate the control of complex and large-scale operations through a range of highly programmed knowledge technologies.[7]

Critical modernism

In contrast, critical modernism stands against the programmatic absolutism of systemic modernism. The main contemporary advocate of this position is Habermas (1972, 1974), whose objective – as we shall see – is to confront the increasing power of instrumental reason in social life and in so doing to recapture the spirit of enlightened rationalism for late modernism. Habermas seeks to decode the repressive dimensions of instrumental reason and to effect the emancipation of social actors (Connerton 1980, Power 1990). For Habermas, discourse is the medium of analysis because language is the medium of reason. Habermas outlines the contradiction between ordinary language, whose foundations lie in the spontaneous actions of the life-world, and the instrumental-calculative language of modern rational systems (Held 1976). Obscured but still active within ordinary langauge is a form of natural reason which communicates itself through instinctive wisdom.

The modern fate of this communicative rationality, however, has been its repression by the discourse of systemic modernism (Cooper and Burrell 1988). Critical reason is urgently required because of this colonization of the life-world by systemic reason. We require Kantian reason to enable us to emancipate social actors from the totalizing control of systemic logic. For Habermas, it is through the 'language of the community' that we will rediscover that lost sense of enlightenment that Kant first revealed to us (Power 1990).

Nevertheless, despite the opposition of systemic and critical forms of modernism – the one championing the mechanization of social order, the other seeking the emancipation of the life-world – they share a commitment to an inherently logical social world constituted by reason (Cooper and Burrell 1988). In systemic modernism the rational subject is the system itself, which acts according to a cybernetic discourse in which reason is a privileged property distinct from its parts.

In critical modernism, on the other hand, it is the knowing subject who, through experiencing a network of meanings, and thus the common sense of ordinary language, reaches the consensus of human understanding. In both positions, therefore, we find the assumption of an underlying unity that provides legitimacy and an authoritative logic. What is criticized, above all, in these two forms of modernism are positions that would fragment the idea of this unity. As Cooper and Burrell state, 'it is such legitimising meta-positions to which postmodernism objects' (p. 98).

Habermas and the 'defence of modernity'

Jameson (1984) has argued that postmodernism should be considered the 'cultural logic of late capitalism'. He champions totalizing Marxian theories as the grand narratives of contemporary social theory, and has relativized postmodernism as another cultural logic within another stage of capitalism.

Other social theorists completely reject the idea of a postmodern break with modernity. Postmodernism is condemned as either a form of intellectual nihilism (Callinicos 1989, Harvey 1989) or a variant of neo-conservative ideology (Aronowitz 1989, Thompson forthcoming).

The most influential critic of postmodernism, however, is Jürgen Habermas (1981, 1987) in the arguments which constitute his well-known 'defence of modernity'. In 'Modernity versus Postmodernity' (1981) Habermas argues that theories of postmodernism represent critiques of modernity which have their ideological roots in irrationalist and counter-Enlightenment perspectives. This line of analysis is continued in his *Lectures on the Philosophical Discourse of Modernity* (1987) in which the object of his critique becomes, specifically, those forms of postmodernist writing associated with modern French philosophers (e.g. Derrida, Foucault, Lyotard). Habermas suggests that as many French writers take their lead from the counter-Enlightenment statements of Nietzsche and Heidegger, this can be interpreted as a disturbing link with fascist thinking (Kellner 1988a). Faced, therefore, with a growing interest in postmodernism, Habermas wishes to defend robustly 'a principle of modernism', which he suggests is an unfinished project that holds great, unfulfilled emancipatory potential.

Above all, Habermas (1981) questions the arguments of those who assert that aesthetic modernism is dead.[8] He raises the issue of whether this cultural decline represents a farewell to modernity and thus by implication a transition into postmodernity. In the process he makes a distinction between aesthetic modernism and societal modernization, the latter of which he defines in the Weberian sense of social differentiation (Power 1990). Habermas gives support to the notion of the differentiation of cultural spheres and in particular to the development of autonomous criteria of rationality in the fields of knowledge, morality, law and art. The development of objective science according to the inner logics of these spheres is for Habermas the true project of modernity (Kellner 1988a).

Although the modernist project has resulted in part in the colonization of the life-world by the logic of scientific-technological rationality, it also for Habermas has unrealized potential for improving conditions of social justice and morality.

It is from this standpoint that Habermas finally criticizes what he calls the 'false programs of the negation of culture', which are those negative attacks on modernity that fail to recognize its potential. Habermas distinguishes between what he terms the anti-modernism of the young conservatives, the pre-modernism of the old conservatives, and the post-modernism of the neo-conservatives. He categorizes Bataille, Derrida and Foucault as critics of modernity who capitulate to the experience of aesthetic modernism and reject the modern world as 'young conservatives' (Kellner 1988a). Habermas expresses the fear that 'ideas of anti-modernity, together with an additional touch of premodernity, are becoming popular in the circles of alternative culture' (1981, p. 14; quoted in Kellner 1988a, pp. 264–5). These in fact are the tendencies to which he is so opposed in the *Lectures on the Philosophical Discourse of Modernity* (1987).

Modernism and organizational analysis

The development of a modernist trajectory in organizational analysis is described by both Gergen (1989) and Clegg (1990). Gergen contrasts an advancing postmodern period for organizational analysis with a retreating modern one.[9] He suggests that modernism has advanced in concert with faith in the notion of progress and our absorption in the machine metaphor. These various assumptions remain central to Western culture and have left a lasting impression on our theories of organization. Not only have modernist principles granted the professional investigator a privileged position in the domain of organizational inquiry, but they have promised that progress can be attained in our understanding of organizational life. Gergen notes how such views are variously represented in

Scientific management theory along with time and motion methodology. General systems theory, its various modifications and extensions, including contemporary contingency theory (e.g. Lawrence and Lorsch). Exchange theorists (e.g. Homans), along with related investigators of equity and bargaining and expectancy value analyses of individual behaviour. Cybernetic theory in which organizations approximate sophisticated mechanical automata. Trait methodology which presumes the stability of individual patterns of behaviour and the possibility of selecting individuals to fit different positions. Cognitive theories of individual behaviour in organizations (see Ilgen and Klein's 1989 review). Theories of industrial society based on rational laws of economic organization and development. (pp. 211–12)

Gergen argues, however, that the paradigm of modernist organization theory may be in decline. While the modernist discourse is far from exhausted, for a great deal of research is still carried out in its name, Gergen feels that it has lost its sense of 'lived validity'. While organization theory has so far drawn its inspiration predominantly from the modernist leitmotif, he suggests that the gains to be acquired from this tradition are diminishing. There is generally a 'yearning for alternatives', the modernist discourse having almost become a 'formalism' or, worse, an 'ideological mystification'. For Gergen, it is this sense of unease which has prompted a growing interest in the 'postmodern turn' in organization studies.

In contrast, Clegg (1990) suggests that rather than notions from the Enlightenment, it is the concept of structural differentiation which represents the motive force behind the modernist theory of organizations. A key part of the sociological enterprise has been the emphasis on processes of differentiation as a basic element of the modern experience. In particular, the division of labour is one of the core concerns of both classical sociology and political economy. It was, for example, one of the key issues which joined the otherwise disparate works of Adam Smith, Karl Marx and Emile Durkheim.[10]

In tracing this trajectory, Clegg argues that the key modernist thesis on organizations is found in Max Weber's work. Indeed the 'modernness' of modern organizations stems from the way they are appreciated 'within a genre of more or less harmonious variations on the theme of Weber's composition of bureaucracy' (p. 176). Clegg suggests that Weber's work on bureaucracy ranks alongside, if not above, Smith's pin factory and Marx's conception of the labour process. It is Weber and his followers who personify organizations as one of the great achievements of modernity. In Weber's work, organizations become the crucible within which processes of differentiation take place.

In Clegg's view, modernity is thus clearly premised on processes of differentiation. In particular, task-differentiation denotes the crucial separation of occupation from organization, or, as Offe (1976) describes it, the move from task-continuous to task-discontinuous operations.[11] When organizations become more complex in their task structures it is increasingly unlikely that any one person can have sufficient knowledge to control all practice adequately. This process sees the mapping of persons on to types of jobs and the control of their discretion once they are in place. Task divisions are no longer related by any normative community: instead, organizational relations become constituted in hierarchical forms.

Clegg argues, therefore, that modernism is premised on an increasing functional differentiation of social phenomena. Organizations are the frameworks which link these differentiations, and the management of modernity involves practices for integrating the core processes of differentiation. It was Weber's achievement, Clegg suggests, to construct a model which codified and formalized the rules for such administrative differentiation. This model saw the managerial function constructed as distinct from that of ownership. Under modernism, organizational relations were mediated through 'mechanisms of market exchange and state regulation rather than through moral sentiment' (p. 11).

Postmodernism: theory and analysis

If a modernist epistemology reflects assumptions of progress, linguistic absolutism and functional differentiation, what are the key characteristics of a postmodern epistemology?[12] Although we seem to be confronted with a diverse set of positions in postmodern writing, and while Habermas (1987) suggests the handling of the postmodern within them is undertheorized, commonalities can be found within sociologically influenced writings on postmodernism. To illustrate this, and to help produce a postmodern epistemology for organizational analysis, we explore the ideas of three leading writers: Jean Baudrillard, Jean-François Lyotard and Jacques Derrida.

Jean Baudrillard and Simulations

Jean Baudrillard was perhaps the first to organize into a postmodern social theory the anticipations of postmodern thought by, for example, Barthes (1957), Debord (1970) and Lefebvre (1971) (Norris 1990, Kellner 1988a). Although Baudrillard did not adopt the term 'postmodernism' until the 1980s, his work of the late 1960s and early 1970s incorporated many prescient themes, notably in the images of the consumer society, the media and its messages, cybernetic systems, and contemporary art and sign culture (see Baudrillard 1968, 1970, 1972).

In Baudrillard's work from the mid-1970s onwards, however, a postmodern form of social theory is developed in *Symbolic Exchange and Death* (1976), *In the Shadow of the Silent Majority* (1983b) and especially *Simulations* (1983a). Baudrillard discusses the end of an era of modernity dominated by production and industrial capitalism and the onset of an epoch of postindustrial postmodernity represented by alternative forms of technology, culture and society (see Kellner 1987). Unlike in modern industrial society, where production was the cornerstone, in the postmodern society simulations structure and control social affairs. Models and codes precede reality and are reproduced unceasingly in a society where the contrast between the real and the unreal is no longer valid (Baudrillard 1983a). As Baudrillard says, 'the real is not only what can be reproduced, but that which is already reproduced, the hyperreal' (1983a, p. 146). In this society, 'simulacra' – that is, copies or representations of objects or events – now constitute 'the real'. Whereas in the modern world we possess meaning in the laws of production, we find in the postmodern world a universe of nihilism where concepts float in a void.

As a postmodern social theory, Baudrillard's work thus operates on a high plane of abstraction. He suggests a break between the modernist epoch and the postmodern one, and develops a set of propositions to conceptualize this transition.[13] While modernist society was characterized by an explosion in the forces of social differentiation – especially through mechanization, market forces and commodification – Baudrillard argues that postmodern society sees an implosion of nearly all those forms of distinction and opposition maintained by orthodox social theory, especially those of high and low culture, and image and reality (Kellner 1988a). This signals the end of the grand positivist statements of traditional social theory, and thus the end of the finalities of social systems analysis. While modernist social theory is characterized by the increasing social differentiation of structural-functionalism, postmodern social theory will be defined as a process of 'de-differentiation' (Lash 1988).

Jean-François Lyotard and The Postmodern Condition

The challenge of developing a specifically postmodern social theory is most commonly associated with the work of Jean-François Lyotard and his book *The Postmodern Condition* (1984).

In this book, Lyotard's goal is to describe 'the condition of knowledge in the most highly developed societies' (1984, p. xxiii). In so doing, he decides to use the word 'postmodern' to describe that situation. This term, he feels, is appropriate to describe 'the state of our culture following the transformations which, since the end of the nineteenth century, have altered the game rules for science, literature, and the arts' (p. xxiii).

Lyotard feels that the term 'postmodern' reflects an epistemology which is appropriate to these new conditions of knowledge. The book's main aim, therefore, is to document the differences between the grand narratives of philosophy and social theory and what he terms 'postmodern science', which represents a preferable form of knowledge to traditional modes of philosophical and scientific inquiry. It is in this context that Lyotard defines postmodern discourse as 'the search for instabilities' (Lyotard 1984, p. 53). New and unpredictable moves are needed for science to make progress, yet these are antithetical to the idea of scientific 'performativity', linked as it is to the notion of a stable enterprise in which inputs and outputs can be regulated and controlled (Power 1990).

This objective, in turn, resonates with Lyotard's associated definition of modernity, which, unlike Baudrillard's, is primarily a form of knowledge rather than a condition of society. Lyotard argues that modernity reflects that dominant form of science which acquires its legitimacy through reference to a 'meta-discourse', that is, through recourse to grand narratives such as the creation of wealth or the emancipation of the subject. In contrast, postmodernism is about the rejection of totalizing meta-narratives. Postmodern knowledge, to quote a popular passage, 'refines our sensitivity to differences and reinforces our ability to tolerate the incommensurable. Its principle is not the expert's homology, but the inventors' paralogy' (1984, p. xxv).

Lyotard's epistemology is a language-games approach in which knowledge is based on nothing more than a number of diverse discourses, each with its own rules and structures. In Lyotard's view, each language-game is defined by its own particular knowledge criteria. Importantly, no one discourse is privileged. The postmodern epistemology concerns knowledge of localized understandings and acceptance of a plurality of diverse language forms. Thus, postmodernism sees the fragmentation of grand narratives and the discrediting of all meta-narratives.

Indeed, Lyotard rejects what he sees as the totalizing master narratives of modern, orthodox social theory, especially those reductionist narratives derived from Marx and Hegel. The postmodern society is one in which actors struggle with an infinite number of language-games within an environment characterized by diversity and conflict (Kellner 1988a). As Lyotard says in the appendix to the English version of *The Postmodern Condition*: 'Let us wage a war on totality; let us be witness to the unpresentable; let us activate the differences and save the honour of the name' (1984, p. 82).

Lyotard's work is not, however, concerned exclusively with epistemological issues. A sociological perspective is also developed in which the status of social knowledge changes as societies enter the postindustrial age and culture enters the postmodern age (Featherstone 1988). Like Baudrillard, Lyotard in many ways associates postmodernity with post-industrialism. He suggests that postmodern society is one of complex and rapid change, as reflected in new advances in science and technology. Above all, it is an information society characterized by an explosion in scientific knowledge. Lyotard clearly sides with the post-industrialists when he defines postmodern society as 'the computerization of society'. He does not, however, like Bell and his followers, suggest that postmodern society is a post-capitalist one. Instead, he suggests that developments in knowledge and technology follow the traditional pattern of the flow of funds in capitalist societies (Kellner 1988a).

Finally, while Lyotard suggests that it is impossible to suggest a new theoretical paradigm for social theory – for this will inevitably involve the construction of another grand narrative – he does, however, offer a new paradigm for the practice of theory. He calls this 'just gaming' (see Lyotard and Thébaud 1986), which is an idea developed from his earlier view of social action as a language-game. The inference is that modern science is founded on 'indeterminacy', and thus it poses a 'dialectic of difference' (Cooper and Burrell 1988). In 'doing' science, we only enter into a number of games with our colleagues. We are in fact involved in a form of 'serious play', which sees us intervene in a variety of language-games, make moves in a number of debates or discussions, and seek to oppose the moves and positions of other players while advancing our own positions. The notion of language-game includes the idea of 'agonistics' or contest, which promotes social action. Domination is realized not through the complete annihilation of one opponent by the other but by maintaining a state of continuous 'difference'. When struggle goes out of the game it loses its potential to motivate social action (Cooper and Burrell 1988).

Jacques Derrida and 'deconstruction'

The notion of 'difference' is more readily associated with the work of Jacques Derrida (1973, 1976, 1978, 1981, 1982). Derrida's postmodernism is founded on a *deconstructive* approach which, on inverting the notion of construction, illustrates how superficial are the normative structures of the social world. Derrida's aim is to show how processes of rationality serve to obscure the logical undecidability which resides at the core of social action (Cooper and Burrell 1988). For Derrida, normative social structures result from systems which privilege unity and identity over separation and difference. In contemporary society this occurs within a modernist arena in which the contest between reason and unreason takes place. Derrida's project is founded on the postmodern notion that knowledge and discourse have to be 'constructed' from a 'chameleonic' world (Cooper and Burrell 1988). Social action is encapsulated by a phenomenological ambivalence, which serves as the motive to organize.

Derrida, however, presents a unique interpretation of ambivalence, one which transcends the psychology and sociology of the actor and locates itself instead in the concept of the 'text'. The text refers both to the interplay of discourses - political, social, philosophical – and the stage upon which the process of deconstruction is enacted (Cooper 1989). In deconstruction theory, Derrida's goal is to expose the inherent contradictions which reside in any text. The general assumption is that texts reflect the notion of language as a medium for the communication of thoughts; that is, thoughts hold primacy, and language is merely the vehicle of transmission. Derrida argues that this is a mental strategy of 'logocentrism', for it pivots social action upon the notion of an original 'logos' or prefixed metaphysical structure (e.g. mind, soul, reason) which validates social action. Logocentrism is a structure with a given point of origin that censors the self-errant tendencies of the text; it specifies a central form of organization with an essential metaphysical origin that guarantees stability and surety (Cooper 1989).

Inherent within this censoring process is a tendency for logocentric 'encapsulation', or a process of prefixed boundary maintenance. To offset this tendency, deconstruction employs the twin movements of 'overturning' and 'metaphorization' (Cooper 1989). The process of overturning assumes that texts are structured around polar opposites (e.g. good–bad, male–female) in which one term dominates the other. Derrida (1981) suggests that to deconstruct the opposition we initially must 'overturn the hierarchy at a given moment' (p. 41, quoted in Cooper 1989, p. 485). He is careful, however, to draw our attention to the trap of simply overturning the superordinate term and replacing it with the subordinate, which in turn becomes the superordinate and is now ready for overturning.

To avoid this, he suggests we activate the second movement of deconstruction, 'metaphorization', which is the distinctive feature of deconstruction as a critical posture. The objective of metaphorization is to prevent the deconstructive process regressing into a simple structure of opposites. Derrida achieves this by demonstrating that there is an essential double-dynamic *within* the opposition. This sees the superordinate term defined only in contrast to the subordinate term, which itself serves to threaten constantly the former's hegemony (Cooper 1989). The relationship between the opposing terms is in fact one of mutual dependence in which each term 'inhabits' the other. Seemingly unique terms submit to a process which sees them combine in a continual exchange of 'undecidable' characteristics. The process of undecidability underpins the dynamic of metaphorization and becomes a medium for textual transportation in which the speaker or writer is simply carried along (Cooper 1989).

Postmodernism and knowledge

Having introduced some basic ideas from leading writers, our aim now is to outline the distinctively postmodern approach to knowledge. In so doing, we take steps towards defining a conceptual framework for postmodern organizational analysis. To realize this, we begin by developing five key epistemological notions which underpin the works of Baudrillard, Lyotard and Derrida: 'representation', 'reflexivity', 'writing', 'differance' and 'de-centring the subject'.

Representation

We have suggested that postmodernism as a theoretical perspective is directed against the idea of a theory-neutral observation language. In particular, it is directed against the 'picture theory' of language in which physical properties of the world are considered fixed while language can be adjusted to meet the needs of their description. Among works which have stimulated a protest against the picture theory approach are Wittgenstein's (1953) analysis of 'language-games', Kuhn's (1962) description of 'scientific revolutions', and Pepper's (1972) analysis of 'world hypotheses'. These writers examine the effects of reality rather than the causes. They argue that our knowledge of the world is constructed as a problem of 'representation' rather than one of factual accuracy.

A first theme of the postmodern approach to knowledge, therefore, is the notion of the replacement of the factual by the *representational* (see also Gergen 1992, Linstead and Grafton-Small forthcoming). This suggests that attempts to discover the genuine order of things are both naive and mistaken. In particular, the modernist objective of determining factual relationships through the empirical method is considered problematic. In the modernist view, the empirical method reflects the assumption that language is a slave to observation and reason. The logic is that through rigorous research we will continuously improve language through a more accurate correspondence with nature.

Under a postmodern approach, however, the empirical process is re-defined. The language which is produced by the empirical process does not equate with an increasingly accurate correspondence with reality. Instead, it represents a process of professional self-justification. Research proceeds on the basis of discourses which are already shared within a particular scientific community. The evidence which is produced is interpreted and justified within a restricted linguistic domain. As the empirical process starts with its theoretical assumptions intact, data produced through experimentation are defined by reference to an existing theoretical spectrum (Gergen 1992). Findings produced through empirical science reflect pre-existing intellectual categories.

Reflexivity

In a postmodern approach to knowledge, we must also possess the ability to be critical or suspicious of our own intellectual assumptions (Lawson 1985). This is achieved through the notion of *reflexivity* (see Platt 1989).

The rationale for reflexivity is that propositions which remove representation from the grasp of the factual are themselves representations. In other words, they treat as real both language and a universe divorced from language. The result is that they beget their own critical analyses.

The reactions of postmodernists to this irony have been varied. Derrida has pursued intentionally ambiguous and self-negating practices in seeking to deconstruct his own propositions. In contrast, Julia Kristeva (1980) has attempted to develop forms of expression which appear nonsensical within traditional conventions but are, she argues, sensible within a primordial semiotic. Others have proposed the less heady alternative of the intellectual playing the fool (Gergen 1992). Uniting all these approaches, however, is the view that we should not portray knowledge as a prestigious and objective estate divorced from the mundane activities of everyday life. Instead, the forms of language we call 'knowledge' should be viewed in a more humble way. Knowledge bases are things which are either more or less interesting to us, but no more than that. They are not the stuff of which ultimate commitments are made.

In Lyotard's terms, therefore, we should beware of subscribing to the grand narrative of progress, for the prime purpose of this discourse is to justify our actions. Above all, we should not subscribe to the seriousness of the progress narrative, for its assumption of unitary and linear progression only serves to supress the possibility of a multitude of alternative voices. We must, though, acknowledge that in everyday affairs our knowledge discourses will be informed by 'serious play'. While we may cease to credit our forms of knowledge with epistemological primacy, we must accept that they are taken seriously on entering society, especially when they may alter patterns of relationships. If theories lend themselves, for example, to repulsive forms of behaviour, we must be able to subject them to criticism. This is reminiscent of Wittgenstein's (1953) view that while language-games are beyond justification, what we say within them is not.

Writing

A postmodern approach to knowledge is concerned with the way we learn to fix the flow of the world in temporal and spatial terms. For Derrida, this is achieved through the notion of 'writing'. Writing is the means by which social actors define order in their environments. It is a universal technology which is concerned with spacing, listing and contrasting (McArthur 1986). In this sense, writing relates to the structure of representations more than to the meaning of messages (Cooper 1989).[14]

Derrida's aim is to overturn a logocentric image of writing which sees language as a sign system for concepts which exist independently in the object world. His concept of writing concerns the physical action of inscribing marks on a surface and not of assuming a logocentric origin beyond those marks. Writing only illustrates how the social actor is materially involved in the world through a process of reflecting. Derrida illustrates the paradoxical – or 'undecidable' – nature of writing in which a term is found to be inhabited by its opposite. Writing is, for example, 'not a direct effect of the stylus' contact with the celluloid surface but is, instead, an indirect effect of the contact between the celluloid and the wax base' (Cooper 1989, p. 485; see also Harland 1987, p. 143). In this view, consciousness comes to us 'on the rebound', as the delayed effect of an involuntary action; it is 'not a direct reflection on the outside world but a relationship made with what has already been inscribed' (Cooper 1989, p. 485). The corollary is that in the process of deconstruction the structured terms of logocentric writing are separated by showing their intrinsic 'supplementarity'. As Cooper (1989) notes,

the various terms of a text point away from themselves to other terms in a continuous, unstoppable movement so that writing appears to be in the grip of an autonomous self-propelling force that lies beyond the intentions of the individual actor. (p. 486)

'Differance'

We have seen how Derrida's notions of deconstruction and writing rely on a denial of conceptual mastery and definition. It is necessary, therefore, for Derrida to develop a strategy of thought which reflects but does not capture this process. He achieves this through the notion of *differance*. In defining *differance* (with an a), we see the extension of Derrida's wish to express writing as a self-deferring process of 'difference' (Cooper 1989).

Cooper (1987) suggests that the concept of difference can be compared to the concept of 'information' in information theory, where it takes the form of a binary structure based on the idea of division. There are two ways of considering division (or difference): by focusing on the two forms that have been separated; or by focusing on the actual process of separating. While the former suggests logocentrism, through emphasizing hierarchical binary oppositions, the latter suggests that division is not simply a static act of separation but can also represent an undifferentiated state where terms are conjoined (Cooper 1990). Division thus both separates and joins: the act of separation also creates the image of something that is whole.

The second sense of the term reflects Derrida's notion of undecidability in which terms inhabit each other. To counter the static logocentrism of hierarchical binary oppositions, and to activate the processual sense of difference, Derrida invents the term *differance*; which is derived, in part, from Saussure's (1974) conception of language as a system of differences (Cooper 1990). In developing the term *differance* he incorporates two senses of the French verb *différer* – to differ (in space) and to defer (in time) – into one designation which both subverts and produces the illusion of presence and consciousness (Johnson 1980). To explain the concept, Derrida outlines how our traditional understanding of the sign is that which we substitute for the absent thing we wish to present. The sign represents the present in its absence – it is 'deferred presence'. Derrida argues against the notion of a fully present reality that is directly available to our understanding. Instead he posits a world that is continually deferred both in space and time. Thus,

the signified concept is never present in and of itself . . . every concept is inscribed in a chain or in a system within which it refers to the other, to the concepts, by means of the systematic play of differences. (Derrida 1982, p. 11: quoted in Cooper 1990, p. 178)

Differance, therefore, can never be grasped in the present. It is an ever-active and essentially prior form of play which cannot be located in a particular place; it is perpetual absence, for the differences of *differance* do not have a specific cause; and it is continuous movement, although not the movement of things. For social theory, Derrida feels that the paradox of social action lies in the censoring of the very dynamic, *differance*, that gives the actor power. Characteristic of our conceptions of agency is an inherent tendency to deny the origins of agency. As a result, the agent necessarily suppresses the forces of its own 'becoming', which arise from the conflict that is differance. Derrida's image of agency is of a field of interactive forces activated by the process of *differance* (Cooper 1989). To reclaim itself as an active agent, the postmodern subject must, therefore,

view itself *in the act of distancing* ... this is exactly the function of deconstruction which shows agency to be an enigmatic process that denies the very thing that gives it life. (Cooper 1989, p. 492)

De-centring the subject

Our final theme in this section develops Derrida's analysis of the deconstruction of presence in terms of its implications for human agency. This is achieved through the notion of *de-centring the subject* as the locus of understanding.

From the logocentric view, the human agent represents an holistic and clearly bounded cognitive universe. Human agency is founded on a personal, subjective core of awareness in which actions and emotions are coordinated from a knowing self. The agent acts within the context of its own dynamic presence.

In contrast, we have seen in Derrida's work that presence is always already mediated by absence. We noted earlier how consciousness is never a direct and unmediated experience but rather comes to us in an indirect way. In this view, agency is an artefact and subjectivity is a process of locating identity in the language of the 'other' (Harland 1987). Agents are constituted through a symbol system which locates them while remaining outside of their awareness (Linstead and Grafton-Small forthcoming).

The process which establishes agency, therefore, is one which takes recourse to the concept of the 'other' (Cooper 1983). The subject is decentred and thus bereft of the logocentric authority it possessed when self-aware and present. The self-conscious agent of modern psychology becomes an image which is no longer sustainable. Derrida (1978) replaces the grand isolation of the modern subject with the notion of agency as a system of relations between strata. The subject is no longer self-directing but is instead a convenient location for the throughput of discourses. As Linstead and Grafton-Small (1991) suggest, subjectivity becomes 'a weave, a texture, fragmented but intertwined rather than hierarchical and integrated, a process and a paradox having neither beginning nor end' (p. 39).

Postmodernism and organizational analysis

We started this chapter by noting the tendency to define postmodernism as representing either an historical periodization (an epoch) or a theoretical perspective (an epistemology). We have since listed five constituent elements of a postmodern approach to knowledge: 'representation', 'reflexivity', 'writing', 'differance' and 'de-centring the subject'. We now discuss, in a modernist way, how these two lines of analysis offer conceptual tools for assessing contributions to a nascent postmodern approach to organization studies.[15]

On the one hand, the epoch–epistemology distinction offers an ideal-type model for interpreting the basic orientation of the analysis. By using this distinction, we can plot the degree to which an investigation is centred upon historical or theoretical concerns. On the other hand, the five knowledge bases offer a guide to the degree of epistemological sophistication present within a study. Whilst not defining intellectual worth, the presence (or absence) of these concepts indicates the extent to which basic concepts have been applied.

Finally, we use this framework to show how, in their 'strong' form, both the epoch and the epistemology positions may actually inhibit theory building for postmodern organizational analysis. We argue, instead, that a position which develops the 'middle ground' between these extremes – and employs the knowledge base to check that postmodern analysis is achieved – offers a more appropriate basis for organization studies.

The epoch position and organizations

A work which reflects the 'epoch' orientation is Clegg's (1990) book *Modern Organizations: Organization Studies in the Postmodern World*. In this work, Clegg advances the periodization position by citing detailed empirical examples of postmodern organizational forms. Declaring his objectivist intentions from the start, Clegg remarks, 'empirical realities are neither imaginary nor whimsical: they cannot be side-stepped' (p. 5). Indeed the tangible description of postmodern organization structures – ones which can be distinguished from the classical modernist form of the bureaucracy – defines this work. Clegg documents the structural properties of postmodern organizations from a review of comparative data. He argues that unlike the highly differentiated and modernist bureaucracy, the postmodern organization is based on a 'de-differentiated' form.

Specifically the postmodern organization has structural characteristics which reflect the socio-economic philosophies of 'flexible specialisation' and 'post-Fordism' (see Piore and Sabel 1984, Pollert 1988, Smith 1989, Hirst and Zeitlin 1991). Clegg argues that examples of the postmodern form are found in the business enterprises of Japan, Sweden, East Asia and the Third Italy. The suggestion is that these are organizational structures in which we find, *inter alia*, a niche-based marketing strategy, a craft-oriented or multi-skilled workforce and a technical core of flexible manufacturing. Although postmodern organizational forms are as yet relatively ill-defined, Clegg suggests they may encourage, as in Sweden, progressive developments in industrial democracy and improvements in the skill levels of labour. He reminds us, however, that the postmodern form, while in certain respects appealing, may also rely upon repressive and elitist industrial practices. Such organizations may be based on a segmented labour force with a clear stratification of privilege, as in Japan.

The epistemological position and organizations

Alternatively, an example of the strong epistemological position is found in the work of Cooper and Burrell (1988: see also Burrell 1988, Cooper 1989). Although, like Clegg (1990), Cooper and Burrell address the modernist assumptions which underpin Weber's work on bureaucracy, they argue that postmodern concepts are appropriate to the theoretical rather than empirical understanding of organizations.

Rather than privilege the functionality associated with increasing levels of differentiation, Cooper and Burrell seek a more abstract understanding of the principles of bureaucratic organization. Their discussion of Weberian modernism centres on the alienating forces of bureaucracy and, in particular, on the notion of bureaucracy as the 'iron cage' which imprisons modern consciousness. Instead of Weber's analysis representing a functional assessment of organizational design, for Cooper and Burrell it is a grand narrative of administrative progress. Although Weber's work emphasizes the processual character of organizational life, modern organizational analysis has seen it de-contextualized and re-written to stress static issues of efficiency and administrative control. Such re-writing has privileged the role of the organizational analyst as a professional observer who possesses the expertise to construct an authoritative meta-narrative of organizational development. The professional observer is able to control the increasing complexity of organizational life by overlaying a template of functional rationality on emergent and perhaps disorderly patterns of social relations. It is the modernist project which reproduces these models of control and allows predictions about organizational activities to be made by the professional cadre of administrative analysts.

Cooper and Burrell argue that the postmodern project emphasizes the futility of such totalizing tendencies. The idea of a superior, objective standpoint is completely rejected, emphasis being placed on the inherent instability of organization. The discourses of organization are no more than changing moves within a game that is never completed. Cooper and Burrell suggest that under postmodernism we should seek to disrupt continuously our normative structures about the organized world. Above all, we should seek to explode the myth of robust structural relations through illustrating the fragile character of organizational life. For Cooper and Burrell, a postmodern analysis should focus on 'the production of organization rather than the organization of production' (p. 106). Under this strategy, we must eschew the idea that organizations are formed and then act themselves to structure relations. We realize, instead, that it is the analysis alone which creates a discourse on organization. The constructs we employ to make sense of organization are moral imperatives which serve to presuppose certain features of organization while excluding the possibility for others. The academic study of organizations is reduced to nothing more than a series of discourses which have no prior claim to an understanding of organizational affairs.

Toward a conceptual framework

Even in an analysis as sophisticated as Cooper and Burrell's, however, it remains difficult to discern any significant movement beyond a 'perspective' on postmodern organization, especially in the direction of a conceptual framework. Although they offer a deeper level of conceptual reflection than, for example, writers who associate postmodern organization with flexible specialization or post-Fordism, it can be argued that Cooper and Burrell have, nevertheless, 'consciously avoided being programmatic' (Parker 1990, p. 9) in their theorizing.

Indeed, when faced with the problem of constructing a postmodern conceptual model at the institutional level we have few exemplars to consult (see Kreiner 1989 on this point). An obvious reason for this difficulty stems from the assumptions of rationality and purpose which underpin the enterprise. Traditional theory construction is founded on belief in the factual nature of a knowable universe. The dominant knowledge bases of social theory thus rest on logocentric foundations. Given these assumptions, it seems that postmodernism must reject the very idea of theory construction at the institutional level. If a factual world is beyond our grasp, what are the grounds for developing such static formulations? Why should we seek to develop formal schemes if the method of deconstruction shows them to be objects for our amusement, elements of 'serious play' at best? Is not theory building a form of intellectual imperialism, and one which fails to acknowledge the basically uncontrollable nature of meaning?[16]

The main postmodern positions in organizational analysis thus appear to be successful in inhibiting formal theory building, albeit in an unconscious way. On the one hand, the epoch position provides positivist descriptions which are developed with scant reflection on the philosophy of postmodern analysis. On the other hand, the epistemological position explodes the myth of the structural form but fails to account for the everyday experiences of social actors. As such, neither develops a framework in which formal organization is acknowledged as a phenomenon which is accessible to postmodern deconstruction.

Developing the middle ground

For those wanting a more robust framework for postmodern organizational analysis, a possible way forward may be offered by Gergen (1989, 1992), who argues that postmodern statements do not necessarily leave us bereft of the potential for theory building. Gergen suggests that the discourses which have historically shaped organization theory – romanticism and modernism – are beginning to lose their lustre, especially when compared with the emergent discourse of postmodernism. Although he does not wish to suggest that postmodernism has greater explanatory power than these older discourses, he feels that it is more closely attuned to the spirit of the times.

Gergen argues, in fact, that the hallmark of an organization theory should be whether or not it supports patterns of relationships we feel have positive rather than negative consequences for social life. He feels that 'if the function of theories is not derived from their truth value, but from their pragmatic implications, then theoretical voice is restored to significance' (Gergen 1992, p. 217). It is suggested that the potential for theory building is in fact greater under postmodernist conditions than under modernist ones. Under modernism, an acceptable theory is constituted by years of 'pure' research by scientists before being 'applied' in the real world by practitioners, that is, by members of a separate culture. Under postmodernism, however, the essence of theory is not its database but its intelligibility.

It is the successful communication of this intelligibility which provides the grounds for its usefulness. Theory and practice are inseparable: there is 'no language of understanding placed beyond the boundaries of potential' (Gergen 1992, p. 217). We should be continuously in the process of absorbing other cultural intelligibilities into our own. Like the postmodern architect, we should feel free to draw from the entire repository of human potentials. As postmodernists, we are concerned not only with the social relationships championed or discredited by particular theories, but also with the potential for theories to offer new possibilities for our culture.

In this analysis, it can be argued that Gergen develops the middle-ground between the 'strong' epoch and epistemology positions. The advantage, for us, is that this quasi-synthetic position maintains in tension the empirical reality of organizations and the fragile nature of their reproduction. As such, it represents a more fertile location for propagating a postmodern approach to organization studies.

The case of the relational theory of power

To demonstrate the power of this position, Gergen has described a deconstructionist theory of organizational power. By re-interpretation we can outline how this work is informed by the concepts of postmodern knowledge outlined above and thus how a conceptual framework for postmodern organization theory can be advanced.

Gergen argues that the concept of postmodern writing can offer new options for organization theory. Indeed it directs him to 'go beyond' speculation about a substantive contribution to postmodern organization theory and to offer one himself, in the form of a 'relational' theory of organizational power. In accepting that a tangible aspect of organization can be addressed from a deconstructionist position it can be argued that the work achieves a tension between the epoch and epistemological approaches to postmodern analysis. Above all, in being a programmatic evaluation, Gergen's work represents an important step towards a postmodern organization theory.

Although Foucault's work plays its part in orienting Gergen's analysis, the project draws more tangibly upon two concerns in Cooper and Burrell (1988) – the 'indeterminacy of meaning' and the tensions which result between forces for 'organization and disorganization' (see Cooper 1990). Gergen wishes to extend these concerns and specifically to erect the 'conceptual scaffolding' for a relational theory. He achieves this by constructing an analysis around the notions of: 'indeterminate rationalities', 'social supplementarity', 'power as social coordination', 'power as self-destructive', and 'heteroglossia and the recovery of efficiency'. Gergen draws inspiration from the ideas of Derrida and Lyotard, and thus the analysis takes recourse to the bases of postmodern knowledge outlined earlier, especially to those of 'differance', 'reflexivity' and the 'de-centred subject'.

For analysing organizational power, Gergen argues that the postmodern 'drama' begins with the realization that the rational sayings available to the manager are in fact of indeterminate meaning. It is here that the concept of differance comes into play for, as Derrida suggests, the meaning of any word is derived from a process of 'deferral' to other words which 'differ' from itself. The strength of the single concept 'differance' is that it reflects both the simultaneous and conflated processes at work in organizational power.

The postmodern plot thickens as it becomes clear that there are multiple meanings for the everyday terms used in organizational power networks. Such terms are polysemous: they have been used in many contexts, and thus bear 'the trace', as Derrida says, of many other terms. The position becomes more complicated still when we discover that each term employed for clarifying an original one is itself obscured until the process of differance is once again set in motion. We also know that these terms subsequently bear the traces of others in an expanding network of significations (see Lash 1988 on this point). Thus, statements which appear to be but simple pieces of organizational rationality, 'on closer inspection can mean virtually anything' (Gergen 1989, p. 20).

This spread of signification is also underpinned by the process of 'ironic self-negation', and thus *reflexivity* is realized. From Derrida we derive the notion that every proposition implies its own contradiction, or in other words that by affirming something we set in motion a chain of significations that confirm its negation. This process finds that each attempt at decoding the original proposition itself becomes another encoding. These encodings are in fact undecidable until constrained by a listener. A speaker may signify, but a supplement, in the form of a listener, is required to determine its meaning. The agent of propositions is therefore a *de-centred subject*. In an organization, 'a manager's words ... are like authorless texts; once the words are set in motion, the manager ceases to control their meaning. They are possessions of the community' (Gergen 1992, p. 220). The rationality of a manager's actions are dependent on the reactions of colleagues and subordinates, for it is they who supply the interpretations of propositions. Managers themselves are never rational. Instead their rationality is a product of collective action.

This postmodern theory of organizational power demonstrates, therefore, that we are empowered only through the actions of others – through 'social supplementarity'. This suggests that textbook theories, which locate power in individual discretion or the structural properties of organization, should be abandoned. Relational theory suggests that managers do not control the fate of their decrees. Instead power is a matter of 'social interdependence'; it is effected through the coordination of actions around specified definitions.

Furthermore, the theory suggests that as sub-units achieve power, so they simultaneously contribute to their own downfall. As a department or function becomes increasingly powerful within itself, so is the organization as a whole devitalized. As the achievement of power at the local level contains within it the negation of power originally sought, so organizations to sustain themselves require means for maintaining a dynamic tension between empowerment and disempowerment. As full consensus within an organization threatens its well-being, so organizational vitality depends on restoring the process of difference. This is true not only for relationships within the organization, but also for that between the organization and those elements which comprise its environment.[17]

Thus Gergen's analysis is informed by key concepts from the postmodern theory of knowledge – especially 'reflexivity', 'differance' and the 'decentring of the subject'. It is also developed from the middle-ground between the 'strong' epoch and epistemology positions. More important still, the analysis is far removed from the modernist one. The grand modernist narrative that suggests we achieve progress through the application of reason and objectivity is rejected. Similarly the image of the ideal organization as a smoothly running machine is viewed as mistaken and dangerous. Instead the relational theory of organizational power suggests that organizational survival depends upon 'the prevalence of creative confusion' (Gergen 1989, p. 26).

Conclusions

In this final chapter, we have moved beyond our earlier discussions of positivism and paradigms and toward a new concern for social and organizational analysis – postmodernism. An overview of the topic has been presented by assessing contributions from philosophers, sociologists and organization theorists alike.

Initially the analysis saw the concept of postmodernism defined and contrasted with its sister term – modernism. We suggested that currently we possess no firm agreed meaning for the concepts of modernism and postmodernism. Instead we find a range of meanings associated with these generic terms and subsequently with the family of terms derived from them.

We attempted to place some structure on the debate by identifying two main orientations within the literature – postmodernism as either an historical periodization or a theoretical position. The former approach suggests that postmodernism is an epoch of cultural and intellectual life: the latter that it is an epistemology. In the former, we can explain cultural change by reference to empirical examples. In the latter, we counter the totalizing tendencies of empiricism by presenting a conceptual alternative.

To establish a conceptual framework, we joined the epoch–epistemology distinction with themes from a 'postmodern approach to knowledge'. This was developed by introducing leading writers on postmodernism and extracting key concepts from their works. Drawing upon Derrida and Lyotard in particular we identified five themes of postmodern knowledge relevant to social theory – 'representation', 'reflexivity', 'writing', 'differance' and 'de-centring the subject'.

Finally, these themes and distinctions formed the structure for a discussion of postmodern organization. Contrasting the epoch and epistemology positions we argued that in their present form neither offers an adequate basis for a postmodern organization theory. Instead we suggested that the middle-ground between these extremes represents a more promising location for theory development. This argument was supported by reference to a case study of Gergen's (1989) 'relational' theory of organizational power. Informed by several themes from the postmodern approach to knowledge, this study deconstructed a tangible issue of organizational life.

Notes

2 THE HEGEMONY OF SYSTEMS

1 Clegg and Dunkerley (1980) suggest that Hage's (1965) 'axiomatic theory of organization' represents an important example of the closed systems approach to organizational analysis. Hage constructs this model around relationships between four organizational goals (adaptiveness, production, efficiency, job satisfaction) and four organizational means to achieve these goals (specialization, centralization, standardization, stratification).

2 The search for such laws is often seen as misguided, as it does not equate with the uniqueness of organizational functioning. The classic expression of this position is March and Simon's (1958) thesis of bounded rationality, where the reality of modern organization resides in attempts to 'satisfice' rather than 'maximise'.

3 Silverman notes how this difficulty is particularly evident in Turner and Lawrence's (1965) development of the 'Requisite Task Attribute' (RTA) Index. In the RTA Index, Turner and Lawrence hypothesize a direct relationship between requisite task attributes and job satisfaction. Their evidence, however, suggests only a qualified relationship between these variables. Silverman notes how, at a very late stage, Turner and Lawrence introduce religious affiliation and place of residence as determinants of the orientation to work. The post-hoc rationalization is that the Protestant ethic is strongest among workers from small towns and rural areas, and that among this group the original hypothesis relating the content of work to job satisfaction is supported. 'City' workers, on the other hand, are predominantly Catholic and interested in maximizing their immediate economic rewards in exchange for a less complex task.

4 Kast and Rosenweig (1973) give the example of a business organization which receives inputs from society in the form of people, materials, money and information. It transforms these into outputs of products, services and rewards to the organization members which are sufficiently large to maintain their participation.

5 Miller and Rice (1967) suggest that the properties of the environment may actually preclude a 'natural coincidence' between the attainment of an organization's goal and the satisfaction of the needs of its members. In such a case a coincidence between the two must be contrived.

6 As details of the various stages of the Hawthorne studies are readily available, we will not recount them here. The reader should consult Roethlisberger and Dickson (1939) and Mayo (1933, 1949) for first-hand accounts, or Rose (1988) for a well-crafted summary.

7 Roethlisberger and Dickson (1939) give weight to the social factors so discounted
in scientific management. Social factors become central elements of their
investigations and form the basis for distinguishing between formal and informal
systems. They conclude from their research that social factors both inside and
outside the workplace influence employee attitudes and hence work effectiveness.
Satisfaction or dissatisfaction must be viewed in light of the individual's status
within the social system of the organization, and especially in regard to 'that
system of practices and beliefs by means of which the human values of the
organization are expressed, and the symbols around which they are organized –
efficiency, service etc.' (1939, p. 374).

3 FROM FUNCTIONALISM TO FRAGMENTATION

1 The literature also suggests several 'scientific' limitations of functionalism. It is
argued, for example, that functionalism fails to present propositions in a form
which leaves them open to falsification (Hempel 1959; Cohen 1968), and that it
produces only teleological explanations, which inhibits the rational and
objective processes of scientific comparison (Dore 1961).
2 Cohen asks, for example, that if a surgeon earns twenty times more than a nurse,
does this mean, necessarily, that the surgeon's skills are twenty times greater or
more valuable to society than those of the nurse?
3 For Allen, the systems theory case study assumes that there are no given causal
relationships, because

only if this assumption is made can the study of social relations as if they constitute an
indeterminate number of separate and relatively independent systems be justified ... as no
causal relationships are given a priori, no order of priority between differing determining
factors is given either. (1975, p. 79)

4 Mayntz (1964) discusses a related issue, that of the kinds of propositions
developed in systems analysis. She focuses on issues of system integration and
centrally the integration of the system (organization) and its environment.
Although commending the systems approach for establishing the notion of
boundary exchange, she notes that – as developed – it fails to do justice to claims
of developing generalizable exchange propositions. Mayntz suggests that for
organizations the process of boundary exchange is necessarily a selective one.
She points out that when we discuss the kinds of regulating mechanisms required
for mediating organizational and environmental demands we are forced to
'leave the level of general propositions valid for all organizations and ... to take
historically specific conditions into account' (1964, p. 113).
5 In developing an attack on what he calls 'American articulated systems
analysis', Allen argues that a consequence of accepting the problems of others as
defined by others is that definitions of terms connected with them have also been
accepted. This, he feels, flies in the face of attempts to develop a science of social
systems. For Allen, the difference between true social scientists and their
'applied' colleagues is that the former are usually scrupulously careful about
their definition of terms, because the manner in which a term is defined can
profoundly influence the subsequent analysis. Allen argues that the act of
defining carries with it conceptual implications, and that this sets limits to the

analysis. Organizational sociologists who act as consultants have breached this professional code. Citing the early socio-technical work of the Tavistock Institute, Allen notes

with an abandon which befitted adolescence rather than scientific maturity ... [they] accepted terms without questioning their relevance, let alone their usefulness. They have made inexcusable breaches of scientific practice. In practice the industry they investigated was a technological phenomenon not a set of social relationships; efficiency was inseparably associated with productivity so that anything which adversely affected productivity could not be efficient; productivity referred to the physical output of industry; morale was related to efficiency so that in some situations and for some types of behaviour it could not be used. They accepted work categories such as skilled, unskilled, manual, professional and non-professional which had no sociological justification and simply mystified behaviour and confounded analysis. They accepted management as an entity which could be usefully analysed because it was said to present problems to employers without questioning whether management was a sociological category or not. (1975, p. 78) (see also Brown 1967).

6 Ritzer also suggests that in the works of the Frankfurt School we see the beginnings of a further influential paradigm – critical theory.

7 Instead of the experiment, many behaviouralists have used the questionnaire – a factist method – as their main research tool.

8 While Evered and Louis (1981) and colleagues (see also Sanders 1982, Martin 1990) concentrate on methodological comparisons, other writers focus on ideological ones. Rather than develop new fieldwork strategies, the aim is to interpret sociological practices from contrasting political perspectives. Examples are Nord's (1974) work on the 'modern human resources paradigm' and Braendgaard's (1978) analysis of 'work humanization' attempts.

9 In developing this analysis, Donaldson (1985) repels the charge that functionalist organization theory is atheoretical. He describes links between empiricism, theory and metatheory in the structural-functionalist framework and states a case for the scientific study of organizations and against charges that organization theory suffers from managerial and conservative bias.

10 Towards the end of his book, Donaldson (1985) returns to the functionalist paradigm to describe the value of contingency theory for designing organizations. He synthesizes some major findings on organization structure and shows how these can be combined to form a coherent decision-making model. The output is a set of taxonomies for illustrating congruent combinations of strategy and structure.

11 Arguing that the professional basis for the study of organizations has changed, Hinings states:

organization theory is no longer the sociology of organizations; it has developed as a discipline in its own right with its own problematics, theoretical structures and methods. It still draws upon sociology, but to an ever decreasing extent. Those who write in *OS* [*Organization Studies*], *ASQ* [*Administrative Science Quarterly*], *AMJ* [*Academy of Management Journal*], *AMR* [*Academy of Management Review*], *JMS* [*Journal of Management Studies*] etc. are not concerned with sociological issues. It seems to me that many of the critiques of organization theory are in actual fact attempts to reclaim it for sociology. (1988, p. 2)

12 Clegg (1988) feels Donaldson's argument is also flawed because it is constructed as a normative orientation to science, rather than one which is naturalistic. As the exercise is based upon Popperian moralism it ends up being 'stipulative'. For Clegg, a credible defence has to be mounted on something other than a critique of taste or preference. Donaldson's preference for organization theory turns out to be simply a preference for what sociologists define as a functionalist version of the genre.

13 Reed (1985) develops this analysis with a description of 'post-interregnum' organizational analysis – a critique of systems theory based on concepts of socio-political consciousness. A renewed emphasis on human agency sees structural determinism rejected in favour of a dialectical conception of structure and action.

14 Donaldson (1989) questions Reed's (1985) treatment of the development of organization theory as a discipline. Although Reed repeatedly chastises various writers for their overreliance on an internalist view of the development of the subject, and their neglect of how the external context has shaped the discipline, there is apparently little in his own history of social science to explain why organizational analysis has moved through the phases described. Donaldson suggests that this neglect is consistent with Reed's overly abstract emphasis and his failure to deal adequately with more concrete levels of analysis.

15 Despite the fact that the practice framework concerns processes of investigation, Donaldson (1989) claims that Reed neglects methodology. Although Reed writes 'winningly' about the virtues of multilevel analysis, he never explains how this is achieved in practice. By remaining at the programmatic level Reed can simply ignore awkward questions about the conduct of empirical inquiry. This is unfortunate, Donaldson feels, because familiarity with research methods leads to a healthy view about what can be known and established about organization, and what limits there are to the empirical base of theorizing.

16 Donaldson (1989) argues that Reed's work thus has three main failings. First, Reed presents an abstract, programmatic overview of general themes without attending to the detailed discussion of theories or empirical research studies. Second, he makes mistaken judgments about past contributions and the history of organization theory. And third, he projects an underdeveloped vision of organization theory's future and retreats into a form of intellectual nihilism that avoids any contact with real world problems.

17 Reed (1989) argues that Donaldson's views of theory development are problematic because they are

mounted from within the assumed epistemological and ethical superiority of a privileged intellectual tradition within organizational analysis – a combination of positivist methodology and functionalist theory geared to the generation of policy science. (p. 256)

In adhering to this tradition, Donaldson is committed to the epistemological principles, theoretical procedures and research methods representative of professional sociology in North America. This strategy sees Donaldson employ tactics that are intended to rebut criticism and re-establish the superiority of the systems theory orthodoxy. First, criticisms are redescribed in the language of structural-functionalism and translated into a form that is compatible with the conceptual idiom provided by the latter. Second, the results of empirical studies that challenge structural-functional analysis are reinterpreted so that they fit the explanatory logic on which the latter rests. And third, fundamental epistemological and theoretical objections to the logic of structural-functionalism and contingency analysis are resolved by treating them as technical hitches that can be ironed out by a further application of functional theory. Thus, by a combination of assimilation, incorporation and rationalization the critics are dismissed and the hegemony of systems theory orthodoxy re-established.

6 POSTMODERNISM AND ORGANIZATION

1 It could be argued that recent chapters have been sympathetic to a postmodern position. Possible evidence for this is the replacement of an absolute approach to social analysis with one that tolerates multiple understandings.

For example, the linguistic essentialism of systems theory has been eroded by philosophies which challenge the proposition that reason and observation can be reflected in language in a direct and objective way. We have described how a transcendent systems metaphor has been confronted by writings which advocate a plurality of methods for making sense of social and organizational issues. The general thrust of the argument has been to dismantle the grand narrative of functionalism and to replace it with localized methods.

Furthermore, the practical outcome of this work, multiple paradigm research (MPR), represents a methodology in which social action is described by several competing narratives. While MPR produces information, this is not in the form of 'hard data', but rather as a set of discourses which are intelligible only in relation to one another. The method is at odds with positivism, in that instead of 'scientific evidence' the production metaphor is 'serious play' (Lyotard and Thébaud 1986). No firm claims are made for the 'truth' of the propositions advanced, and no single interpretation is privileged above the rest. Instead, the approach resonates with the notion of 'de-centring' (Derrida 1978, Cooper 1989) the subject. The MPR researcher, for example, is the medium through which discourses are processed, not the core of intellectual authority. Reality is located in the language of the 'other' (Cooper 1983), not in external objects.

We must, however, make two qualifications to this argument. The first is that we reject a key aspect of the 'collective action' position (Gergen 1989, Shotter 1980) – that language-games are 'incommensurable'. While the professional work of scientific communities may signal that discrete language practices are being adopted, we find porosity within the meta-discourses of their production. The image of hermetically sealed surface languages belies the essentially screen-like properties of their deep-seated technical languages. This argument, like the notion of 'supplementarity' (Cooper 1983, 1989), suggests that an hermetically sealed language can never 'know itself'.

The second qualification relates to the actual practice of multiple paradigm research. Although we advocate an epistemological position which is in sympathy with postmodern sociology, we do not wish to guarantee the production of an associated research tool. While it could be argued that multiple paradigm research implies the 'de-centring' of the researcher, it cannot be regarded as a postmodern data-gathering technique, for this is a contradiction in terms. We cannot define as postmodern an enterprise which is based on the logic of linear accumulation. Such an approach will be exclusively modernist in its trajectory.

2 Featherstone (1988) notes, however, that Lyotard changes register from one use of postmodernism to the next. In his more recent works (especially Lyotard 1986) there is the emphasis that the postmodern is to be regarded as part of the modern. Lyotard writes:

> 'postmodern' is probably a very bad term because it conveys the idea of a historical 'periodization'. 'Periodizing', however, is still a 'classic' or 'modern' ideal. 'Postmodern' simply indicates a mood, or better a state of mind. (Lyotard, 1986–7, p. 209, quoted in Featherstone, 1988, p. 198)

3 Through this process, 'social relations become saturated with shifting cultural signs to the extent that we can no longer speak of class and normativity and are faced by "the end of the social"' (Featherstone, 1988, p. 201).

4 Influential figures here are: in painting – Picasso, Matisse, Braque, Cézanne and the futurist, expressionist, Dada and surrealist movements; in literature – Joyce, Yeats, Gide, Proust, Kafka, Lawrence and Falkner; in poetry – Pound, Eliot, Rilke, Lorca and Valéry; in drama – Strindberg, Pirandello and Wedekind; and in music – Stravinsky, Schoenberg and Berg (see Bradbury and McFarlane 1976).

5 Parker (1990) feels that such postmodern writing would have no obvious practical benefits, for it would describe only the limits of social projects. This holds true for academic work as much as for that of any other social sphere. The attempts by academics to codify and systematize are just as susceptible to the 'myth of the grand narrative of the Enlightenment'.

6 Although the Standing Conference on Organizational Symbolism started life as a sub-group of the European Group for Organization Studies (EGOS) its membership is now larger than the parent body.

7 The concept of systemic modernism is also found in the work of Luhmann (1976). Addressing the 'new systems theory', he outlines the rational dynamic of systemic modernism and suggests that Kant's notion of the 'critically rational subject' is repressed in favour of developing a mechanistic system of social functionality (Cooper and Burrell 1988). Society is treated as just another, albeit macro, form of organization. The system goal is the global optimization of input and output relations, or, to use Lyotard's (1984) term, universal 'performativity'. Performativity assumes a central role in systemic modernism, for it takes precedence over thought itself in the social mind. Luhmann argues that in post-industrial societies the normativity of laws is superseded by the legitimation of performativity. The source of legitimation becomes the system's ability to control its immediate environment (Cooper and Burrell 1988).

8 Habermas argues that from the classical period onwards the modern has represented 'the new' and has served to distinguish the present epoch from that of antiquity. Following the Enlightenment, the modern was signified by scientific and technological advance, especially in relation to industrialism. In contrast, the aesthetic modernism of the nineteenth century equated the modern with various forms of artistic novelty. Aesthetic modernism represented an extreme, radical assault on traditional artistic values which prized dynamism, singularity and intense presence (Kellner 1988a, Power 1990).

9 Gergen (1989) suggests that modern organization theory was shaped not only by modernist notions from the Enlightenment but also by the romanticist discourse of the nineteenth century. Examples of the continuing legacy of romanticism in organization theory are found in:

> Work emanating from the Tavistock Institute (including Bion, Jaques, Menzies and Bridger) along with other psychoanalytically based theories of the organization (e.g. Zaleznick) in which unconscious dynamics furnish the explanatory fulcrum. Theoretical work inspired by Jung's theory of archetypical bases of action (e.g. Denhardt, Mitroff); Theory and research presuming fundamental human needs, including human resource management and human potential perspectives (e.g. Mayo, Maslow, McGregor). Positions emphasizing the personal resources essential for successful leadership (e.g. Fiedler, Hollander). Aspects of Japanese management theory, as made intelligible in the West, emphasizing organizational commitment, bonds between organizations and their members which transcend market exigencies. And inquiries into executive appreciation that emphasize the workers' needs for positive regard and the significance of empathy to organizational success (e.g. Cooperider and Srivastva). (pp. 5–6).

Gergen feels that although a romanticist vocabulary still underscores much of Western culture, it is a vocabulary in remission – romanticist voices now speak increasingly from the margins. He suggests that the chief replacement for the romanticist worldview is the modernist.

10 Differentiation is similarly a core concept of structural-functionalism (especially in the work of Talcott Parsons, where it is synonymous with more modern and essentially better societies).

11 This thesis implies that when tasks were less differentiated, and more likely to be appreciated as successive phases in a single career, they were more or less coterminous in terms of the managerial hierarchy.

12 Throughout the 1970s and 1980s, claims were made for a new postmodern epistemology to replace the redundant Cartesian tradition. The trajectory of modern philosophy was considered to be faltering in its attempt to establish an absolute foundation for philosophical systems (Rorty 1979). Derrida (1976), for example, argued that modern Western philosophy was condemning itself through its system of binary conception, its logocentrism, and its privileging of speech over writing. The binary system only succeeded in ensnaring practitioners within hopeless metaphysical traps (see Kellner 1988a). A complete deconstruction of philosophy, and thus a new philosophical practice, was required to remedy this situation.

13 Kellner (1988a and 1988b) suggests that Baudrillard's account is flawed in that he takes trends in the present social situation for finished states. Kellner (1988a) argues that his work is 'good science fiction but poor social theory' (p. 248). As the theory is not adequately contexualized, it tends to be blind to a number of continuities between modernism and postmodernism. As Kellner notes, Baudrillard 'reproduces certain trends of the present age which he projects into a simulation model of postmodernism as the catastrophe of modernity' (1988a, p. 248).

14 Derrida (1976) argues further that Western history shows that writing has always been subordinate to speech. Speech is considered prior to writing, which is awarded only the status of a vehicle for the spoken word. As speech, the

superordinate term, is the medium through which the mind expresses thought, Derrida feels the real significance of writing is suppressed (Cooper 1989).

15 We suggested earlier that the academic study of organizations has witnessed considerable recent interest in postmodern ideas. We have seen assessments of the contributions of key writers on postmodernism to the study of organizations (e.g. Burrell 1988 on Foucault; Cooper 1989 on Derrida); the analysis of specific organizational issues from a postmodern perspective (e.g. Linstead and Grafton-Small 1991 on culture; Carter and Jackson forthcoming on motivation; Björkegren forthcoming on art); and critiques of the value of postmodernist concepts for organizational analysis (e.g. Ackroyd 1992, Parker forthcoming, Thompson forthcoming).

16 As Kreiner (1989) argues,

it would be futile for an organization theory to propose new and alternative reifications of a 'reality' which is probably complex, paradoxical, ambiguous and superficial, and which thus escapes ultimate reification. If we succeed in marketing such alternative reifications, they would only be new costumes for the masquerade of knowledge. (p. 6)

17 Gergen goes as far as to suggest two 'practical' implications from this analysis: that 'the localized realities of the organization must be pressed into the public sphere' (p. 24), and that 'the organization must open its doors to alien or alternative realities' (p. 25).

Bibliography

Ackroyd, S. (1989) 'The Development of Metatheory in Organizational Analysis'.
Paper presented at 'Rethinking Organization: New Directions in Organizational Research and Analysis Conference', Lancaster, September
(1992) 'Paradigms Lost: Paradise Regained', in M. Reed and M. Hughes (eds.)
(1992)
Acton, H. (ed.) (1972) *John Stuart Mill*, London: Everyman (new edition: originally
published 1908)
Adair, J. (1968) *Training for Leadership*, London: Macdonald
(1973) *Action-Centred Leadership*, London: McGraw-Hill
(1983) *Effective Leadership*, Aldershot: Gower
(1984) *The Skills of Leadership*, Aldershot: Gower
Adler, F. (1977) 'Factory Councils, Gramsci and the Industrialists', *Telos* 31: 67–90
Allen, V. L. (1975) *Social Analysis: a Marxist Critique and Alternative*, London:
Longmans
Allison, G. T. (1971) *Essence of Decision: Explaining the Cuban Missile Crisis*,
Boston: Little Brown
Althusser, L. (1969) *For Marx*, Harmondsworth: Penguin
(1972) *Lenin and Philosophy and Other Essays*, London: New Left Books
Andreski, S. (1974) *The Essential Comte*, London: Croom Helm
Aron, R. (1968) *Main Currents in Sociological Thought*, Vol. 1, Harmondsworth:
Penguin
(1970) *Main Currents in Sociological Thought*, Vol. 2, Harmondsworth: Penguin
Aronowitz, S. (1989) 'Postmodernism and Politics', in A. Ross *Universal Abandon:
the Politics of Postmodernism*, Edinburgh University Press
Atkinson, D. (1972) *Orthodox Consensus and Radical Alternative*, London:
Heinemann
Baran, P. and Sweezy, P. (1968) *Monopoly Capital*, Harmondsworth: Penguin
Baritz, L. (1960) *Servants of Power*, Middletown, Conn.: Wesleyan University Press
Barthes, R. (1957) *Mythologies*, Paris: Editions du Seuil (trans. New York: Hill and
Wang, 1962)
Baudrillard, J. (1968) *Le Système des objects*, Paris: Denoel-Gonthier
(1970) *La Société de consommation*, Paris: Gallimard
(1972) *Pour une critique de l'économie politique du signe*, Paris: Gallimard
(translated as *For a Critique of the Political Economy of the Sign*, St Louis:
Telos Press, 1981)
(1976) *L'Echange symbolique et la mort*, Paris: Gallimard

(1983a) *Simulations*, New York: Semiotexte

(1983b) *In the Shadow of the Silent Majority*, New York: Semiotexte

Bauman, Z. (1988a) 'Viewpoint: Sociology and Postmodernity', *Sociological Review* 36 (6): 790–813

(1988b) 'Is there a Postmodern Sociology?', *Theory, Culture and Society* 5 (2): 217–37

Bell, D. (1973) *The Coming of Post-Industrial Society*, New York: Basic Books

Benson, J. K. (1977a) 'Innovation and Crisis in Organizational Analysis', *Sociological Quarterly* 18 (2): 229–49

(1977b) 'Organizations: a Dialectical View', *Administrative Science Quarterly* 22 (1): 1–21

(1983) 'A Dialectical Method for the Study of Organizations', in G. Morgan (ed.) (1983)

Bertalanffy, L. von (1950) 'The Theory of Open Systems', *Science* 3: 23–9

Beynon, H. (1973) *Working for Ford*, Harmondsworth: Penguin

Bion, W. (1950) 'Experiences in Groups', *Human Relations* 3 (1): 55–67

(1961) *Experiences in Groups*, London: Tavistock

Björkegren, D. (forthcoming) 'Postmodernism and Art', in J. Hassard and M. Parker (eds.) (forthcoming)

Blackstone, G. (1957) *A History of the British Fire Service*, London: Routledge and Kegan Paul

Bottomore, T. (1975) 'Competing Paradigms in Macrosociology', in A. Inkeles (ed.), *Annual Review of Sociology*, New York: Annual Reviews

Bradbury, M. and McFarlane, J. (1976) *Modernism: 1890–1930*, Harmondsworth: Penguin

Braendgaard, A. (1978) 'Cultural-Normative Change or Interest Politics in Disguise? Two Different Interpretations of Recent Efforts in Work Humaniza-tion'. Paper presented at 'E.I.A.S.M. Seminar on Cultural and Normative Change in Organizations', Brussels, April

Braverman, H. (1974) *Labor and Monopoly Capital*, New York: Monthly Review Press

Brown, R. K. (1967) 'Research and Consultancy in Industrial Enterprises', *Sociology* 1 (1): 167–78

Buckley, W. (1958) 'Social Stratification and the Functional Theory of Differentia-tion', *American Sociological Review* 23: 369–75

Burns, T. and Stalker, G. (1961) *The Management of Innovation*, London: Tavistock

Burrell, G. (1988) 'Modernism, Postmodernism and Organizational Analysis 2: the Contribution of Michel Foucault', *Organization Studies* 9 (2): 221–35

Burrell, G. and Morgan, G. (1979) *Sociological Paradigms and Organizational Analysis*, London: Heinemann

Callinicos, A. (1989) *Against Postmodernism*, Cambridge: Polity

Carchedi, G. (1977) *On the Economic Identification of Social Classes*, London: Routledge and Kegan Paul

Carter, P. and Jackson, N. (forthcoming) 'Modernism, Postmodernism and Motivation', in J. Hassard and M. Parker (eds.) (forthcoming)

Clark, D. L. (1985) 'Emerging Paradigms in Organization Theory', in Y. Lincoln (ed.) (1985)

Clegg, S. (1975) *Power, Rule and Domination*, London: Routledge and Kegan Paul

(1988) 'The Good, the Bad and the Ugly', *Organization Studies* 9 (1): 7–13

(1990) *Modern Organizations: Organization Studies in the Postmodern World*, London: Sage

Clegg, S. and Dunkerley, D. (1975) *Critical Issues in Organizations*, London: Routledge and Kegan Paul

(1980) *Organizations, Class and Control*, London: Routledge and Kegan Paul

Cohen, P. (1968) *Modern Social Theory*, London: Heinemann

Comte, A. (1844) *Trait philosophique d'astronomie populaire*, Paris: Carilian-Geoury et Dalmont

(1853) *The Positivist Philosophy*, Vol. 1, London: Chapman

(1865) *A General View of Positivism*, London: Trubner

Connerton, P. (1980) *The Tragedy of Enlightenment: an Essay on the Frankfurt School*, Cambridge University Press

Connor, S. (1989) *Postmodern Culture*, Oxford: Blackwell

Cooper, R. (1983) 'The Other: a Model of Human Structuring', in G. Morgan (ed.) (1983)

(1987) 'Information, Communication and Organization: A Post-Structural Revision', *Journal of Mind and Behaviour* 8 (3): 395–416

(1989) 'Modernism, Postmodernism and Organizational Analysis 3: The Contribution of Jacques Derrida', *Organization Studies* 10 (4): 479–502

(1990) 'Organization/Disorganization', in J. Hassard and D. Pym (eds.) (1990)

Cooper, R. and Burrell, G. (1988) 'Modernism, Postmodernism and Organizational Analysis: an Introduction', *Organization Studies* 9 (1): 91–112

Crozier, M. (1964) *The Bureaucratic Phenomenon*, London: Tavistock

Cousins, C. (1984) 'Labour Processes in the State Service Sector'. Paper presented at the 'Organization and Control of the Labour Process 2nd Annual Conference', Aston University, March

Cunningham, Sir Charles (Chairman) (1971) *Report of the Cunningham Inquiry into the Work of the Fire Service*, London: HMSO (Home Office and Scottish Home and Health Department)

Dahrendorf, R. (1959) *Class and Class Conflict in Industrial Society*, London: Routledge and Kegan Paul

Debord, G. (1970) *The Society of the Spectacle*, Detroit: Black and Red

Denisoff, R. *et al.* (1974) *Theories and Paradigms in Contemporary Sociology*, New York: Peacock

Derrida, J. (1973) *Speech and Phenomena*, Evanston: Northwestern University Press

(1976) *Of Grammatology*, Baltimore: Johns Hopkins Press

(1978) *Writing and Difference*, London: Routledge and Kegan Paul

(1981) *Positions*, University of Chicago Press

(1982) *Margins of Philosophy*, Brighton: Harvester

Dex, S. (1986) *The Sexual Division of Work*, London: Wheatsheaf

Disco, C. (1976) 'Ludwig Wittgenstein and the End of Wild Conjectures', *Theory and Society* 3 (2): 265–87

Donaldson, L. (1985) *In Defence of Organization Theory: a Reply to the Critics*, Cambridge University Press

(1988) 'In Successful Defence of Organization Theory: a Routing of the Critics', *Organization Studies* 9 (1): 28–32

(1989) 'Review Article: *Redirections in Organizational Analysis* by Michael Reed', *Australian Journal of Management* 14 (2): 243–54

(forthcoming) 'The Liberal Revolution and Organization Theory', in J. Hassard and M. Parker (eds.), *Towards a New Theory of Organizations*, London: Routledge

Dore, R. (1961) 'Function and Cause', *American Sociological Review* 26 (4): 843–53

Driggers, P. (1977) 'Theoretical Blockage: a Strategy for the Development of Organization Theory', *Sociological Quarterly* 18 (1): 143–59

Durkheim, E. (1915) *The Elementary Forms of Religious Life*, London: Allen and Unwin

(1938) *Rules of Sociological Method*, Glencoe, Ill.: Free Press

(1947) *The Division of Labour in Society*, Glencoe, Ill.: Free Press

(1951) *Suicide*, Glencoe, Ill.: Free Press

Eagleton, T. (1983) *Literary Theory*, Oxford: Blackwell

Eckburg, D. and Hill, L., Jr. (1979) 'The Paradigm Concept and Sociology: a Critical Review', *American Sociological Review* 44 (4): 925–37

Effrat, A. (1973) 'Power to the Paradigms', in A. Effrat (ed.), *Perspectives in Political Sociology*, New York: Bobbs-Merrill

Eldridge, J. and Crombie, A. (1974) *A Sociology of Organizations*, London: George Allen and Unwin

Emery, F. and Trist, E. (1960) 'Socio Technical Systems', *Management Sciences Models and Techniques* 5

(1965) 'The Causal Texture of Organizational Environments', *Human Relations* 18 (1): 21–33

(1972) *Toward a Social Ecology*, New York: Plenum

Evered, R. and Louis M. (1981) 'Alternative Perspectives in the Organizational Sciences', *Academy of Management Review* 6 (3): 385–95

Featherstone, M. (1988) 'In Pursuit of the Postmodern: an Introduction', *Theory, Culture and Society* 5 (2–3): 195–215

Feyerabend, P. (1970a) *Against Method*, Minnesota Studies in the Philosophy of Science 4

(1970b) 'Consolations for the Specialist', in I. Lakatos and A. Musgrave (eds.) (1970)

Fire Brigades Union (1968) *Fifty Years of Service*, London: Fire Brigades Union

Fleron, F. and Fleron, L. (1972) 'Administrative Theory as Repressive Political Theory', *Telos* 12 (1): 63–92

Foster, H. (1983) *Postmodern Culture*, London: Pluto

Foucault, M. (1977) *Discipline and Punish: the Birth of the Prison*, Harmondsworth: Penguin

(1980) *Power/Knowledge*, Brighton: Harvester

Friedheim, E. A. (1979) 'An Empirical Comparison of Ritzer's Paradigms and Similar Metatheories', *Social Forces* 58 (1): 59–66

Friedrichs, R. (1970) *A Sociology of Sociology*, New York: Free Press,

Garfinkel, H. (1967) *Studies in Ethnomethodology*, Englewood Cliffs, N.J.: Prentice-Hall

Gergen, K. J. (1989) 'Organization Theory in the Postmodern Era'. Paper presented at 'Rethinking Organization Conference', Lancaster, September

(1992) 'Organization Theory in the Postmodern Era', in M. Reed and M. Hughes (eds.) (1992)

Giddens, A. (1976) *New Rules of Sociological Method*, London: Hutchinson
  (1978) *Durkheim*, London: Fontana
Goldman, P. and Van Houten, P. (1977) 'Managerial Strategies and the Worker',
  Sociological Quarterly 18 (1): 108–25
Goldthorpe, J. (1969) 'Herbert Spencer', in T. Raison (ed.) (1969)
Goodrich, C. (1920) *The Frontier of Control*, London: Bell and Sons (republished by
  Pluto Press, 1975)
Gospel, H. and Littler, C. (eds.) (1983) *Managerial Strategies and Industrial
  Relations*, London: Heinemann
Gouldner, A. W. (1954) *Wildcat Strike*, New York: Antioch Press
  (1959) 'Reciprocity and Autonomy in Functional Theory', in L. Gross (ed.)
  (1959)
  (1965) 'Explorations in Applied Social Science', in A. W. Gouldner and S. M.
  Miller (eds.), *Applied Sociology*, New York: Free Press
  (1970) *The Coming Crisis of Western Sociology*, London: Heinemann
Gramsci, A. (1977) *Selections from the Prison Notebooks*, London: Lawrence and
  Wishart
Griffiths, D. (1983) 'Evolution in Research and Theory: a Study of Prominent
  Researchers', *Educational Administration Quarterly* 19 (2): 210–21
Gross, L. (ed.) (1959) *Symposium on Social Theory*, New York: Row Peterson
Guba, E. (1985) 'The Context of Emergent Paradigm Research', in Y. Lincoln (ed.)
  (1985)
Habermas, J. (1972) *Knowledge and Human Interests*, London: Heinemann
  (1974) *Theory and Practice*, London: Heinemann
  (1979) *Communication and the Evolution of Society*, London: Heinemann
  (1981) 'Modernity Versus Postmodernity', *New German Critique* 22: 3–14
  (1987) *Lectures on the Philosophical Discourse of Modernity*, Cambridge, Mass.:
  MIT Press
Hackman, R. and Oldham, G. (1975) 'Development of the Job Diagnostic Survey',
  Journal of Applied Psychology 60 (1): 159–70
  (1976) 'Motivation Through the Design of Work', *Organizational Behaviour and
  Human Performance* 16 (2): 250–79
  (1980) *Work Redesign*, Reading, Mass.: Addison-Wesley
Hage, J. (1965) 'An Axiomatic Theory of Organizations', *Administrative Science
  Quarterly* 10 (4): 289–320
Hall, R. (1972) *Organizations: Structure and Process*, Englewood Cliffs, N.J.:
  Prentice-Hall
Hall, S. and Jacques, M. (eds.) (1989) *New Times*, London: Lawrence and Wishart
Hampshire, S. (1959) *Thought and Action*, London: Chatto and Windus
Hanson, N. R. (1958) *Patterns of Discovery*, Cambridge University Press
Harland, P. (1987) *Superstructuralism*, London: Methuen
Harvey, D. (1989) *The Condition of Postmodernism*, Oxford: Blackwell
Hassard, J. (1985) 'Multiple Paradigms and Organizational Research: an Analysis
  of Work Behaviour in the Fire Service'. Ph.D. thesis, Aston University
  (1988) 'Overcoming Hermeticism in Organization Theory: an Alternative to
  Paradigm Incommensurability', *Human Relations* 41 (3): 247–59
  (1991a) 'Multiple Paradigm Analysis: a Methodology for Management
  Research', in C. Smith and P. Dainty (eds.), *Handbook for Management
  Researchers*, London: Routledge

(1991b) 'Multiple Paradigm Research in Organizations: a Case Study', *Organization Studies* 12 (2): 275–99

Hassard, J. and Parker, M. (eds.) (forthcoming) *Postmodernism and Organizations*, London: Sage

Hassard, J. and Pym, D. (eds.) (1990) *The Theory and Philosophy of Organizations*, London: Routledge

Held, D. (1976) *Introduction to Critical Theory: Horkheimer to Habermas*, London: Hutchinson

Hempel, C. (1959) 'The Logic of Functional Analysis', in L. Gross (ed.) (1959)

Heydebrand, W. (1977) 'Organizational Contradictions in Public Bureaucracies: Toward a Marxian Theory of Organizations', *Sociological Quarterly* 18 (1): 83–107

Hinings, R. (1988) 'Defending Organization Theory: a View from North America', *Organization Studies* 9 (1): 2–7

Hirst, P. and Zeitlin, J. (1991) 'Flexible Specialisation Versus Post-Fordism: Theory, Evidence and Policy Implications', *Economy and Society* 20 (1): 1–56

Holland, R. (1990) 'The Paradigm Plague: Prevention, Cure and Innoculation', *Human Relations* 43 (1): 23–48

Holroyd, Sir Ronald (Chairman) (1970) *Report of the Departmental Committee on the Fire Service*, London: HMSO (Home Office and Scottish Home and Health Department)

Hopper, T. and Powell, A. (1985) 'Making Sense of Research into the Organizational and Social Aspects of Management Accounting', *Journal of Management Studies* 22 (5): 429–65

Husserl, E. (1931) *Ideas: a General Introduction to Pure Phenomenology*, New York: Macmillan

Ilgen, D. and Klein, H. (1989) 'Organizational Behaviour', in M. Rosenweig and L. Porter (eds.), *Annual Review of Psychology* 40: 327–52

Jackson, N. and Carter, P. (1991) 'In Defence of Paradigm Incommensurability', *Organization Studies* 12 (1): 109–27

Jameson, F. (1984) 'Postmodernism: the Cultural Logic of Late Capitalism', *New Left Review* 146: 53–93

Jaques, E. (1951) *The Changing Culture of a Factory*, London: Tavistock

Jarvie, I. (1964) *The Revolution in Anthropology*, London: Routledge

Jick, T. (1979) 'Mixing Quantitative and Qualitative Methods: Triangulation in Action', *Administrative Science Quarterly* 24 (4): 602–11

Johnson, B. (1980) *The Critical Difference*, Baltimore: Johns Hopkins Press

Karpik, L. (1988) 'Misunderstandings and Theoretical Choices', *Organization Studies* 9 (1): 25–8

Kast, F. and Rosenweig, J. (1970) *Organization and Management*, New York: McGraw Hill

(1973) *Contingency Views of Organization and Management*, Chicago: Science Research Associates

Katz, D. and Kahn, R. (1966) *The Social Psychology of Organizations*, New York: John Wiley

Keat, R. and Urry, J. (1975) *Social Theory as Science*, London: Routledge and Kegan Paul

Kellner, D. (1987) 'Baudrillard, Semiurgy and Death', *Theory, Culture and Society* 4 (1): 125–46

(1988a) 'Postmodernism as Social Theory', *Theory, Culture and Society* 5 (2–3): 239–69

(1988b) *Jean Baudrillard: from Marxism to Postmodernism and Beyond*, Cambridge: Polity

Kenny, A. (1973) *Wittgenstein*, London: Allen Lane

Knights, D. and Willmott, H. (eds.) (1986) *Gender and the Labour Process*, Aldershot: Gower

Knights, D., Willmott, H. and Collinson, D. (1985) *Job Redesign: Critical Perspectives on the Labour Process*, Aldershot: Gower

Koontz, H. and O'Donnell, C. (1974) *Management: a Systems and Contingency View of Managerial Functions*, New York: McGraw-Hill

Kreiner, K. (1989) 'The Postmodern Challenge to Organization Theory'. Paper presented at 'Postmodern Management: the Implications for Learning Conference', Barcelona, September

Kristeva, J. (1980) 'Postmodernism', *Bucknell Review* 25: 136–41

Kuhn, T. S. (1962), *The Structure of Scientific Revolutions*, Chicago University Press

(1970a), *The Structure of Scientific Revolutions*, Chicago University Press (second edition with postscript)

(1970b) 'Reflections on My Critics', in I. Lakatos and A. Musgrave (eds.) (1970)

(1974) 'Second Thoughts on Paradigms', in F. Suppe (ed.), *The Structure of Scientific Theories*, Chicago: University of Illinois Press

(1977) *The Essential Tension*, University of Chicago Press

Lakatos, I. (1970) 'Falsification and the Methodology of Scientific Research Programmes', in I. Lakatos and A. Musgrave (eds.) (1970)

Lakatos, I. and Musgrave, A. (eds.) (1970) *Criticism and the Growth of Knowledge*, Cambridge University Press

Lammers, C. (1974) 'Mono- and Poly-Paradigmatic Developments in the Natural and Social Sciences', in R. Whitley (ed.), *Social Processes of Scientific Development*, London: Routledge and Kegan Paul

Lash, S. (1988) 'Discourse or Figure? Postmodernism as a "Regime of Significa-tion"', *Theory, Culture and Society* 5 (2–3): 311–35

(1990) *The Sociology of Postmodernism*, London: Routledge

Lash, S. and Urry, J. (1987) *The End of Organised Capitalism*, Cambridge: Polity

Lawrence, P. and Lorsch, J. (1967) *Organization and Environment*, Cambridge, Mass.: Harvard University Press

Lawson, H. (1985) *Reflexivity: the Postmodern Predicament*, London: Hutchinson

Lefebvre, H. (1971) *Everyday Life in the Modern World*, New York: Harper and Row

Lehmann, T., and Young, R. (1974) 'From Conflict Theory to Conflict Methodo-logy: an Emerging Paradigm for Sociology', *Sociological Inquiry* 44 (1): 15–28

Lewin, K. (1951) *Field Theory in Social Science*, London: Tavistock

Lincoln, Y. (ed.) (1985) *Organizational Theory and Inquiry*, Beverly Hills: Sage

Linstead, S. and Grafton-Small, R. (1991) 'On Reading Organizational Culture'. Working paper, University of Lancaster

(forthcoming) 'On Reading Organizational Culture', *Organization Studies*
Lockwood, D. (1956) 'Some Remarks on "The Social System"', *British Journal of Sociology* 7 (1): 134–43
Louis, M. R. (1983) 'Organizations as Culture Bearing Milieux', in L. Pondy *et. al.* (eds.) (1983)
Low-Beer, A. (1969) *Spencer*, London: Collier-Macmillan
Luhmann, N. (1976) 'A General Theory of Organized Social Systems', in G. Hofstede and M. Kassem (eds.), *European Contributions to Organization Theory*, Amsterdam: Van Gorcum
Lukes, S. (1973) *Emile Durkheim: His Life and Works – An Historical and Critical Study*, Harmondsworth: Allen Lane
Lunn, E. (1985) *Marxism and Modernism*, London: Verso
Lyotard, J.-F. (1977) 'The Unconscious as Mise-en-Scène', in M. Benamou and C. Caramello (eds.), *Performance in Postmodern Culture*, Wisconsin: Center for Twentieth-Century Studies and Coda Press
    (1984) *The Postmodern Condition: a Report on Knowledge*, Manchester University Press
    (1986) *Le Postmoderne expliqué aux enfants*, Paris: Galilee
Lyotard, J.-F. and Thébaud, J.-L. (1986) *Just Gaming*, Manchester University Press
Malinowski, B. (1932) *The Sexual Life of Savages in North-Western Melanesia*, London: Routledge and Kegan Paul
    (1944) *A Scientific Theory of Culture*, Charlotte: University of Carolina Press
March, J. and Simon, H. (1958) *Organizations*, New York: John Wiley
Martin, J. (1990) 'Breaking Up the Mono-Method Monopolies in Organizational Research', in J. Hassard and D. Pym (eds.) (1990)
Maruyama, M. (1974) 'Paradigms and Communication', *Technological Forecasting and Social Change* 6: 3–32
Marx, K. (1867) *Capital: a Critique of Political Economy*, Harmondsworth: Penguin (1976 edition)
Mayntz, R. (1964) 'The Study of Organizations', *Current Sociology* 13: 95–156
Mayo, E. (1933) *The Human Problems of an Industrial Civilisation*, New York: Macmillan
    (1949) *The Social Problems of an Industrial Civilisation*, London: Routledge and Kegan Paul
McArthur, T. (1986) *Worlds of Reference*, Cambridge University Press
Merton, R. (1940) 'Bureaucratic Structure and Personality', *Social Forces* 18 (5): 560–8
    (1949) *Social Theory and Social Structure*, Chicago: Free Press
Miliband, R. (1973) *The State in Capitalist Society*, London: Quartet Books
Mill, J. S. (1866) *Auguste Comte and Positivism*, London: Trubner
Miller, E. (1959) 'Technology, Territory and Time: the Internal Differentiation of Complex Production Systems', *Human Relations* 12 (2): 243–72
Miller, E. and Rice, A. K. (1967) *Systems of Organization: the Control of Task and Sentient Systems*, London: Tavistock
Morgan, G. (ed.) (1983) *Beyond Method: Strategies for Social Research*, Beverly Hills: Sage
Morgan, G. (1986) *Images of Organization*, Beverly Hills: Sage

(1989) *Creative Organization Theory*, Beverly Hills: Sage

(1990) 'Paradigm Diversity in Organizational Research', in J. Hassard and D. Pym (eds.) (1990)

Mouzelis, N. (1975) *Organizations and Bureaucracy*, London: Routledge and Kegan Paul

Nichols, T. (ed.) (1980) *Capital and Labour*, London: Fontana

Nord, W. (1974) 'The Failure of Current Applied Behavioural Science', *Journal of Applied Behavioural Science* 10 (4): 457–78

Norris, C. (1990) 'Lost in the Funhouse: Baudrillard and the Politics of Postmodernism', in R. Boyne and A. Rattansi, *Postmodernism and Society*, London: Macmillan

Nyland, C. (1989) *Reduced Worktime and the Management of Production*, Cambridge University Press

O'Connor, J. (1973) *The Fiscal Crisis of the State*, New York: St. Martin's Press

Offe, C. (1976) *Industry and Equality*, London: Edward Arnold

Oldham, G., Hackman, J. and Stepina, L. (1979) 'Norms for the Job Diagnostic Survey', Journal Supplement Abstract Service (JSAS) *Catalogue of Selected Documents in Psychology* 9 (14)

Parker, M. (1992) 'Post-Modern Organizations or Postmodern Organization Theory?', *Organization Studies* 13 (1): 1–13

(forthcoming) 'Life After Jean-François', in J. Hassard and M. Parker (eds.) (forthcoming)

Parkes, M. S. (1976) 'A Generalized Model for Automating Judgemental Decisions', *Management Science* 16 (4): 841–51

Parsons, T. (1937) *The Structure of Social Action*, Chicago: Free Press

(1951) *The Social System*, Chicago: Free Press

(1956) 'Suggestions for a Sociological Approach to the Theory of Organizations', *Administrative Science Quarterly* 1: 63–85, 225–39

(1960) *Structure and Process in Modern Societies*, Chicago: Free Press

(1965) 'An Outline of the Social System', in T. Parsons (ed.), *Theories of Society*, New York: Free Press

(1967) 'A Paradigm for the Analysis of Social Systems and Change', in N. Demerath and R. Peterson (eds.), *System, Change and Conflict*, New York: Free Press

Pascale, R. (1990) *Managing on the Edge*, New York: Simon and Schuster

Pascale, R. and Athos, A. (1982) *The Art of Japanese Management*, Harmondsworth: Penguin

Pepper, S. (1972) *World Hypotheses*, Berkeley: University of California Press

Perry, N. (1977) 'Recovery and Retrieval in Organizational Analysis'. Working paper, University of Strathclyde

Peters, T. (1988) *Thriving on Chaos*, London: Macmillan

Peters, T. and Waterman, R. (1982) *In Search of Excellence*, New York: Harper and Row

Phillips, D. (1977) *Wittgenstein and Scientific Knowledge*, London: Macmillan

Pinder, C. and Bourgeois, V. (1982) 'Borrowing and the Effectiveness of Administrative Science'. Working paper No. 848, University of British Columbia

Piore, M. and Sabel, C. (1984) *The Second Industrial Divide*, New York: Basic Books

Platt, R. (1989) 'Reflexivity, Recursion and Social Life: Elements for a Postmodern Sociology', *Sociological Review* 37 (4): 636–67

Pollert, A. (1988) 'Dismantling Flexibility', *Capital and Class* 34 (1): 42–75

Pondy, L. and Boje, D. (1981) 'Bringing Mind Back In', in W. Evan (ed.), *Frontiers in Organization and Management*, New York: Praeger

Pondy, L., Frost, P., Morgan, G. and Dandridge, T. (eds.) (1983) *Organizational Symbolism*, Greenwich, Conn.: JAI Press

Popper, K. (1968) *The Logic of Scientific Discovery* (translation of *Logik der Forschung*), London: Hutchinson

—— (1970) 'Normal Science and its Dangers', in I. Lakatos and A. Musgrave (eds.) (1970)

Power, M. (1990) 'Modernism, Postmodernism and Organization', in J. Hassard and D. Pym (eds.) (1990)

Pugh, D. and Hickson, D. (1976) *Organization Structure in its Context: the Aston Programme 1*, Farnborough: Saxon House

Radcliffe-Brown, A. R. (1952) *Structure and Function in Primitive Society*, London: Cohen and West

Raison, T. (ed.) (1969) *Founding Fathers of Social Science*, Harmondsworth: Penguin

Reed, M. (1985) *Redirections in Organizational Analysis*, London: Tavistock

—— (1989) 'Deciphering Donaldson and Defending Organization Theory: a Reply to Lex Donaldson's Review of Redirections in Organization Theory', *Australian Journal of Management* 14 (2): 255–60

Reed, M. and Hughes, M. (eds.). (1992) *Rethinking Organization: New Directions in Organization Theory and Analysis*, London: Sage Publications

Rex, J. (1969) 'Emile Durkheim', in T. Raison (ed.) (1969)

Rice, A. K. (1958) *Productivity and Social Organization: the Ahmedabad Experiment*, London: Tavistock

—— (1963) *The Enterprise and Its Environment*, London: Tavistock

Ritzer, G. (1975) *Sociology: a Multiple Paradigm Science*, New York: Allyn and Bacon

Roethlisberger, F. and Dickson, W. (1939) *Management and the Worker*, Cambridge, Mass.: Harvard University Press

Rorty, R. (1979) *Philosophy and the Mirror of Nature*, Princeton University Press

Rose, M. (1975) *Industrial Behaviour: Theoretical Developments Since Taylor*, Harmondsworth: Penguin

—— (1988) *Industrial Behaviour: Research and Control*, Harmondsworth: Penguin (revised edition)

Salaman, G. (1981) *Class and the Corporation*, London: Fontana

Sanders, P. (1982) 'Phenomenology: a New Way of Viewing Organizational Research', *Academy of Management Review* 7 (3): 353–60

Saussure, F. de (1974) *Course in General Linguistics*, London: Fontana/Collins

Schutz, A. (1967) *The Phenomenology of the Social World*, Evanston, Ill.: North Western University Press

Selznick, P. (1943) 'An Approach to a Theory of Bureaucracy', *American Sociological Review* 8 (1): 47–54

(1948) 'Foundations of the Theory of Organizations', *American Sociological Review* 13 (1): 25–35

(1949) *TVA and the Grass Roots*, Berkeley: University of California Press

Shapere, D. (1971) 'The Paradigm Concept', *Science* 17: 706–9

Shotter, J. (1980) 'Action, Joint Action and Intentionality', in M. Brenner (ed.), *The Structure of Action*, Oxford: Blackwell

Siehl, C. and Martin, J. (1988) 'Measuring Organizational Culture: Mixing Qualitative and Quantitative Methods', in M. Jones, D. Moore, and R. Snyder (eds.), *Inside Organizations*, Beverly Hills: Sage

Silverman, D. (1970) *The Theory of Organizations*, London: Heinemann

Silverman, D. and Jones, J. (1976) *Organizational Work*, London: Collier Macmillan

Simon, H. (1947) *Administrative Behavior*, New York: Free Press

Skinner, B. F. (1953) *Science and Human Behavior*, New York: Macmillan

Smith, C. (1989) 'Flexible Specialisation, Automation and Mass Production', *Work, Employment and Society* 3 (2): 203–20

Snizek, W. (1976) 'An Empirical Assessment of "Sociology: A Multiple Paradigm Science"', *American Sociologist* 1 (2): 217–19

Sofer, C. (1975) *Organizations in Theory and Practice*, London: Heinemann

Spencer, H. (1852) *A Theory of Population*, London: Westminster Review

(1857) *Progress: its Law and Causes*, London: Westminster Review

(1864) *Reasons for Dissenting from the Philosophy of A. Comte*, London: Westminster Review

(1872) *The Principles of Psychology*, London: Williams and Norgate

(1893) *Principles of Sociology*, London: Williams and Norgate

Steinle, C. (1983) 'Organization Theory and Multiple Plane Analysis', *Management International Review* 23: 31–46

Storey, J. (1983) *Managerial Prerogative and the Question of Control*, London: Routledge and Kegan Paul

Thomas, W. (1985) *Mill*, Oxford University Press

Thompson, P. (1983) *The Nature of Work*, London: Macmillan

(forthcoming) 'Fatal Distraction: Postmodernism and Organizational Analysis', in J. Hassard and M. Parker (eds.) (forthcoming)

Trist, E. and Bamforth, K. (1951) 'Some Social and Psychological Consequences of the Longwall Method of Coal-Getting', *Human Relations* 4 (1): 3–38

Trist, E., Higgin, G., Murray, H. and Pollock, A. (1963) *Organizational Choice*, London: Tavistock

Tumin, M. W. (1953) 'Some Principles of Stratification: a Critical Analysis', *American Sociological Review* 18 (4): 387–94

Turner, A. and Lawrence, P. (1965) *Industrial Jobs and the Worker*, Cambridge, Mass.: Harvard University Press

Turner, B. (ed.) (1990) *Theories of Modernity and Postmodernity*, London: Sage

Van den Berge, P. (1963) 'Dialectics and Functionalism: Toward a Theoretical Synthesis', *American Sociological Review* 28 (5): 695–705

Watkins, J. (1970) 'Against Normal Science', in I. Lakatos and A. Musgrave (eds.) (1970)

Weber, M. (1947) *The Theory of Social and Economic Organization*, New York: Free Press

(1949) *Methodology of the Social Sciences*, New York: Free Press
Weick, K. (1969) *The Social Psychology of Organizing*, Reading, Mass.: Addison Wesley
  (1974) 'Amendments to Organizational Theorising', *Academy of Management Journal* 17 (4): 487–502
Weider, L. (1974) 'Telling the Code', in R. Turner (ed.), *Ethnomethodology*, Harmondsworth: Penguin
Wells, R. and Picou, J. (1981) *American Sociology: Theoretical and Methodological Structure*, Washington D.C.: University of America Press
White, O. (1983) 'Improving the Prospects for Heterodoxy in Organization Theory', *Administration and Society* 15 (2): 257–72
Whyte, W. (1964) 'Parsons' Theory Applied to Organizations', in M. Black (ed.), *The Social Theories of Talcott Parsons*, Englewood Cliffs, N.J.: Prentice-Hall
Willmott, H. (1990) 'Beyond Paradigmatic Closure in Organizational Inquiry', in J. Hassard and D. Pym (eds.) (1990)
Winch, P. (1958) *The Idea of a Social Science*, London: Routledge and Kegan Paul
Wittgenstein, L. (1922) *Tractatus Logico-Philosophicus*, London: Kegan Paul
  (1953) *Philosophical Investigations*, London: Blackwell
  (1958) *The Blue and Brown Books*, London: Blackwell
Wood, S. (ed.) (1982) *The Degradation of Work?*, London: Heinemann
Woodward, J. (1958) *Management and Technology*, London: HMSO
Zimbalist, A. (ed.) (1979) *Case Studies in the Labor Process*, New York: Monthly Review Press

Author index

Ackroyd, S., 69–70, 146
Acton, H., 8
Adair, J., 103
Adler, F., 102
Aldrich, H., 63, 71
Allen, V. L., 54–5, 102, 140–1
Althusser, L., 60, 68, 105
Andreski, S., 6, 7
Aron, R., 5, 6, 15
Aronowitz, S., 119
Athos, A., 47
Atkinson, D., 57

Bamforth, K., 38, 54, 55
Baran, P., 105
Baritz, L., 56, 102
Barthes, R., 122
Bataille, G., 120
Baudrillard, J., 3, 111, 113, 114, 122–3, 124, 126, 145
Bauman, Z., 115
Bell, D., 114, 115, 117, 124
Benson, J. K., 62, 69, 70
Bertalanffy, L. von, 39, 46
Beynon, H., 102
Bion, W., 38, 145
Bjökegren, D., 146
Blackstone, G., 106
Blau, P., 57, 63
Boje, D., 62, 63–4, 78, 81, 87, 88
Bottomore, T., 60–1
Bourgeois, V., 68
Bradbury, M., 144
Braendgaard, A., 141
Braverman, H., 105
Bridger, J., 145
Brown, R. K., 141
Buckley, W., 53
Bukharin, N., 105
Burns, T., 43, 45
Burrell, G., 30, 34, 37, 40, 42, 62, 63, 65–9, 70, 72, 73, 78, 87, 88, 89–90, 109, 116–19, 125, 132–3, 134, 136, 144, 145

Callinicos, A., 115, 119
Carchedi, G., 106, 107
Carter, P., 78, 146
Child, J., 71
Clark, D. L., 62, 65
Clegg, S., 27, 31, 47, 69, 70, 71–2, 73, 102, 112, 120, 121–2, 132, 139, 142
Cohen, P., 20, 52, 53, 140
Colletti, L., 105
Collinson, D., 105
Comte, A., 2, 4–7, 8, 9, 13, 14, 16, 17, 18, 19, 117
Connerton, P., 118
Cooper, R., 116–19, 125, 126, 128–31, 132–3, 134, 136, 143, 144, 145, 146
Cooperider, S., 145
Cousins, C. 106
Crombie, A., 105
Crozier, M., 73

Dahrendorf, R., 66, 105
Darwin, C., 10, 11
Debord, G., 122
Denhardt, J., 145
Dennisoff, R., 59
Derrida, J., 3, 111, 114, 119, 120, 122, 125–6, 127, 128–31, 136, 138, 143, 145, 146
Dickson, W., 33–8, 139, 140
Disco, C., 83, 84
Donaldson, L., 69–74, 76, 88, 91, 141, 142
Dore, R., 140
Douglas, J., 57
Driggers, P., 62
Dunkerley, D., 27, 31, 47, 69, 70, 72, 102, 139
Durkheim, E., 2, 4, 13–16, 17, 18, 19, 21, 37, 52, 61, 121

Eckburg, D., 59, 78
Effrat, A., 59–60
Einstein, A., 80
Eldridge, J., 105
Emery, F., 39, 42–3
Etzioni, A., 63

Evered, R., 62, 65, 141

Featherstone, M., 112, 113, 114, 115, 124,
    144
Feyerabend, P., 76, 80, 85, 112
Fiedler, F., 63, 64, 145
Fleron, F., 102
Fleron, L., 102
Foucault, M., 119, 120, 145
Friedheim, E. A., 62, 68, 69, 78
Friedrichs, R., 57–9, 60, 64

Garfinkel, H., 57, 101
Gergen, K. J., 120–1, 127, 128, 134–7, 138,
    143, 145, 146
Giddens, A., 14, 15, 69, 81, 83, 86, 87
Goffman, E., 57
Goldman, P., 70
Goldthorpe, J., 10, 12
Goodrich, C., 102
Gospel, H., 106
Gouldner, A. W., 53–4, 56, 57, 58, 60, 73
Grafton-Small, R., 127, 131, 146
Gramsci, A., 60, 101, 102
Griffiths, D., 65
Gross, L., 57
Guba, E., 62

Habermas, J., 111, 114, 116, 118, 119–20,
    121
Hackman, R., 63, 93, 94, 97, 98
Hage, J., 63, 139
Hall, R., 45, 63
Hall, S., 115
Hampshire, S., 82
Hanson, N. R., 76, 85, 86
Harland, P., 129, 131
Harvey, D., 115, 119
Hassan, I., 114
Hassard, J., 62, 92
Hegel, G., 124
Heidegger, M., 119
Held, D., 118
Hempel, C., 140
Heydebrand, W., 70
Hickson, D., 45
Higgin, G., 38–9, 54, 55
Hill, L. Jr., 59, 78
Hinings, R., 71, 141
Hirst, P., 105, 132
Hobbes, T., 10
Holland, R., 65, 87
Hollander, E., 145
Homans, G., 57, 120
Hopper, T., 65
Hulin, R., 63
Husserl, E., 61, 99

Ilgen, D., 120

Jackson, N., 78, 146
Jacques, M., 115
Jaques, E., 54, 145
Jameson, F., 114, 119
Jarvie, I., 20
Johnson, B., 130
Jones, J., 99

Kahn, R., 45–6
Kant, I., 116, 117, 118, 144
Karpik, L., 49, 71
Kast, F., 45, 139
Katz, D., 45–6
Keat, R., 5, 6, 8, 9, 11, 12
Kellner, D., 119, 120, 122, 123, 124, 125,
    144, 145
Kenny, A., 82
Klein, H., 120
Kohler, W., 86
Koontz, H., 45
Knights, D., 105
Kriener, K., 134, 146
Kristeva, J., 128
Kuhn, T. S., 1, 2, 49, 56–7, 59, 62, 65, 76–
    87, 88, 127

Laing, R. D., 57
Lakatos, I., 77, 79
Lamarck, C., 11
Lammers, C., 76
Lash, S., 115, 123, 136
Lawler, E., 63
Lawrence, P., 43–5, 63, 64, 120, 139
Lawson, H., 127
Lefebvre, H., 122
Lehmann, T., 59
Lewin, K., 38
Lincoln, Y., 62
Linstead, S., 127, 131, 146
Littler, C., 106
Lockwood, D., 66
Lorsch, J., 43–5, 63, 64, 120
Louis, M. R., 62, 65, 141
Low-Beer, A., 10, 11, 12
Luhmann, N., 144
Lukács, G., 60, 101
Lukes, S., 14, 15
Lunn, E., 114
Lyotard, J.-F., 3, 111, 112, 113, 114, 119,
    122, 123–5, 126, 128, 136, 138, 143,
    144

Malinowski, B., 16, 19–20, 21
March, J., 27, 28, 63, 64, 139
Marshall, A., 21
Martin, J., 78, 88, 141

Maruyama, M., 69, 85
Marx, K., 57, 58, 60, 61, 68, 69, 105, 106, 121, 124
Maslow, A., 103
Matza, J., 57
Mayntz, R., 30, 140
Mayo, E., 33–8, 139
McArthur, T., 128
McFarlane, J., 144
McGregor, D., 145
Menzies, I., 145
Merton, R., 16, 26–28, 29, 30
Michels, R., 29
Miliband, R., 105
Mill, J. S., 2, 4, 7–9, 13, 16, 18, 19
Miller, E., 41–2, 139
Mitroff, I., 145
Morgan, G., 30, 34, 37, 40, 42, 62, 63, 65–9, 70, 72, 73, 78, 81, 87, 88, 89–90, 108, 109
Mouzelis, N., 69, 105
Murray, H., 38–9, 54, 55
Musgrave, A., 79

Newton, I., 80
Nichols, T., 105
Nietzsche, F., 119
Nord, W., 102, 141
Norris, C., 122
Nyland, C., 106

O'Connor, J., 106
O'Donnell, C., 45
Offe, C., 121
Oldham, G., 93, 94, 97, 98
Onis, F. de, 114

Pareto, V., 21, 22, 29, 37
Parker, M., 115, 116, 134, 144, 146
Parkes, M. S., 76
Parsons, T., 2, 16, 21–6, 46, 47, 50–2, 54, 57, 61, 145
Pascale, R., 47
Pepper, S., 127
Perrow, C., 63
Perry, N., 69
Peters, T., 47
Pfeffer, J., 63
Phillips, D., 83, 84, 85, 86, 87
Picou, J., 62
Pinder, C., 68
Piore, M., 105, 115, 132
Plato, 10
Platt, R., 127
Pollert, A., 132
Pollock, A., 38–9, 54, 55
Pondy, L., 62, 63–4, 78, 81, 87, 88

Popper, K., 2, 79–81, 85
Porter, L., 63
Powell, A., 65
Power, M., 111, 112, 116, 118, 119, 124, 144
Pugh, D., 45, 63, 64

Radcliffe-Brown, A. R., 16, 19, 20–1
Reed, M., 69, 72–4, 142–3
Rex, J., 15, 105
Rice, A. K., 40–2, 54, 55, 139
Ritzer, G., 61–2, 63–4, 68, 78, 87, 141
Roethlisberger, F., 33–8, 139, 140
Rorty, R., 145
Rose, M., 34, 55, 139
Rosenweig, J., 45, 139

Sabel, C., 105, 115, 132
Saint-Simon, H. de, 5, 8, 117
Salaman, G., 65
Sanders, P., 141
Saussure, F. de, 130
Schutz, A., 61, 99, 101
Selznick, P., 26, 28–30, 73
Shapere, D., 81, 86
Shotter, J., 143
Silverman, D., 31, 32, 33, 51, 52, 62, 63, 68, 69, 70, 99, 139
Simon, H., 27, 28, 63, 64, 139
Skinner, B. F., 68
Smith, A., 121
Smith, C., 132
Snizek, W., 62
Sofer, C., 32
Spencer, H., 2, 4, 9–13, 13, 14, 16, 17, 18, 19, 37
Srivastva, S., 145
Stalker, G., 43, 45
Steinle, C., 81
Stepina, L., 94, 98
Stirner, M., 101
Storey, J., 106
Sweezy, P., 105

Thébaud, J.-L., 112, 125, 143
Thomas, W., 8
Thompson, P., 119, 146
Trist, E., 38–40, 54, 55
Tumin, M. W., 53
Turner, A., 139

Urry, J., 5, 6, 8, 9, 11, 12, 115

Van den Berge, P., 51, 52
Van Houten, D., 70
Vroom, V., 63

Waterman, R., 47
Watkins, J., 69, 86, 87

Weber, M., 9, 21, 26, 57, 61, 105, 113, 121, 122, 132, 133
Weick, K., 63
Weider, L., 100
Wells, R., 62
White, O., 65
Whyte, W., 51
Willmott, H., 69, 105
Winch, P., 87

Wittgenstein, L., 2, 81, 82–7, 127, 128
Wood, S., 105
Woodward, J., 43, 45, 63, 64

Young, R., 59

Zaleznick, A., 145
Zeitlin, J., 105, 132
Zimbalist, A., 105

Subject index

absolutism, 122
Academy of Management Journal, 109, 141
Academy of Management Review, 141
action frame of reference, 68, 92
action research, 35
action theory, 61, 63, 68, 70, 71, 72
administrative man, 64
administrative science, 102
Administrative Science Quarterly, 23, 25,
    47, 109, 141
affective outcomes, 94, 97
agency, 112, 130, 131
AGIL model, 22, 24–25, 46
'agonistics', 125
alienation, 89
anarchism, 101
anomaly, Kuhnian, 58
anthropology, 19–21, 65, 71
anti-organization theory, 101
Aston School, 45, 63, 64, 74
autonomy, 94, 95, 96, 97; functional, 53–4

behaviourism, 61, 62, 64, 68, 141
belief matrix or system, 59, 64
biological analogy, 7, 10–13, 18, 20–1, 27,
    29–31, 40–1, 43, 46, 47, 55
boundary maintenance and relations, 23–6,
    32–3, 40–3, 47, 126, 140
bureaucracy, 29–30, 53, 72, 92, 105, 121;
    French, 73; as an 'iron cage', 132;
    modernism and 132–3
business schools, 71, 92

capitalism, 89; flow of funds in, 125;
    ideology of, 102; late, 119; post-, 115,
    124
Cartesian tradition, 144
central value system, 22–6, 51–2
class(es), action, 57; conflict, 55; dominant,
    72
classical administrative theory, 27, 32, 33,
    34, 36, 92
clinical methods, 65
'collective conscience', 17

collective action position, 143
collectivists, French, 60
commodification, 123
common sense, 102
conflict theory, 58, 61, 68, 105
consensus–conflict debate, 66–8
consultancy, 92
contingency theory, 33, 43–5, 48, 63, 71, 92,
    120, 141, 143; design approach of, 72
contradictions, structural, 55; in the 'text',
    126
control-resistance dialectic, 106
conventionalism, 76, 85
correlations, inter-, 97–8
craft history, 106
crisis model *see* social science
critical theory, 72, 90, 91, 101–5, 141;
    Frankfurt School, 60, 101, 141
cultural/institutional level, 24
culture, 27, 47, 123; alternative, 120, 122;
    art and sign, 122; high and low, 123;
    mass and popular, 115; and
    modernism, 114–15; negation of, 120;
    and personality school, 60; and
    postmodernism, 114–15, sign and
    signifying, 114, 144; 116; Western, 120,
    144
Cunningham Report, 106
cybernetics, 60, 117, 118, 120, 122

'dare to know' (*aude sapere*), 117
Darwinian biology, 18
dealing with others, 95, 96
decentring the subject, 130–1, 136, 137,
    138, 143
decision theory, 117
deconstruction, 111, 125–6, 128, 130, 134,
    138, 144
deduction, 8–9, 17, 65
delegation, 28
de-skilling thesis, 105
determinism, 57; environmental, 51–2;
    managerial, 106; political, 70;
    structural, 142

163

dialectic, of difference, 125; of nature and language, 83, 86; of structure and action, 142
differance, 129–30, 131, 136, 137, 138
'difference', 125, 129
differentiation, 10–13, 44, 56, 121, 122, 145; of cultural spheres, 119; de-, 123, 132; functional, 121; social, 119, 121, 123; structural, 63, 121; task, 121
disciplinary matrix, 65, 85
disorganization, 115, 136
division of labour, 17, 53, 121; bureaucratic, 29
domination, 125
dramaturgy, 57
Durkheimians, 60
dynamic equilibrium, 33
dysfunctions, 27, 29–30, 48, 56

Einstein's paradigm, 80
elites, professional, 53
empiricism, dogma of, 54–5
employment relations, 91, 106–7
Enlightenment, 121, 144; counter, 119; grand narrative of, 144; notion of reason, 112, 116
environment(s), 28, 32–3, 36, 39, 40–1, 50, 51, 137, 140; causal texture of, 42–3; enterprise and, 40–2, 44
epistemological break, 68
epistemology, 65–6, 73, 110
epoche, 99
equifinality, 39, 46
equity theory, 120
essentialism, 143
ethnography, 98–101, 103–4
ethnomethodology, 57, 60, 61, 65, 72, 91, 98
event-structure theory, 45
evolution, 9–13; paradigm, 62; social, 59; typology of, 17
exchange theory, 57, 60, 61, 120; post-, 63
existential presuppositions, 68
existentialism, 108; French, 101
expectancy theory, 93, 120
experienced meaningfulness, 94, 95, 96, 97
experienced responsibility, 94, 95, 96

factor analysis, 64
facts of nature, 83, 85
false consciousness, 105
falsificationism, 77, 140; sophisticated, 77
feedback; from job, 94, 95, 96, 97; from agents, 95, 96, 97
fill-in work, 100
Fire Brigades Union, 106
firefighter(s); attitudes of, 94–8; careers of,

94; probationary, 94; qualified, 94; strike in 1977–8, 106
Fire Service, British, 88, 90, 92–109; groups, 94–7
fiscal crisis theory, 106
flexible specialization, 105, 132, 134
Fordism, and Americanism, 102; post-, 105, 115, 132, 134
form of life, 82
Frankfurt School *see* critical theory
Freudians, 60
frontier of control, 102
functional alternatives, 27
functional imperatives, 22–3
functionalist paradigm, 66–8, 73, 89, 90, 91, 92–8, 109
functionalist sociology, 16–18, 21–30, 50–3, 58, 59; challenges to, 73, 76; decline of, 50–3, 58, 60; and endogenous change, 51; and exogenous change, 51; ideology of, 52–3; method of, 16; and organizations, 23–30, 71, 141; origins of, 4–18; as paradigm, 18, 57–62, 69, 71; scientific limitations of, 140; substantive problems of, 50–2

game theory, 117
'gaming', 125
general systems theory, 30–3, 38, 39, 45–6, 50, 54, 56, 76, 120
German idealists, 60
gestalt-switch, 69, 77, 78, 85
Gestalt theory, 38
grand narrative(s), 119, 123, 124; of administrative progress, 133; of the Enlightenment, 144; fragmentation of, 124; of functionalism, 143; of modernism, 137; of progress, 128
growth need strength, 94, 97; job choice, 95, 96, 97; total, 95, 96; 'would like', 95, 96, 97
gypsum plant, 73

Harvard group/school, 37
Hawthorne studies, 33–8, 39, 139
hegemony, 126; ideological, 102–105; reproduction of, 108; of systems, 19–48, 74, 143
heteroglossia, 136
historical materialism, 105
Hobbesian problem of order, 22,
Holroyd Report, 107
homeostasis, 33, 46
human action science, 65
human relations psychology, 44, 45, 92

ideology, 30; dominant, 55; neo-conservative, 119

imperialism, 72
incommensurability see paradigms and
    incommensurability
indeterminacy, 125
induction, 8, 17, 77
industrial psychology, 36, 63
industrial relations see employment
    relations
information society, 124
'inquiry from the inside', 65
'inquiry from the outside', 65
instant-paradigm thesis, 69, 80, 85
integration, 10–13, 44, 56; integrationism,
    72
intensification of labour, 107
interorganizational; networks and relations,
    63, 64
interpretive paradigm, 66–8, 73, 89, 90, 91,
    98–101, 109
isolationism, 72

job characteristics model and theory, 93–8
job diagnostic survey (JDS), 93–8
Journal of Management Studies, 141
Jubilee Calico Mills, 40

knowledge of results, 94, 95, 96
Kohler drawing, 86
Kruskal–Wallis test, 94–8
Kuhn–Popper debate, 79–81

labour process; in firefighting, 105–8; and
    gender, 105; in Marxism, 121;
    sociology, 91; and time, 105
language(s), 78, 80, 116, 118, 128, 135; of
    the community, 118; discrete, 143;
    instrumental-calculative, 118;
    ordinary, 85, 118; philosophy of, 60;
    picture theory of, 127; surface, 143; as
    a system of differences, 130; and
    thought communication, 126;
    translation of, 80–1
language-game(s), 81, 82–7, 116, 127, 128,
    143; everyday, 84–6; of organization,
    85; primitive, 84; and postmodernism,
    124; of science, 84; social action as,
    125; special, 84–6; technical, 84–6, 143;
    of truth, 85
'law of the three stages', 5–6
life-space, 38
life-world, 101; colonization of, 119
logocentrism, 126, 128–9, 130, 131, 134,
    145

McKinsey 7-S model, 46–7
machine check, 100–1
managerialism, 72
Marxism, 45, 55, 60, 68, 70, 72, 73, 108;

and humanism, 58, 60, 68;
    Mediterranean, 105; and
    postmodernism, 119; and
    structuralism, 60, 68, 90, 105; unity in,
    68
Maslow's 'ladder of needs', 103
mechanical analogy, 7
mechanical equilibrium model, 29, 34, 35–
    6, 38–9
meta-discourse/narrative, 124, 143
metalanguage in use, 85, 86
metaphorization, 126
metatheory, 65–9, 73, 90
methodological unity, 111
methodology of the social sciences, 8
middle-class careers, 102
middle-range theories, 27
Mill's methods, 8–9
moderator variables, 94
modernism, 111, 116–22, 124, 134, 138;
    aesthetic, 119, 120, 143; anti-, 120;
    artistic, 114; critical, 111, 117, 118–19;
    defence of, 111, 116; high, 114; and
    organizational analysis, 120–2; and
    postmodernism, 114–15; pre-, 120;
    systematic, 111, 117–18; trajectory,
    111, 112
modernity, 112, 113; defence of, 119–20; as
    epoch, 113
modernization, 112, 113–14
mono-method approaches, 88
motivation, job and work, 91, 92–8;
    internal, 94; potential score (MPS), 97
multiple paradigm research, 63, 75, 81, 87,
    88–110, 142, 143
myth of the structure, 116

natural selection, 10
negotiated order theory, 72
network of meanings, 119
New Deal, 29
New Times, 115
Newtonian mechanics, 8–9, 18
Newtonian paradigm, 80
non-capitalist state apparatus, 106
normal working day, struggle for, 106–7

objectivism, 92
observation, non-participant, 98;
    participant, 61; theory dependence of,
    86
observation-language, theory neutral, 86,
    127
Omega, 109
ontology, 66, 68; non-standard use of, 68
operations, task continuous, 121; task
    discontinuous, 121

order–conflict debate, 66–7
organic analogy *see* biological analogy
organization(s); axiomatic theory of, 139;
    and control, 28; deconstructionist
    theory of, 135–7; formal, 29; needs, 28,
    48; postmodernism and, 131–7;
    rational, 53; sociology of, 70–1, 83,
    141; sub-units of, 28; values, 24
Organization Studies, 71, 141
organization theory; community structure
    of, 49–50, 63, 65, 77, 142; crisis model
    of, 62; critics of, 70–5, 76, 91; defence
    of, 69–71; democracy in, 110; hallmark
    of, 134; Marxian, 70; paradigm status
    of, 74; as policy science, 74; as poly-
    paradigmatic, 76; postmodern, 131–7,
    138; sociology of, 76
organizational climate, 63
organizational design, 63
organizational goals, 24
organizational roles, 63
orthodoxy, administrative science, 30;
    critique of, 74; intellectual, 74;
    sociological, 7, 9, 12, 16, 23; systems,
    16, 32, 34, 37–8, 90, 92
'other', 131, 143

paradigm(s), 49–75, 77–81, 85–6, 88–110;
    apartheid, 72; blindness, 69; bridges,
    61, 69; closure, 69–70, 74;
    communication, 77–87; communities,
    49, 63, 91; competition, 79; evolution,
    62; exemplars, 64, 65; first and second
    order, 58; heterodoxy, 49, 74; and
    incommensurability, 68, 69, 72, 74–87,
    90; individual's, 76; mediation, 79, 81,
    85; and organization theory, 62–75;
    and relativism, 68, 69, 74–87, 110;
    social behaviour, 61, 62, 63–4; social
    definition, 61, 62, 63–4; social facts,
    61, 62, 63–4; switches/transitions, 69,
    71
paradigm research *see* multiple paradigm
    research
Paretian mechanics, 39
Pearson product-moment correlation
    method, 98
performativity, 123, 144
phenomenology, 60, 61, 70, 90, 108; and
    ambivalence, 125; and organization,
    101; and sociology, 60
philosophy of consciousness, 112
pin factory, Smith's, 121
play, action as, 112; serious, 125, 128, 134,
    143
pluralism, 72, 73, 92
political economy, 105, 121

positivism, 4–18; Comtean, 4–7;
    Durkheimian, 13–16; and evolution,
    12; Millian, 7–9; and the organic
    metaphor, 12; and pragmatism, 6; and
    sociological method, 13–14;
    Spencerian, 9–13; truth claims of, 88
postindustrialism, 113, 115, 117, 122, 124,
    144
postmodern(ism), 111–38; aesthetic, 112;
    age, 113, 124; architect, 135; and art,
    112, 146; condition, 123; critiques of,
    146; and culture, 146; definition of,
    111–12, 144; as epistemology, 111,
    115–16, 122, 131, 132–3, 134, 135, 138;
    as epoch, 111, 115–16, 131, 132, 134,
    135, 138; and knowledge, 126–31, 136,
    138; mood, 144; and motivation, 146;
    and organizational analysis, 131–8;
    and paradigms, 111, 116; science, 123;
    sensibility, 115; society, 113; and
    sociology/social theory, 111, 115, 123;
    'turn', 121; writing, 116
postmodernity, 112, 113, 122
postmodernization, 112, 113–14
poststructuralism, 115
power, networks, 136; relational theory of,
    135–7, 138; as self-destructive, 136;
    servants of, 56; as social coordination,
    136; structures, 63
pragmatism, 6, 92, 109, 135
primary task, 40–1, 48
Protestant ethic, 139
psychoanalysis, 38, 143

qualitative vs. quantitative methods, 64–5
Question of Loyalties, 103

radical change, sociology of, 66
radical humanist paradigm, 66–8, 89, 90,
    101–5, 108
radical organization theory, 105
radical structuralist paradigm, 66–8, 70, 72,
    89–90, 91, 105–8
radical Weberianism, 105
rationality, bounded, 139; indeterminate,
    136; instrumental, 117; of
    organizational analysis, 53; purposive,
    53; scientific-technological, 129;
    subjective, 64
realism, 107
reason, 118, 125, 137; critical, 118; death
    of, 111; Enlightenment notion of, 112;
    instrumental, 118; Kantian, 118;
    systemic, 118; and unreason, 125
'recipes', 99
reflexivity, 127–8, 131, 136, 137, 138
regulation, sociology of, 66

reification, 54, 146
relativism *see* paradigms and relativism
reliabilities, internal consistency, 98
Renaissance, 113
representation(s), 127, 128, 131, 138; autonomous, 112; of objects/events, 123
Requisite Task Attribute (RTA) Index, 139
revolutionary movements, 52
romanticism, 134, 144

Sandhurst package, 102
satisfaction, general, 94, 95, 96; growth, 94, 95, 96, 97; pay, 94, 95, 96; security, 94, 95, 96; social, 94, 95, 96; supervisory, 94, 95, 96
science, communication in, 69, 81; in crisis, 57, 59; history of, 76; inorganic, 7; normal, 62, 77–81; philosophy of, 56, 77, 87; organic, 7; reductionism in, 7; revolutions in, 59, 77–81, 127
scientific management, 27, 32, 34, 44, 120, 136
self-negation, ironic, 136
'simulacra', 123
simulation(s), 122–3; model, 143; world, 114
skill variety, 94, 95, 96, 97
Skinnerian psychology, 61, 62, 68
social, construction, 99–101; dynamics, 7–8; facts, 8, 14–15; kaleidoscopes, 57; physics, 5–7, 17–18; statics, 7–8; supplementarity, 136, 137, 143; trends, 15–17; world, 90
social action theory *see* action theory
social-practice framework, 72, 73
social science, community structure of, 49–50, 57; crisis model of, 49–87; developmental status of, 56; nature of, 66–7, 89; as pluri-paradigmatic, 81
society, theory of, 66–7, 89
'sociologist as priest', 58, 64
'sociologist as prophet', 58, 64
sociology, 'clinical', 56; departments, 71; of development, 113; 'engineering', 56; frame of reference of, 62; historical, 60; as immature science, 59; of knowledge, 57; laws of, classic, 62; micro-, 59; paradigms models in, 57–62; as preparadigmatic, 59; sociology of, 56, 57–9
socio-technical systems, 33, 34, 38–43, 54–5, 63, 92, 141
solidarity, 15, 21, 37; mechanical, 17; organic, 17
solipsism, 83
sophisticated falsificationism *see* falsification

Spearman rank-order correlation method, 98
state, 106
stocks of knowledge, 99
strategic choice thesis, 70
stratification, 52–3
structural-functionalism, 16, 21–30, 45–6, 47, 50–2, 57, 61, 68, 70, 123, 141, 142–3, 144
subject-matter, images of the, 61, 62, 64, 68, 108
subject–object debate, 66–8, 89
superorganisms, 10–11
supplementarity, 129
'survival of the fittest', 10
symbolic interactionism, 57, 60, 61
système de la Mediterranee, 117
systems approach, 30–48, 53–6, 58, 143; applied, 54–6; and case studies, 54–5; closed, 31–2, 139; criticisms of, 55–6; hegemony of, 19–48, 74; natural, 53–4; 'new', 144; open, 32–3, 39–43, 45, 51, 54; origins of, 4–18; as a paradigm, 30–48, 58; partially open, 32; task and sentient, 41–2

task identity, 94, 95, 96, 97
task significance, 94, 95, 96, 97
Tavistock Institute, 38–43, 55, 141, 145
Taylorism *see* scientific management
technocracy, 72
Tennessee Valley Authority (TVA), 28–9, 73
'text', 125, 129
Third Italy, 132
totality, 16–17, 124
Tower of Babel, 59
'trace', 136
training, management, 91, 102–5
Trobriand society, 20
truth, consensus theory of, 85

undecidability, 125–6, 128, 129, 136
upper-quartile agreement, 106
utilitarians, 60

verstehen, 61
voluntarism, 70

Weberian(s), 60, 61
Weltanschauung, 76
Western Electric Company *see* Hawthorne studies
work routines, 91, 99–101
world hypotheses, 127
world view, 64
'writing', 128–9, 131, 138

Cambridge Studies in Management

1 John Child and Bruce Partridge *Lost managers: supervisors in industry and society*
2 Brian Chiplin and Peter Sloane *Tackling discrimination in the workplace: an analysis of sex discrimination in Britain*
3 Geoffrey Whittington *Inflation accounting: an introduction to the debate*
4 Keith Thurley and Stephen Wood (eds.) *Industrial relations and management strategy*
5 Larry James *Power in a trade union: the role of the district committee in the AUEW*
6 Stephen T. Parkinson *New product development in engineering: a comparison of the British and West German machine tool industries*
7 David Tweedie and Geoffrey Whittington (eds.) *The debate on inflation accounting*
8 Paul Willman and Graham Winch *Innovation and management control: labour relations at BL Cars*
9 Lex Donaldson *In defence of organisation theory: a reply to the critics*
10 David Cooper and Trevor Hopper (eds.) *Debating coal closures: economic calculation in the coal dispute 1984–85*
11 Jon Clark, Ian McLoughlin, Howard Rose and Robin King *The process of technological change: new technology and social choice in the workplace*
12 Sandra Dawson, Paul Willman, Alan Clinton and Martin Bamford *Safety at work: the limits of self-regulation*
13 Keith Bradley and Aaron Nejad *Managing owners: the national freight consortium in perspective*
14 David Hugh Whittaker *Managing innovation: a study of Japanese and British factories*
15 Bruce Ahlstrand *The quest for productivity: a case study of Fawley after Flanders*
16 Chris Smith, John Child and Michael Rowlinson *Reshaping work: the Cadbury experience*
17 Howard Gospel *Markets, firms and the management of labour in modern Britain*
18 Mari Sako *Prices, quality and trust: inter-firm relations in Britain and Japan*
19 Paul Willman, Tim Morris and Beverly Aston *Union business: trade union organisation and reform in the Thatcher years*
20 John Hassard *Sociology and organization theory: positivism, paradigms and post-modernity*
21 Andrew Scott *Willing slaves? British workers under human resource management*
22 John Kelly and Edmund Heery *Working for the union: British trade union officers*
23 John Child *Management in China during the age of reform*
24 Anthony Hopwood and Peter Miller (eds.) *Accounting as social and institutional practice*